Strategic Arms Control
after SALT

Strategic Arms Control after SALT

Stephen J. Cimbala
Editor

A Scholarly Resources Imprint
WILMINGTON, DELAWARE

Acknowledgments

The author is grateful to Carolyn Travers and Richard Hopper of Scholarly Resources for their assistance and encouragement. Acknowledgment also is made to Diane Wolf, Jeanette Rieck, and Edward Tomezsko of Pennsylvania State University.

The paper used in this publication meets the minimum requirements of the American National Standard for permanence of paper for printed library materials, Z39.48, 1984.

Scholarly Resources Inc.
104 Greenhill Avenue
Wilmington, DE 19805-1897

Library of Congress Cataloging-in-Publication Data
Strategic arms control after SALT / Stephen J. Cimbala, editor.
    p. cm.
    Includes index.
    ISBN 0-8420-2290-2
    1. Nuclear arms control— United States. 2. Nuclear arms control— Soviet Union. 3. Strategic Arms Limitation Talks II.
JX1974.7.S79 1989   88-35254
327.1'74 — dc19   CIP

To David and Chris

Contents

vii

Introduction

THE LITERATURE OF arms control is primarily one of advocacy, instead of analysis. Although advocacy has its place, it also has its dangers. Polarized debates lead to policy misconstructions and language ábuse. The rhetoricians for and against arms control agreements, of various kinds, have not helped to clarify the relationship between arms control and U.S. national strategy. At one extreme, there are those who believe that U.S.-Soviet negotiations are all part of a Soviet deception plan. At the other, it is perceived that the world will not survive without formal agreements.

As the contributors to this volume will make clear, the place of arms control in U.S. strategy and in strategic thought is not settled. The overall verdict is elaborated upon in the concluding chapter, but the gist is that arms control is eufunctional for stability—provided issues of timing and content can be handled skillfully. It has not always been the case that they have. The U.S. domestic audiences for arms control initiatives include, among others, the media, Congress, the public at large, arms control lobbyists and their opponents, and the academic community. Each of these audiences has a partial or segmental view of what arms control ought to accomplish. Behind these views lie images of America's role in the world and of Soviet political and military objectives as well.

George Quester contends that we should focus on the outputs of arms control and on what it accomplishes compared to disarmament or the status quo. The pertinent outputs are to reduce the probability of war, to reduce the consequences of war if deterrence fails, and to limit peacetime military expenditures. By these standards, arms control is not a poor substitute for disarmament, as is sometimes argued, but possibly better. A world of general and complete disarmament might be less stable than the present world, with or without agreements. According to Quester, arms control is not identical to formal negotiations about armaments. Such negotiations are sometimes helpful if the appropriate objectives of arms control are the yardstick. Formal negotiations can descend into propaganda exchanges. They can be exploited by the bargaining-chip ploy, in which both sides build forces so that they can be traded away later.

Even those who accept a more correct definition of arms control objectives might be dissatisfied with the contribution of arms control to solving the problem of crisis stability. Destabilizing forms of weaponry such as MIRV or improved accuracies for hard target-killing weapons have increased the chances that crisis stability might be eroded. Arms control logic would suggest that the United States should not match Soviet deployments of potentially destabilizing weapons systems; instead, it unilaterally should take initiatives to protect its retaliatory forces and other assets so as to avoid fanning the flames.

According to Louis René Beres, arms control by itself is destined to fail. Washington's efforts will not succeed unless the American public and its leaders first detach themselves from primitive fixations and ideological misconceptions. Among these, misperceptions of the Soviet Union are very important, and contributory negligence in this regard can be ascribed to policymakers with ideological agendas. Furthermore, Beres contends that our political institutions have failed to provide an authentic national identity for the public at large. Instead, mass publics relate to government as cheerleaders for the absurd. Because Americans cannot find meaning as individuals, they are driven to find significance in antipathy for foreign adversaries. Beres argues that, before U.S. arms control policy can accomplish anything meaningful, Americans will have to recover a truer sense of state or public consciousness. Successful arms control must be built on a new social harmony in which citizens are not disconnected from public policy and from one another and so may feel secure in a perilous world.

Alvin Weinberg and Jack Barkenbus contrast two points of view about active defenses, including ballistic missile defense (BMD) and its mission in superpower strategic planning. The first perspective is deontological, meaning that defenses may be morally justifiable in their own right regardless of their consequences. The second perspective is consequentialist; it determines the value of defenses on the basis of their actual consequences, regardless of the intentions of the parties building and deploying them. There is some overlap between the deontological and consequentialist perspectives; it is a matter of relative emphasis.

Weinberg and Barkenbus contend that, from both deontological and consequentialist perspectives, a defense-dominant world might be preferable to an offense-dominated one. However, the burden of proof in terms of consequences lies with those favoring defenses, since they can argue that deterrence based on offenses has worked, at least until now. On the other hand, placed against this might be the consequences of deterrence failure, which could approach ultimate costs in an offense-dominated world. Some theorists, moreover, believe that it is a MAD world in fact regardless of preferred theories of deterrence.

It may be possible, according to the Weinberg-Barkenbus study, to separate more efficient and morally defensible uses for BMD from less preferred ones. The consequentialist perspective could abide BMD if it contributed to deterrence stability by protecting retaliatory forces against first strikes. This and other selective deployments could be supportive of stability as the U.S. defense establishment and mainstream deterrence theory now define stability. However, there is the downside risk that the progression from limited to unlimited BMD deployments will regenerate a defense-offense arms race, with the superpowers jointly increasing their shared losses.

Donald Snow is dubious about the prospects for a defense-dominant world, supposing it to be at all possible. Ronald Reagan's arms control program is centered on an expectation that the Strategic Defense Initiative (SDI) can provide a basis for reconstruction of the U.S.-Soviet deterrence relationship. So far, this vision has not been an appealing one to the Moscow leadership. The Reagan strategic concept envisions a first phase in which large reductions in offensive forces take place, a second during which limited defenses are deployed, and a third in which territorial defenses are deployed and offenses reduced to nearly zero. Moreover, U.S. defenses must meet the criteria of survivability and marginal cost effectiveness before they are deployed.

The Reagan administration did not take Moscow's objections to SDI at face value. It interpreted them as subterfuge, while the Soviets' real agenda was to limit SDI and to preserve their preeminence in BMD. There are several possible interpretations for the Soviets' view, according to Snow: they believe what they say, that SDI is an offensive weapons system in purpose if not in technology; their depictions of SDI mirror their own hopes and research efforts, but they fear that the United States may succeed first; they also fear not being able to afford the costs of an SDI competition; or, fourth, they fear a U.S. dominance of space for military purposes across the board and interpret SDI as one step in that strategy.

For Snow, there are three possible outcomes to this U.S.-Soviet impasse over BMD: 1) that one side or the other will change its position; 2) that continued stalemate will preclude agreement; and 3) that one or both sides will compromise. If the USSR fears that SDI is a species of space-strike weapon mated to a U.S. strategy of preemption, then compromise on its part seems unlikely. A possible path to compromise is to limit defense to those weapons that are unambiguously defensive in purpose, such as those which are tasked to defend retaliatory forces and based terrestrially. Space-based systems are almost certain to lend themselves to ambiguous interpretation.

Michael Altfeld and Stephen Cimbala examine the controversy over SDI and BMD from another perspective. Much of the arms control debate posits two antithetical concepts of strategic stability. One is based on mutual assured destruction (MAD), the other on mutual assured survival. MAD, according to some proponents of its logic, requires that deterrence be based solely on offensive retaliation; in this vision, defenses are destabilizing in principle. Mutual assured survival is parallel to the Reagan strategic concept, discussed by Snow, in which nuclear offenses are gradually built down and replaced by nonnuclear strategic defenses.

According to Altfeld and Cimbala, the actual impact of any SDI deployment may be to strengthen MAD instead of weakening it. Contrary to some arms control theology, defenses may have this effect because they will be much more effective in protecting retaliatory forces than in protecting cities. The two authors show that the deployment of moderately effective layered defenses improves significantly the survivability of strategic forces, but it cannot prevent a devastating countercity attack by the USSR.

How we conceptualize the problem of strategic defense is extremely important. It is not very useful for analytic purposes to assume that defenses will work perfectly, or not at all. Instead, we assume that any defense will have some leakage, and the task is to describe the process by which leakage will occur. The approach taken by Altfeld and Cimbala is not the traditional "pure price of entry" in which the defenses absorb a certain number of warheads and, after reaching saturation, collapse. An alternative is to use a Bernoulli process in which the parameters of defense effectiveness, numbers of attacking warheads, attacker confidence requirements, and the number of warheads that the attacker wants to assign to a given target are factored into the equation. The analysis shows that, instead of undermining MAD, defenses may help to preserve a situation in which victory is impossible.

If the problem of ballistic missile defense is solved through arms control, it is only part of the problem. As David Sorenson notes, cruise missiles and advanced cruise missiles pose their own unique threats to deterrence stability. Again, this is contrary to some conventional wisdom, which supposes that slow-moving (compared to ballistic missiles) cruise missiles pose no preemptive threats and therefore contribute to stable deterrence. However, the picture is more complicated than this. Newer or advanced cruise missiles will be designed to foil improved Soviet radar detection by using enhanced low observable technology. Improved aerodynamics, engine modifications, and more efficient fuel consumption will increase the ranges of advanced cruise missiles compared to present generations. Future cruise missiles also will have better guidance including updates from satellite-deployed systems. These technological "improvements" have implications for their contributions to stability.

Among these implications are some that are immediately problematical for Washington's deterrence requirements. Cruise missiles fired from Soviet submarines far from U.S. shores or from aircraft equally distant might be difficult for present or even future atmospheric defenses to detect and intercept. Air- and sea-launched advanced cruise missiles—if they escape detection—will have the accuracies to destroy hard targets, including ICBM silos, with plausible launch trajectories. However, they would be even more useful in attacking mobile ICBMs, which would offset gains in survivability derived from making land-based missiles road or rail mobile, as both superpowers are now planning to do. Incorporating advanced cruise missiles into future superpower arms control agreements creates the need to deal with asymmetries of technology and strategic risk, with the former asymmetries favoring the United States and the latter, the Soviet Union.

Cruise missiles of the present and near-term future pose difficult problems for arms control monitoring and verification. Present generations of strategic cruise missiles can be enumerated indirectly by counting the carriers that bring them within range of their targets. Advanced cruise missiles with longer ranges could not be monitored so easily. Range could be verified by using telemetry derived from observation of tests, but cruise missile telemetry may be harder to interpret than similar information about ballistic missile testing. Possible approaches to limitation of cruise missile threats to stability include bans on testing of advance cruise missiles, limitations on production and on their attributes such as speed and range, or controls on launch platforms.

Keith Payne contends that U.S. arms control efforts are often pursued with no regard for much of the pertinent context, including deterrence requirements and arms control commitments. He examines the linkages among arms control, SDI, deterrence requirements for nuclear and conventional forces, and the U.S. guarantee to NATO.

The Reagan-Gorbachev discussions at Reykjavik resulted in much criticism of Washington's position from many quarters. American allies in Europe were publicly cautious and privately pleased that SDI appeared to preclude an agreement which might remove many nuclear weapons from the Continent. Opponents of SDI criticized the president for missing an opportunity to bring about deep reductions in strategic offensive forces. After Reykjavik, Mikhail Gorbachev agreed to decouple the issue of reductions in long- and short-range intermediate nuclear forces (LRINF and SRINF) from the SDI impasse. Europeans reacted to this, too, with ambivalence.

According to Payne, the promise of Reykjavik is the promise of a new approach to arms control which includes rather than excludes strategic defense. Arms control under a defense transition would be a radical departure from previous U.S. policy. However, the "traditional" approach, in which defenses are excluded as components of stable deterrence, has not worked. Traditional arms control (for example, SALT) has not been able to stabilize the balance of strategic offensive forces by persuading the USSR that survivability for both sides' forces was the key to stability. At Reykjavik, the superpowers finally moved away from the notion that arms control and BMD are incompatible.

If a defense transition is to come about, it will have to take into account the indivisibility of the U.S.-Canadian relationship. According to Cynthia Cannizzo, issues of geography, culture, economics, politics, and military strategy tie the two countries' fates together, to the occasional frustration of both parties. The U.S.-Canadian alignment is formalized in two organizations: NATO and NORAD. Through NATO, Ottawa is involved in MBFR/CSCE and nuclear space talks. Some sentiment exists within the Canadian public for withdrawal of their troops from the Central Front, and other sentiment favors nonalignment or neutrality in the East-West conflict. Canadian governments have favored MAD doctrine as an expedient approach to stability and war prevention. They also endorse the concept of flexible response in the sense of providing for flexible nuclear options if deterrence fails (although before it does, the threat of escalation should be quite emphatic). A major shift in Washington's doctrine, including one toward SDI and defense dominance, would meet with Ottawa's skepticism and resistance.

Canada's commitment to NORAD involves a number of sensitive issues, of which the most sensitive may be sovereignty. This is apparent in the country's reactions to U.S. testing of cruise missiles over its territory. Another sensitive issue is the possible American expectation that Soviet cruise missile-firing submarines could be attacked by U.S. submarines in Canadian arctic waters. SDI is also sensitive in this regard. According to Cannizzo, Canadians fear strategic "entanglement" with SDI on account of the "roof and walls" relationship between ballistic and atmospheric defenses: one makes little sense without the other. Thus, Canadians could find themselves pressured to deploy enhanced air defenses that contribute to the SDI program objectives. Warning systems now channeled through NORAD logically would be connected to SDI's alerting and response systems, and surveillance systems incorporated within SDI also could be used for detection of bombers and cruise missiles.

The prospects for successful U.S.-Soviet arms control agreements are in some measure dependent upon the relationship between intelligence and verification. According to Charles Gellner, verification is a special form of intelligence consisting of several elements: acquiring information, appraising that information in the context of arms control agreements, and assessing decisions by officials with regard to compliance of the signatory with the treaty provisions. Each of these processes is subjective, especially the last.

According to Gellner, the use of intelligence methods in the verification process has evolved through three major stages since World War II. In the first stage from 1946 until the 1960s, the United States proposed ambitious arms control and disarmament schemes which included intrusive on-site inspections. The USSR rejected many of these as covers for intelligence-gathering operations. During the second stage, from the 1970s to the mid-1980s, the superpowers agreed to legalized safeguards for monitoring by national technical means (satellite observation). The transition to a third stage began in the mid-1980s and is still under way. In this stage, more prominence has been given to cooperative and intrusive methods of monitoring in U.S. arms control proposals. Examples are the Threshold Test Ban and Peaceful Nuclear

Explosion treaties of 1974 and 1976. Intrusive methods of monitoring recently have been emphasized in arms control proposals by President Reagan and General Secretary Gorbachev. Trends in this most recent stage of verification include the spread of satellite and other technical forms of monitoring to countries other than the superpowers; the growing acceptance of international verification organizations; and, third, the potential linkage of satellite-monitoring technology with those international organizations.

The United States generally has proposed only arms control agreements that it determined, through interagency staffing, that it could monitor. Sometimes, though, a more restrictive limitation is included in an agreement despite the fact that a less restrictive guideline would be easier to monitor (an example is the clause in the SALT II Treaty permitting five-percent ICBM modernization). Criteria for threat assessment are much more vague and judgmental than criteria for verifying noncompliance with an arms control agreement. Thus, concluding such agreements might require some reallocation of intelligence resources in order to monitor them. The intelligence community also can obtain valuable benefits from verification provisions in arms control agreements. The provisions in the ABM and SALT II treaties permitting both superpowers to use national technical means to monitor compliance with the treaty also allowed, in fact if not in theory, for the collection of other information on defense capabilities. In addition, the numerical ceilings imposed on Soviet military forces by SALT II were helpful to U.S. intelligence efforts to track those forces, necessary with or without the treaty.

However, we must be cautioned against getting overly concerned with the details of monitoring and verification and therefore losing sight of first principles. Patrick Morgan raises this concern with regard to the issue of strategic surprise, that we have based arms control on the weapons in our arsenal instead of attempting to shape the arms control context for our own purposes. According to Morgan, strategic surprise is the starting point. The relationship between arms control and strategic surprise, moreover, is a complicated one. In the twentieth century, strategic surprise has become more attractive to policymakers and more feasible with conventional and nuclear weapons. It is defined by Morgan as a surprise military attack meant to alter decisively the military situation and perceived by the defender as a serious blow to his national strategy.

Although studies usually depict deterrence as the key to prevention of war, Morgan sees deterrence as a species of arms control and argues that the key to success in deterrence has been the avoidance of strategic surprise strategies. Where strategic surprise cannot succeed, deterrence holds. This is true for both nuclear and conventional deterrence and shows up in the negotiations over SDI and MBFR in Europe. And the avoidance of strategic surprise is not a concern of the great powers alone: Arab-Israeli relations have always been marked by reciprocal fears of surprise attack. As applied to the superpowers, Morgan's analysis of deterrence as strategic surprise avoidance suggests that "assured destruction" was never the key to deterrence. Instead, the prospect of nuclear retaliation cancels strategic surprise by eliminating the incentives for it. His approach directs our attention to the cost-benefit calculus of strategic planners conceived in terms of their expectations about *decisive* success, compared to anything less than that. He also notes that improvements in U.S.-Soviet political relations are the key to reducing the risks of nuclear war. Neat arrangements for arms reductions are best seen as contributing to improved political climates.

Surprise by definition points to the unexpected, and there are many kinds of military surprises. But strategic nuclear surprise has been considered unlikely because it could only happen in the aftermath of a superpower crisis, or grow out of a conventional war, and in either case it would not be surprising.

However, nuclear surprise is more probable if we think of it as a continuum of expectations, including expectations about how crisis might slip out of control, or how nuclear war might be fought, after deterrence has failed. In this more process-oriented concept of surprise, one can distinguish among preventive war, anticipatory preemption, retaliatory preemption, and launch under attack. Following this distinction, anticipatory preemption occurs when one side expects the other to attack although the offensive of the second side has not actually been launched. Retaliatory preemption is similar to launch on warning and occurs after the second side has launched its forces but before those forces impact on the territory of the first side. Launch under attack means that retaliation takes place after the weapons of the second side have begun to detonate on the targets of the first. Thus the "positive control launch" of the U.S. strategic bomber force might be described as preparation for retaliatory preemption or for launch under attack, depending upon the decision of the U.S. National Command Authorities.

Preemption strategies combined with active defenses change the relationship between error probabilities and disutilities in estimates of crisis stability. Combined with defenses, preemption might seem less dangerous because the costs of error are presumably less catastrophic. Defenses might make the defender overconfident of successfully riding out an attack, or the attacker too optimistic about avoiding a retaliatory strike. U.S. or Soviet policymakers might be emboldened to attack, or deterred from attacking, on the basis of the same range of values for given variables. The best evidence may suggest that preemption pays because the options of policymakers seem to have narrowed to those which involve only desperate choices. The inner logic of deterrence choice thus may defeat itself, requiring that the micrologic of choice among options leads to national defeat and international chaos. Political realism may be incompatible with strategic rationality; the more improbable nuclear surprise seems, the more appealing it may be once policymakers are persuaded (wrongly) that the opportunity for other choices has passed.

The editor argues against the conventional wisdom that arms control has failed to limit significantly the U.S.-Soviet arms race. Arms control can provide contributory processes toward resolution of political differences between superpowers, when and if their leaders want to improve their political relations. Moreover, complaints about the ineffectiveness of arms control understate the obstacles it faces. Changes in technology, command and control issues, and alliance cohesion are some of the subject matter which confound efforts to obtain superpower arms agreements. Moreover, the Reagan administration changed the agenda with its declaration of a new "strategic concept" involving the build-down of nuclear offenses and the buildup of nonnuclear defenses. The post-Reykjavik and post-INF climate for superpower arms agreements may be better or worse than the pre-Reykjavik and pre-INF one, but leaders need to remain mindful of the distinction between arms control and disarmament. Proposals for drastic reductions in offensive arsenals may lower the probability of successful arms control if they lower the threshold of NATO alliance disagreement. Nuclear force reductions in Europe may need to be offset by improvements in conventional forces tasked for the defense of NATO.

About the Contributors

Michael F. Altfeld is a graduate of Northeastern Illinois University and earned his Ph.D. in political science at the University of Rochester. He has taught at several universities and currently holds the post of strategic policy analyst at the U.S. Army War College Strategic Studies Institute. Dr. Altfeld has written extensively in the fields of international conflict and nuclear strategy and is the author of "Strategic Defense and the 'Cost-Exchange Ratio,'" *Strategic Review* (Fall 1986).

Jack N. Barkenbus is a political scientist with the Institute for Energy Analysis, Oak Ridge Associated Universities. He has extensive research experience in examining the interface of technology, institutions, and policy. He is the coeditor of *The Nuclear Connection: A Reassessment of Nuclear Power and Nuclear Proliferation* (1985) and joint author of *A Second Nuclear Era* (1985).

Louis René Beres, a professor of political science and international law at Purdue University, lectures and publishes widely on issues relating to nuclear war, nuclear strategy, and human rights. Born in Zurich, Switzerland, he received his Ph.D. from Princeton and is the author of many books, monographs, and articles in his field. He also contributes regular guest editorials to such newspapers as the *New York Times, Los Angeles Times, Christian Science Monitor, Cleveland Plain Dealer, Washington Post, Chicago Tribune, Newsday Baltimore Evening Sun, St. Louis Post Dispatch, USA Today, Louisville Courier Journal,* and *Dallas Morning News*. Professor Beres's most recent book is *America Outside the World: The Collapse of U.S. Foreign Policy* (1987).

Cynthia A. Cannizzo received her Ph.D. from the University of Michigan. An assistant professor of political science and research associate at the Mershon Center, Ohio State University, from 1976 to 1980, she worked as a postdoctoral research fellow at the Centre for Arms Control and International Security, University of Lancaster, England, in 1980–81. Currently she is assistant director of the Strategic Studies Program and an associate professor of political science at the University of Calgary. Her publications include *The Gun Merchants* (1980); articles in *Orbis, Armed Forces and Society*, and the *Journal of Peace Research;* and several edited books.

Stephen J. Cimbala teaches political science at Pennsylvania State University and has contributed to the field of national security studies for many years. His recently published works include *Rethinking Nuclear Strategy* (1988), *Nuclear Strategy: Unfinished Business* (1988), and various edited volumes on U.S. national defense policy.

Charles R. Gellner is senior specialist in international affairs for the Congressional Research Service (CRS) at the Library of Congress. He was chief of the Foreign Affairs and National Defense Division of CRS (1966–1975), where he dealt with a variety of national security and defense issues; chief of the reference and research staff, U.S. Arms Control and Disarmament Agency (1961–1966); and a staff member of the Subcommittee on Disarmament, Senate Foreign Relations Committee (1956–1959). Gellner has written numerous reports for the CRS on defense and foreign policy matters. His current interests are in arms control and national defense.

Patrick M. Morgan is a professor of political science at Washington State University. He is the author of *Theories and Approaches to International Politics* (1981) and *Deterrence: A Conceptual Analysis* (1977), and coauthor of *Strategic Military Surprise: Incentives and Opportunities* (1982). His articles have appeared in various journals and edited collections. He has taught at the University of Washington, and in Belgium at the Catholic University of Louvain and the College of Europe.

Keith B. Payne, an analyst specializing in U.S. and Soviet strategic and defense policy, international security affairs, and Soviet foreign policy, is executive vice president of the National Institute for Public Policy. He is the coauthor of *Nuclear Strategy: Flexibility and Stability* (1978) and author of numerous works, including *Nuclear Deterrence in U.S.-Soviet Relations* (1982), *Why SDI?* (1985), and *A Just Defense: The Use of Force, Nuclear Weapons and Our Conscience* (1987). He is also the editor and a contributor to *Laser Weapons in Space* (1983) and *Missiles for the Nineties: ICBMs and Strategic Policy* (1984).

George H. Quester is chairman of the Department of Government and Politics at the University of Maryland, where he teaches courses on defense policy and arms control and American foreign policy. Previously he has taught at Cornell and Harvard universities, the University of California at Los Angeles, and the National War College. He is the author of *The Politics of Nuclear Proliferation, American Foreign Policy: The Lost Consensus* (1982), and *The Future of Nuclear Deterrence.*

Donald M. Snow is a professor of political science and the director of international studies at the University of Alabama. He served as one of the first Secretary of the Navy Senior Research Fellows at the U.S. Naval War College, and he also has been visiting professor of National Security Affairs at the Air Command and Staff College. His most recent books include *The Last Frontier: An Analysis of the Strategic Defense Initiative* (with Gary L. Guertner), *National Security: Enduring Problems of U.S. Defense Policy*, and *The Necessary Peace: Nuclear Weapons and Superpower Relations.*

David S. Sorenson is an associate professor of political science at Denison University and senior research associate at the Mershon Center, Ohio State University. He has published in the areas of nuclear strategy and technology, superpower defense expenditures, and arms race stability. Professor Sorenson also has done contract research on ballistic missile defense for the U.S. Air Force. He currently serves as the chair of the Section on Military Studies of the International Studies Association.

Alvin M. Weinberg is a Distinguished Fellow with the Institute for Energy Analysis, which he was instrumental in establishing at Oak Ridge Associated Universities. From 1955 to 1973 he was director of the Oak Ridge National Laboratory, where he had worked since 1945. The originator of the pressurized water reactor, Weinberg has played an active role in the development of nuclear energy. In recent years he has examined public policy issues involving energy and technology and the contribution of nuclear power to the energy mix. He is a member of the National Academy of Sciences and the National Academy of Engineering.

Fundamental Questions about Arms Control

Recovering Our Bearings on Arms Control

GEORGE H. QUESTER

"ARMS CONTROL" WAS hardly at the peak of its public acceptance for most of the 1980s. The phrase is attacked by the Left and by the Right, amid scholarly discussions of why arms control has failed. The Left tends to see arms control as an alternative to disarmament—as a dangerous alternative, because well-intentioned people somehow will be tricked into settling for less than the best.[1] The Right instead sees arms control as synonymous with disarmament; it often uses the terms almost interchangeably and attacks all such moves as naive and gullible, in face of the hostile and aggressive intentions of the Soviet Union.[2] Furthermore, the press often identifies arms control with disarmament or with formal negotiations about disarmament, or perhaps with formal disarmament agreements only after they have been signed and ratified—that is, seeing no arms control until negotiations have been successfully completed.[3] It will be argued here that none of these definitions is correct or particularly helpful. The usual criticisms of arms control often stem from these kinds of conceptual blurrings.

Arms control might be defined more helpfully as a way of looking at decisions about weapons with a view to outputs and with a concern about the impact on the likelihood of war, the damage inflicted if war breaks out, and the costs in peacetime of being prepared for war.[4] Disarmament is good only if it serves these ends. Can any advocate of disarmament argue that swords should be beaten into plowshares if this causes a war to erupt which otherwise would have been avoided, or even if it makes wars more horrible when they break out? Formal negotiations are similarly good only if they make war less likely or less horrible, or if they at least help to curb the economic drains of the arms race.

Arms control is to disarmament as program budgeting is to line-item budgeting. Any student of systems analysis recognizes that this is a clear way of looking at military preparation decisions if we wish to be happy with the policies we adopt. Disarmament thus is an input rather than an output. It is a means rather than an end, and the inputs and the means constantly have to be judged and analyzed. Do they really serve the outputs and ends we have identified for ourselves?

Arms Control versus Disarmament

We can think of many cases where disarmament serves the purposes of U.S. foreign policy by the rubric of arms control, so that it hardly is appropriate for liberals to conclude that they are being offered an alternative or substitute for what they always have intuitively endorsed. If pressed as to why they support disarmament, such advocates might respond that it must be because arms make wars more likely and more horrible, while wasting mankind's resources in a useless arms race. Yet there are some forks in the road here, points where disarmament does not improve our human situation any further.

Some of the proposals for deep cuts in our nuclear arsenal would make no difference in the crisis stability of the two superpowers. We can easily envisage cuts of 50 percent in the major nuclear arsenals, or perhaps even 75 percent, with no threat to the assured retaliatory capabilities of each side—and with a beneficial political tonic if such cuts were made. At some point, however, we would have to be concerned lest any further reductions in the U.S. and Soviet strategic nuclear arsenals cause each country to worry about the other's sneak attack, as well as cause each one to contemplate the possibilities of launching such a sneak attack itself.

At the very least, any simple focus on quantitative disarmament would lose the analytical advantages of sorting out kinds of weapons by their stability—whether they are more or less stabilizing for future crisis situations. Doing away with multiple-warhead missiles thus should take precedence over doing away with single-warhead missiles, and doing away with land-based missiles comes ahead of disarming submarine-based missile forces. If we admit that some kinds of weapons are worse than others in terms of the goals that any humane analyst would have to endorse, then it is a simple step to conclude that some kinds of weapons may be desirable, rather than undesirable; that these kinds of weapons should not be reduced in quantity even when others are dismantled and eliminated; and that some kinds of weapons might even be increased in quantity.

Questions about the desirability of deep cuts apply all the more to what the superpowers endorse ritualistically at sessions of the UN General Assembly (what the normal advocate of disarmament tends to describe as his ultimate goal): general and complete disarmament (GCD). Would the world really be more secure, would wars really be less likely if we committed ourselves to GCD and approached a fulfillment of commitments to such total disarmament?[5] Or would there not then be a flurry of rumors that the other side might be cheating, might have hidden away some nuclear warheads and missiles, or might have secretly trained some kinds of police or gymnasts as a conventional fighting force? Would not the rumors emerging about the other side then prod our side to do some prudential and precautionary cheating just in case those rumors proved to be true? And any precautionary moves we made would amount to a confirmation of the worst fears entertained by the other side about us.

It is sadly true that there is some persistent and irreducible risk of nuclear war in the status quo of current alliance structures and armament levels. Yet any move toward total disarmament, or even toward very substantial disarmament, would greatly increase these risks of "a war nobody wanted," precisely because the interactions of the rumors outlined above would work in a self-confirming way to produce distrust and preemption. Crisis stability refers to whether rumors of war are likely to be self-confirming. The world of total or substantial disarmament probably would offer much less crisis stability than current arrangements. The massive overkill of today's nuclear arsenals rightly offends all observers for the damage they could do to all mankind if an all-out war were ever to happen. But the same horrendous arsenals drastically reduce any real or perceived advantages to striking first in a crisis—advantages that could loom into sight again if this overkill were to be eliminated.

Arms Control versus Formal Negotiations

If arms control is neither the opposite of nor identical to disarmament, it also is not identical to formal negotiations about armaments. The world tends to take hope whenever negotiations begin. "At least, they are talking to each other again." And the world tends to regard it as bad news whenever arms negotiations between the two superpowers are terminated. We have to contend here with intuitions that lead liberals and press commentators to focus on an input and to assume that it is rigidly coupled with improvements in output. Again, there are many cases where negotiations are productive and where their initiation is a good sign. Much can be accomplished by formal and careful negotiations that might not be achievable otherwise. Misunderstandings can be cleared up, and possibilities of confusion can be avoided. A contract can be signed with the entire world as a witness, with the likelihood therefore increased that each side will adhere to the contract. The witnessing neutrals would impose various disutilities on whichever side had brazenly failed to stick by the agreed plan, and each side could worry less that the other would plunge ahead with increases in its arsenal.

There are many instances, however, where formal negotiations can be counterproductive, where a better service might have been done for arms control if negotiations had not been under way. The same neutral gallery of witnesses also can lead each of the adversaries to play to that gallery during the negotiating process, with a view to scoring propaganda points. When formal negotiations about arms decisions descend into a propaganda exchange, with each side trying to win over the public opinion of Western Europe or the Third World, it might be better for the superpowers and for the whole world if no formal negotiations had ever begun. Another drawback of formal negotiations emerges in the bargaining-chip ploy: the project or weapons system that neither side wishes to pursue but which is retained and funded, simply on the expectation that the other side might be willing to give up something in exchange for it. We may even hold back on changes that we ourselves desire, if we sense that the other side desires them even more.

It has been argued that there might have been lower levels of arms spending in the USSR and the United States in the 1970s and 1980s if the Strategic Arms Limitations Talks (SALT) process had never begun. Moreover, some weapons systems (for example, the B-47) that were scrapped in the early 1960s, in the days when Moscow and Washington could not bring themselves to initiate formal negotiations, might have been retained if negotiations had been under way, to be used as bargaining counters for concessions.

If it is true that arms control should not be seen as identical to arms reductions or to formal agreements, we have to be wary of the interaction of the phrase "formal disarmament agreements." For us to say that arms control has failed simply because formal agreements have been rejected prior to ratification, or because no such formal limits on armaments have been negotiated, is to give a wrong analytical bent to our assessments of whether we are making progress.

Arms Control versus the Economic Burden of Defense

Reductions in armaments, whether they are arrived at formally or not, tend to be linked closely to the last of our categories of output: the reduction of the peacetime burdens, economic and otherwise, of international tension. In general, arms cost money; disarmament, therefore, saves the taxpayers some money. It is difficult to think of any exceptions to this last generalization which has nourished the intuitions of those who equate arms control with disarmament. Yet a few possibilities come to mind.

The military often tries to downplay the costs of weapons procurements by touting all the spin-offs that stem from the research and development of weapons. Would we have Teflon frying pans if we had not developed the heat shields needed to allow missile warheads to reenter the atmosphere without burning up? Yet, if this example is somewhat bogus— frying pans could have been developed more cheaply in a dedicated civilian effort, without burdening the world with arrays of ICBMs in the process—a dangerous counterpossibility does emerge, from time to time, of a spin-off in the opposite direction, whereby civilian economic ventures would produce weapons naturally and relatively cheaply.

One possibility, occupying our concerns for the present, is that nuclear weapons can be assembled as the by-product of the production of electricity by nuclear reactor power plants.[6] Another such possibility comes in the easy derivation of chemical weapons from civilian research on pesticides. Where Mother Nature has been so unkind as to burden hostile states with these kinds of temptations toward spin-off weapons, it may be very hard for two of these states to reassure each other that no such weapons are being developed. Assurances from our neighbor that nuclear weapons are not being produced or that chemical weapons are not being stockpiled may entail abstaining generally from nuclear or chemical industry, with substantial costs to the civilian economy.

These cases violate the intuition that disarmament is always a relief to the burdened civilian sector, for the only meaningful disarmament may be the kind that can be surely and reliably verified. A total abstinence from some valuable dual-purpose industries might be necessary, if anything reliable in the way of disarmament were to be instituted here.

Crisis Stability

There also are commentators who conclude that arms control has failed, without equating arms control to formal agreements that reduce or limit arms totals. These would-be analysts recognize the logic of what a precise concept of arms control may amount to but question whether this logic has been accepted by many people who matter. The important test of the acceptance of the arms control logic may come through whether enough attention is directed to crisis stability when we are designing and purchasing weapons, and when we are deciding how to respond to the weapons decisions made by our adversaries.

A good portion of our decisions and enunciations of doctrine on the nuclear confrontation shows an acceptance of this part of the arms control logic. In addition to assuring ourselves that we will not be caught by some kind of Soviet sneak attack, keeping us from retaliating against whatever the Kremlin leadership values, we must assure the Soviets against their having to worry about a counterforce attack on our part. The advantages of secure command-and-control arrangements are addressed in a bilateral way, as are the advantages of secure basing modes (especially the submarine).

There also have been numerous decisions and developments in the strategic area which cast doubt on whether the logic of crisis stability has been digested and accepted as widely as we need. The addition of multiple warheads (MIRV) to land-based missiles should have been foreseen to be upsetting to stability in any future crisis, especially when coupled with improved accuracies in the guidance of warheads. However accurate nuclear missiles may be, however small the circular error probable (CEP) around the target at which they are fired, without multiple warheads we never would have encountered a situation where both sides would be better off militarily by firing their ICBM forces first after a crisis had put peace in doubt. With MIRV, such a situation, at least with regard to the land-based components of the two superpowers' nuclear forces, is much more possible.[7]

The most severe test of whether an understanding of crisis stability has been achieved comes when the opposite side makes a move toward acquiring a destabilizing form of weaponry. What are we to do, then, except to follow suit? If the Soviets invest in very accurate intercontinental ballistic missiles, is it not necessary for the United States to do the same in order to restore the balance? If the Soviets have acquired a counterforce capability for the fighting of some future nuclear war, does it not follow that the West also must possess such capabilities? An analyst immersed in arms control reasoning would quickly spot the flaws in these intuitive responses, for a Soviet investment in destabilizing counterforce weaponry combined with a matching Western procurement of such weaponry would make the situation far worse, loading all decisions when there are rumors of war (a "crisis" by the most practical of definitions) toward policies and decisions which make war actually happen.

Rather than match Soviet counterforce capabilities with counterforce capabilities of our own, arms control logic dictates that we try to blunt the effectiveness of such Soviet counterforce capabilities by making our own retaliatory forces more secure and survivable.[8] Rather than seek antisubmarine warfare (ASW) capabilities, whenever the Soviet Navy seems to be pursuing such capabilities—and in this area the U.S. Navy seems to be far ahead of the Soviet Navy—we should augment the silence and security of our own submarines.

All in all, our record of "success" or "failure" in arms control, in the sense of whether the logic has been understood and accepted, has been uneven during the past two decades of American policy on strategic nuclear weapons. Now far more military officers, executive branch officials, and Congressmen really understand the concept of crisis stability, the prerequisites of such stability, and the fuller logic of mutual assured destruction (MAD). It has to be part of the American national interest not to cause the Soviet leadership to panic over nuclear war threats from the United States, since the price of such a panic may be a nuclear war one day that neither side wants. Yet there are also man, Americans in each of the three groups who either fail to understand or reject this logic of arms control and concern for crisis stability.

Many of the deployment decisions made on U.S. strategic weapons illustrate a clear acceptance of arms control reasoning, including the heavy investment in submarine-launched ballistic missile (SLBM) submarines, in command and control links, and in the deep concern addressed to psychological screening for the personnel who fire nuclear missiles. Other decisions, including the installation of multiple warheads on land-based missiles, the perfection of accuracies, and the enunciation of new war-fighting doctrines in case deterrence should fail, amount to less of a success for the arms control logic.

Conventional Arms Decisions

The same logic for assessing the impact of weapons decisions, with reference to the crucial outputs of whether wars become more likely and more destructive, also should apply to preparations for conventional war; here our record may be still more uneven. Ever since the Maginot Line failed to prevent the German conquest of France in 1940 (perhaps simply because it had not been extended along the French frontier with Belgium), military officers of the United States and its allies have been reluctant to sort any weaponry into categories of offensive and defensive. They particularly have been reluctant to be identified with the defensive and thus be accused of a Maginot mentality. Yet the same logic that has been accepted more fully for strategic nuclear weapons also should apply to tanks, troop carrier aircraft, and naval vessels. These kinds of weapons systems make it more desirable to attack whenever we are in doubt about what the adversary is about to do; other weapons systems make it more advisable to wait, offering the military advantage to the side that sits still.

The distinction between military offense and defense probably refers to this, if the words are to have any meaning anymore.[9] The nomenclature has been used and abused for political purposes, as every regime wishes to pretend that it never attacks and only defends against the attacks of others. When such distinctions were explored in the past, every nation insisted that its own favorite weapons systems were defensive, while those of their adversaries were offensive.

Leaving the political propaganda aside, logic tells us that any change in military technology either makes it less attractive, or more attractive, to strike first in a battle than before the new technology was introduced. Whenever a weapon makes it less attractive to strike and more attractive to wait, we should regard it as defensive and crisis-stability supporting—and also as good arms control. Tanks tend to favor the offensive, and antitank weapons thus tend to favor the defensive. Fixed fortifications are less use to an aggressor and more use to the one side standing and waiting, in case the other side is feeling aggressive. No one can argue that this is an easy distinction to apply to the continual flow of new conventional weapons systems, but we still should accord more attention to this distinction. We need to bring arms control reasoning, defined not simply as disarmament and arms restraints, more fully to bear on the nonnuclear side of the picture.

Such analysis occasionally is folded under the category of confidence-building measures (CBM) along with improved communication links between the command centers of the two sides, regularized procedures for notifications of maneuvers, and so forth.[10] Unfortunately, the analysis sometimes has been regarded as naive, as if it depended on high confidence in the motives and good intentions of our Soviet adversaries.

Together with the consideration of crisis stability on the nuclear sphere, we ought to understand that these approaches do not require or presuppose any flattering impressions of Moscow's intentions. Regardless of the hostility between the two sides, some kinds of nuclear and conventional weapons reduce the likelihood of war, simply because they leave each side more secure against the worst that the other side may plan to inflict. Quick reaction forces and rapid deployment forces may panic each state into striking or intervening in some region, because it dreads what may happen if the other side moves first. By contrast, the kinds of weapons which punish mobility may make the bitterest of enemies wait and see during some crisis, rather than initiate war.

The most frightening model of a war between societies which were not deeply hostile to each other came with the outbreak of World War I. Our retrospective arms-control reasoning would not prescribe total disarmament as the antidote to what occurred in 1914 but rather would stress a move away from the mobilization systems and military harnessing of railroads—the rapid deployment forces of the time, which allowed neither the kaiser nor the czar nor the French government to rest easy once the major issues had been raised after Sarajevo.

As a more positive sign that not everyone is shrugging off all considerations of defense or crisis stability at the conventional level, some West German and other Democratic Socialists have begun seriously to explore a notion of "defensive defense." The finding of any good answers here is hardly a certainty, but the mere pursuit of answers is an encouraging sign on "whether arms control can succeed."[11]

Attention is being directed toward whether the Swiss or Swedish or Austrian models of territorially based reserve systems can be adopted to enhance the West German ability to repel an attack from the East, without increasing (or even decreasing) the Bundeswehr's ability to attack across the Elbe. Other studies have stressed the technological possibilities of antitank weapons, especially antitank guided missiles (ATGM), some of which promise to have much higher kill ratios than comparable weapons of the past. More broadly, there are prospects for the use of very accurate cruise missiles, or even ballistic missiles, with conventional warheads, hypothetically knocking down every bridge in Poland in response to a Soviet invasion of West Germany, thus slowing the Soviet armored advance when supplies and logistical support are not forthcoming.

Other kinds of reform proposals pertain to larger issues of force structure and of maneuver style once a battle begins. Not all such proposals, however, are so fully directed to an emphasis on defense over offense—that is, to an emphasis on stability.[12] As often, the dominant theme becomes the achievement of a victory if a conventional war breaks out, a victory sparing all sides any escalation in the use of nuclear weapons and assuring that little or no territory in West Germany falls under Communist control—but not reassuring the Soviet and East German authorities that no attack need ever be feared from the West. As in the nuclear area discussed earlier, we have neither a clear success nor a clear failure here, in the intellectual battle of getting important output considerations of arms control incorporated into weapons planning for conventional war.

Other Senses of Stability

Crisis stability is not the only measure of arms control, since analysts also refer to "arms race stability" and "deterrence stability." These three notions of stability might be assessed and compared. Crisis stability refers to whether weapons, by their very existence, ever cause wars to happen. By comparison, arms race stability refers to whether weapons, by their very existence, cause other weapons to be purchased by the opposite side, which in turn causes more weapons to be acquired on our side, all at great expense to the taxpayers of the states involved. This is clearly directed to the third important output listed above, whether the costs in peacetime of being prepared for war are raised or lowered by any particular policy decision. While few people would doubt that this is indeed an important consideration, it also might be contended that this arms race stability is hardly ever as important as crisis stability, even if it tends to capture more attention among the traditional advocates of disarmament.

The third term, deterrence stability, pertains to whether weapons (in particular, nuclear weapons) by their very existence keep wars involving lesser kinds of weapons from starting, that is, whether some weapons prevent wars that otherwise would have occurred. This also has to be an important consideration in any military policy decision, for the world cares about peace, whether it is achieved by disarmament or by armaments. Indeed, the extended nuclear deterrence question is the stimulus for most of what is interesting and alive about the subject of military policy and arms control. If there were no inherent threat of an invasion by Soviet conventional ground forces (with only the continuing escalation in U.S. nuclear weapons having warded off that threat since 1950), there would be much less for analysts to argue and worry about. To put it another way, if West Germany and Western Europe were as shielded geographically as Japan—if the Elbe River were as wide as the Sea of Japan—then many political scientists and engineers now would be free to devote their time and energies to other issues far removed from the possibilities of war.

Because we are concerned about deterrence stability (and have to be, as long as Americans continue to care about the future of Europe), we take more chances with crisis stability and worry less about arms race stability. To place a priority on any of these three terms, however, is hardly to shrug off the others. Serving the national interest well entails applying the fullest assessment of consequences to any decisions made about weapons and dropping the blinders and narrowness imposed by the traditional approaches: "traditional" disarmament or "traditional" strategy.

Burdens to an Intellectual Acceptance of Arms Control

How can we account for the delays in winning acceptance for the logic and maxims of arms control, if they are as clear and persuasive as has been contended here? If the "failure of arms control" is to be viewed as an intellectual failure, are most of the people who matter in this policy field somehow deficient in their intelligence, unable to learn the lessons that have confronted them for more than forty years? We can stipulate several factors that might bias the discussion in ways which do not disparage the intelligence or competence of the military officers and civilian defense planners who make policy for both superpowers but which explain how arms control may consist of good ideas and still not be accepted.

To begin, there is the bias of most military professionals against the offensive. To advocate the defensive is to be accused of a Maginot mentality, of being insufficiently aggressive, and of having no initiative, no get-up-and-go. Defensive preparations suggest a smugness and a commitment to the status quo, while the offensive implies courage and innovation.[13] Stressing the offensive also can bring increased appropriations for one's branch of the service, when the threat posed by the enemy and the opportunities for counterattack loom large. And faster promotions come with larger appropriations. As the military officers of the United States and their Soviet counterparts assign more prestige to the offensive side of military possibilities, the risk emerges that considerations of crisis stability will be neglected and that opportunities for a simultaneous easing in both sides' situations will be missed. Beyond this traditional professional military commitment to the offensive, we can identify another intellectual barrier to a fuller acceptance of arms control. The moral intuitions of most ordinary people are dead set against any full resignation to MAD, any simple contentment withholding the civilian population of the other side hostage for the good behavior of its governing regime.

Professional military officers and moral civilians thus agree that nuclear weapons should be governed by the rules which more generally govern weapons, that the object of using a weapon should be the winning of a victory, that only military targets should be aimed at, and that civilian targets should be spared as much as possible. What Robert Jervis has labeled "the conventionalization of nuclear weapons" produces planning for war-fighting uses of such weapons, on the (possibly wrong) premise that the side-effect collateral damage to civilian populations in any use of nuclear weapons can be reduced and made manageable.[14]

The traditional morality of Western societies is quite contrary to the logic of the arms control we are espousing here. The arms control approach is results-oriented: anything that works to prevent war or to reduce its destructiveness is desirable. Traditional morality is means-oriented: we cannot pursue a good end by a bad means. If the retention of various kinds of armaments or the threatening of civilian lives is a bad means, then such traditional perspectives will not be relaxed by our calculations that human purposes are being served.

Americans and others who uphold a more traditional view of the proper military approach draw reinforcement from what we are able to read of Soviet pronouncements on the subject. Over the past four decades these texts also have typically upheld the traditional view, stating that the military forces of the other side, and not the opposing civilian population, should be attacked if war breaks out. They declare that the protection of the civilian population is the highest calling of the military professional, and they generally extol the initiative and the offensive in combat.[15]

It is easy to overrate the importance of the training documents and public speeches that emerge from the Soviet military, for some of this material amounts to a morale booster for young officers; free and open discussion of the choices and issues is not allowed to surface in the USSR. Yet any American analyst who contends that the Soviets have fully accepted the necessity and desirability of mutual deterrence and MAD, including notions of crisis stability and a welcoming of adversary retaliatory capabilities, still has an uphill battle in documenting this, in finding relevant quotations and citations among all those of a more traditional variety that can be extracted from Soviet sources.

It is entirely plausible to this author that the Soviet views of the outputs that need to be pursued in arms policy and of the linkages that inescapably bind inputs to outputs are not very different from what we have been putting forward here as a sensible Western assessment of arms control. However, the Soviet Union has the luxury of thinking at one level and conducting open discussions at a very different level. There have been times when Moscow has been able to reap some advantage from conducting its true strategic debate in privacy, thus forcing the West to guess whether or not Soviet leaders are bluffing. Yet their ability to disguise and hide their true thinking has also worked to hinder a fuller Western acceptance of arms control logic. Moscow simply has played dumb too long on some of the issues here, and in the process it has caused confusion in the West on the same issues. It even has caused the West to be somewhat dumb as well.

Conclusion

As a final barrier to the success of arms control, we can return to the conceptual confusions with which we started—the analyses by which any failure to achieve a formal agreement or to pursue formal negotiations is seen as a failure of arms control. If we misinterpret what we are doing and then draw our senses of optimism or pessimism from these very misinterpretations, we then doom ourselves to fail by more serious measures of Soviet-American relations and to fail as part of a self-confirming hypothesis.

Arms control, it must be stressed, does not require extensive love or trust between the two sides and does not have to be the result of some fundamental improvement in political relations between Moscow and Washington. Rather, arms control is simply a sophisticated and elementary recognition that the relationship between the superpowers is not a zero-sum game, that there may be military improvements which ease the situation of both sides. Each state prefers peace to war, even if the two superpowers disagree substantially about what would be the nicest form of peace. An improvement in the world situation can take place with or without a substantial reduction in the weapons inventories of the two sides and with or without any signed and sealed treaty or formal negotiations between them. When policy is discussed and interpreted today, we tend to scoff at arms control, but this is a tendency which we should be able to overcome.

Notes

[1] For an earlier example of criticism of arms control from the Left see Elizabeth Young, *A Farewell to Arms Control?* (London: Penguin, 1972)

[2] An illustration of this kind of hawkish criticism can be found in Seymour Weiss, "The Case against Arms Control," *Commentary* 77, no. 11 (November 1984): 19–23

[3] See Leslie Gelb, "A Glass Half Full," *Foreign Policy* 36 (Fall 1979): 21–31, for an illustration of this kind of definition by a press analyst.

4 The original formulation of this is found in Thomas Schelling and Morton Halperin, *Strategy and Arms Control* (New York: Twentieth Century Fund, 1961), p. 2.

5 See Hedley Bull, *The Control of the Arms Race* (New York: Praeger, 1965), on the inherent problems of GCD

6 On the nuclear proliferation spin-off see Albert Wohlstetter et al., *Swords from Plowshares* (Chicago: University of Chicago Press, 1979).

7 The particular problems caused by MIRVs are outlined in Herbert Scoville, *MX: Prescription for Disaster* (Cambridge: MIT Press, 1981).

8 For some very level-headed analyses here see Peter Clausen, Allan Krass, and Robert Zirkle, *In Search of Stability: An Assessment of New U.S. Nuclear Forces* (Cambridge: Union of Concerned Scientists, 1986).

9 For the author's more extended views on the subject see George H. Quester, *Offense and Defense in the International System* (New York: Wiley, 1977).

10 Confidence-building measures are discussed in William J. Lynn, "Existing U.S.-Soviet Confidence-Building Measures," in Barry Blechman, ed., *Preventing Nuclear War: A Realistic Approach* (Bloomington: University of Indiana Press, 1985), pp. 24–51.

11 For some examples of this kind of analysis of a "defensive defense" see Horst H. Afheldt, *Verteidigung und Frieden-Politik mit Militarichen Mitteln* (Defense and peace-politics through military means) (Munich: Hanser, 1976); Horst H. Afheldt, *Defensive Verteidigung* (Defensive defense) (Reinbek bei Hamburg: Rowohlt, 1983); Labour party, *Defense and Security for Britain* (Manchester: Labour party, 1984); and G. Brossollet and E. Spannocchi, *Verteidigung ohne Schlacht* (Defense without battle) (Munich: Hanser, 1976).

12 See Andrew J. Pierre, ed., *The Conventional Defense of Europe* (New York: Council on Foreign Relations, 1986), for some general proposals on reforms of NATO preparations for conventional war.

13 The professional military bias against the offensive is discussed in Stephen Van Evera, "The Cult of the Offensive and the Origins of the First World War," *International Security* 9, no. 1 (Summer 1984): 58–107; and Jack Snyder, "Civil-Military Relations and the Cult of the Offensive, 1914 to 1984," ibid., 108–46.

14 Robert Jervis, *The Illogic of American Nuclear Strategy* (Ithaca: Cornell University Press, 1984).

15 For a pessimistic view of Soviet sophistication about stability and arms control see Donald G. Brennan, "Commentary," *International Security* 3, no. 3 (Winter 1978–79): 193–98. Brennan was responding to Raymond L. Garthoff, "Mutual Deterrence and Strategic Arms Limitation in Soviet Policy," ibid., no. 1 (Summer 1978): 112–47. A later version was reprinted in *Strategic Review* 10, no. 4 (Fall 1982): 36–51. See also Richard Pipes, "Soviet Strategic Doctrine: Another View," *Strategic Review* 10, no. 4 (Fall 1982): 52–58.

Arms Control, Ideology, and Self-Affirmation: Exploring the Linkages

LOUIS RENÉ BERES

TAKEN BY ITSELF, arms control between the superpowers is destined to fail. No formula, whether offered by the United States or the Soviet Union, can succeed on its own. This is true even for the most promising and generous proposals. Before arms control can work, moreover, this country will have to reject its all-consuming hatred of the other country. Discovering that ideological anti-Sovietism is not an authentic creed but an untruthful prescription for despair, we will have to progress beyond the desolate metaphysics of permanent international hostility. In the final analysis, this will require a profound change in the lives of individual Americans.

Self-liberation is the key to national liberation in America. Taken by themselves, indictments of Sovietophobia are inadequate to the task of creating a purposeful U.S. arms control policy. Rather, these indictments must be founded upon an authentic understanding of America's ritualized hatred of the USSR, an understanding that points toward essential transformations of personal and collective life within the United States.

Let us listen. What do we hear? The sounds of "happiness" and "success" in today's America are manufactured. They are the dull vibrations of rehearsed gaiety, of false communion, of flight to the herd for meaning and for self-esteem. This reign-of-the-herd instinct flows from a far-reaching assembly of nonpersons, one that mistakes the images of a surreal world politics for reality, never permitting the world within to assert itself. It should not be surprising, then, that almost an entire nation now accepts gibberish as truth and that a state that seems outwardly powerful and vital is actually decayed, rotten, and about to collapse.

Perhaps we are made for oblivion! But if we are not—if in the end we are creatures of authentic longevity—then current U.S. nuclear strategy portends a terrible evil. Rejecting even the remotest tilt toward lucidity, this strategy now proceeds with the abrogation of all remaining barriers between safety and necropolis. On November 28, 1986, the Reagan administration intentionally violated SALT II provisions ending all agreed-upon numerical limits on U.S. and Soviet missiles and on bombers carrying nuclear weapons. And to proceed with its orbiting Maginot Line called Strategic Defense, it is about to terminate illegally our obligations under the Anti-Ballistic Missile (ABM) Treaty.

At the same time, the administration has gone ahead with the development and deployment of such highly accurate, hard-target, multiple-warhead missiles as MX and the Trident II submarine (SLBM) missile—weapons that threaten the Soviet Union with a first-strike attack. Taken together with the president's "countervailing strategy" that calls for policy wherein "U.S. nuclear capabilities must prevail even under the conditions of a prolonged war," these uniquely provocative steps bring us unbearably close to the outer limits of misfortune. In this connection, matters have been worsened considerably by the administration's insistence upon continued nuclear testing and by a very dangerous rejection of General Secretary Mikhail Gorbachev's offer to negotiate an end to all nuclear tests.

Ronald Reagan tells us that we must seek "peace through strength" and that he must be trusted to ensure stable patterns of deterrence. Yet, nuclear war, not peace, is the only possible outcome of a system designed to remove U.S. vulnerability to Soviet nuclear forces while it maintains Soviet susceptibility to our own nuclear strikes. Faced with an adversary that thinks only in starkly caricatural terms and that deploys new nuclear weapons with no plausible deterrence role, Moscow's incentive to strike first may soon prove compelling. While the U.S. response to such preemption would likely be devastating, the Soviets still may calculate that they would suffer less than if they merely waited to be struck first by an America now perceived as veering out of control.

Let us look more closely. What do we see? From Washington and Madison Avenue we witness the endless recitation of fantasy dressed up as fact, the steady naturalistic presentation of an imaginary world rendered believable through repetition: War is peace. A deterrence strategy of "nuclear warfighting" will make us safe from nuclear war. Our European allies must continue to "love the bomb." Civilian populations in America can survive a nuclear war by following government directives for "crisis relocation." Shipping U.S. arms to state sponsors of terrorism will combat anti-American terrorism. Terrorism is counterterrorism.

With its plans to prevail in a protracted nuclear war with the Evil Empire, Washington's nuclear strategy now also resembles an eschatological scheme for the Final Battle. Since all apocalyptic belief is a way of overcoming the terror of uncertainty, this strategy issues forth without regard for truth. Unwilling to be confused by an overwhelming array of facts, the president embraces megadeath in the search for collective immortality. As for telling the American public the full range of his plans for oblivion, there is really no point to disturbing our sleep. Our leaders certainly know best. And (no small matter, to be sure), God is entirely on *our* side.

The Reign of the Herd

Today, not long after the bicentennial year of the Constitution, only schizophrenics seem to be suffering from the truth. With very few exceptions, other Americans are content to live with imposture, even when the policies of their government point fixedly toward the end of the world. Although the truth is scandalous and silence brings very special rewards, the price of complicity with current strategic thinking can only be a permanent rendezvous with extinction.

Where can we turn? Shouted down by leaders who still make verses among the tombs, how can we end the nightmare that masquerades as a prophetic dream? To begin, a curious aspect of nightmares is that they always have a precise topography. A sense of déjà vu is ever present. Let us remember that hundreds of generations have been enfeebled and destroyed by similar falsehoods and that there is still time to learn from their mistakes. Led by those who casually transform truth into politics, we must recall that America displays the same fragility as an individual life, and that only by caring for honesty and courage can we care for our country. Recognizing that the visible earth can be made into ashes and that ashes signify something momentous, we must learn that the most terrible, infinite sighs are not those for lost possessions or disabled career prospects but for something far more grave—for lost arms control opportunities to prevent an entire species from becoming a corpse.

Jorge Luis Borges, the Argentine writer, tells us: "If we attend the theater, we know that, amid the scenery, there are costumed people speaking the words of Shakespeare or Ibsen or Pirandello, which have been put in their mouths. But we accept that these people are not costumed, that the man in the ante-chamber slowly talking to himself of vengeance really is Hamlet, Prince of Denmark."[1] We lose ourselves in the theater. Sadly, we also lose ourselves as playgoers attending the absurd drama of politics. Taking actors as authentic leaders, we allow them to play their parts without interference. Acknowledging its willful suspension of disbelief, America forfeits both its interests and its ideals. *Exeunt omnes.*

It is time for a new cast of characters, for *dramatis personae* who must remain recognizable as performers. Before this can happen, however, the audience must change, transforming itself from passive observer to active director. And this, in turn, requires a wholly new view of the drama itself, one wherein every important cue has its origins in the individual, in the person.

According to Thomas Hobbes's *Leviathan,* "A PERSON is he, *whose words or actions are considered, either as his own, or as representing the words or actions of another man.* . . . When they are considered as his own, then he is called a *Naturall Person:* And when they are considered as representing the words and actions of another, then is he a *Feigned* or *Artificiall person*" (chap. 16). Today's American is only rarely a "Naturall Person." Rather, taking cues from the obligatory discourse of a ritualized public world, he willingly accepts being "Artificiall" as the price of belonging. Rejecting the essential pact between mind and collectivity, he surrenders both himself and his country to defilement and disappearance.

For the moment, the I, as subject, has vanished. For now, the state preempts thought. No one can criticize seriously without first protesting his patriotism. This leads to a reminder of just how fortunate the critic is to live within this state, bringing dishonor upon the criticism and depriving the critic of his work as the author of a decent activity. In the end, the state itself falls victim to this syndrome, its dire circumstances an ironic mirror image of the individuals formerly crushed by governmental machinery or by its unwitting servants.

Who governs in America today? Who speaks for the people? Let us be frank. It is the mass man or woman who celebrates conformity—a creature of the herd with huge ambitions but normally little talent, of skillful oratory but no substance, of great energy (who forever reminds us of the responsibilities of citizenship) but no imagination. For these people the truth must always sing in an undertone and vision must always be unbearable. Significantly, these herd-persons who govern today are not all in public positions. "Politics," as José Ortega y Gasset understood, "is a second-level occupation," and it is in business, in education, in the professions, and even in the arts that many of our governors earn their daily living. Spreading the Constitution's gospel of liberty, justice, and democracy, they are ever ready to lionize the people with balloons and bravado, but when serious matters are at hand, they are quick to exclude all but themselves.

As James Madison feared in *The Federalist No. 10*, addressed to the people of the State of New York two hundred years ago, we have fallen victim to "the violence of faction." As far as the visible composition of this faction is concerned (Madison described such groups that are "adverse to the rights of other citizens" as both majorities and minorities), it is a tiny elite indeed, but when one probes beneath the surface its claims are virtually all-inclusive. Two hundred years after the birth of the Constitution, the herd reigns supreme in America, and—in realization of Madison's apprehensions—"measures are too often decided not according to the rules of justice and the rights of the minor party, but by the superior force of an interested and overbearing majority."

What is the "minor party"? And what is "an interested and overbearing majority"? The minor party is that very small number of citizens who have steadfastly refused to become a herd, those masterless individuals who elect to discover self-worth within themselves and who understand that the people can govern and survive only where they are first allowed to become persons. They are the proprietors of awareness, the authentic heirs of the Founding Fathers who stand at the edges of the grazing herd. People of strong appetites but not of omniverous tastes, they abhor the herd's obscene subjugation of science to the technology of annihilation, a defilement signaling the triumph of fools over reason and of death over life.

The interested and overbearing majority, on the other hand, comprises a burlesque chorus of national cheerleaders, applauding their membership in the larger society as they rummage for meaning in a frenzy of incantations: "We're Number One! We're Number One! Coke is it! Coke is it!" Terrified to imagine themselves as genuine persons, because that would risk vulnerability and insignificance, they are imprisoned by the deception that personal esteem flows meaningfully from an exchange of things for silence. Not surprisingly, in abandoning the obligations of personhood—obligations that make "We the people" a wellspring of promise—we the people have turned from the eighteenth-century possibilities of wisdom and understanding to a desolate panorama of manipulation and belonging.

Our leaders have distanced themselves greatly from the framers of America's Ark of the Covenant. Two hundred years ago the Founding Fathers displayed persistent fear of the mob. In the words of the young Gouverneur Morris: "The mob begin to think and reason, Poor reptiles! . . . They bask in the sun, and ere noon they will bite." Today, our public officials have themselves become part of the mob—not, to be sure, the mob feared by Morris and Alexander Hamilton and Roger Sherman—but a dangerous mob nonetheless.

Who are the members of this mob? Significantly, they are drawn from every corner of the nation. They are rich and poor, black and white, easterner and westerner, educated and uneducated, young and old, Jew and Christian. It is, as so many of the founders feared, a restless mob, but its distinguishing criterion is not poverty and low station. It is the absence of individuality and authentic thought.

How shall we change? How can we identify and select leaders who are not drawn from the mob? In view of the structure of our democratic institutions, there can be only one answer: the mob itself must be transformed. We should return to the Greek belief—a belief that figured importantly among the founders—that persons must be honored for individual worth. In the words of the Athenian statesman, Pericles: "Each single one of our citizens, in all the manifold aspects of life, is able to show himself the rightful lord and owner of his own person, and do this, moreover, with exceptional grace and exceptional versatility." This must be our objective. For now we live not with the Greeks, but with the Hegelian residue. The freedom granted to citizens in America is routinely transmuted into obedience. The state is taken as the true self in which the mere individual must be absorbed.

This is the problem of American foreign policy. All else is shadow. We display incoherence as a nation because we celebrate impotence as persons. Before we reveal collective power we first will have to create a society that nurtures individuality, a society that puts an end to deification of the herd. As the source of a purposeful arms control policy, America can exist only in the shadow of eroded divinities. For now, there is nothing more distasteful for America than to take the path that leads to itself, to its principles, to those purposes for which the authors of the Declaration of Independence pledged "to each other our Lives, our Fortunes, and our sacred Honor." Yet, it is only by taking this path that we can hope to endure. Exploding the closed universe of a foreign policy that indefatigably patronizes itself, we must recognize *ourselves* as the vital starting point for a primary victory as a nation, the victory of not perishing.

For the moment, America needs to despise the Soviet Union because such hatred reaffirms goodness in the United States. The value of our crowd is established dialectically by the evil of another crowd. In a sense, we love to hate the Soviet Union because the Evil Empire guarantees the potency of the Free World, and doubts cast upon the Devil undermine faith in God. Yet, if Americans were able to draw meaning as individuals, there would be no need to cultivate hatred of the Soviet Union. Reconstructing ourselves upon the ruins of crowd theology, we could begin to distance ourselves from loyalties that acknowledge only self-contempt, loyalties that demand hatred and ultimately oblivion. A result of such acknowledgments of imagination could be a new and auspicious U.S. arms control policy, one wherein this country would be liberated from its still-incessant preparations for the Apocalypse.

It follows that before the United States can extricate itself from the predatory embrace of anti-Sovietism, individual Americans will need to discover alternative and more authentic sources of reassurance. To a certain extent this process is already under way, animated by the manifestly contrived dualism offered by our leaders. Yet, the benefits of this process will accrue only to those people who display some measure of political awareness; they will be lost upon the many millions of others who are unmoved by reason.

What is to be done about those people for whom the angst of our time is only the newest form of hubris? Although their politics is a lie, confirming a total disjunction between problem and solution, it is a politics that confers essential ego satisfaction and self-esteem. Where are there appropriate substitute forms of such satisfaction?

To answer these questions we first must understand that the journey from ubiquitous conformity to personhood begins with myth and ends with apprehension. For this journey to succeed, the individual traveling along the route must learn to substitute a system of uncertainties for what he has always believed; he must encourage doubt as a replacement for the comforting woes of clichés and slogans. Induced to live against the grain of our shallow civilization, he must become not only conscious of his singularity but also satisfied with it. Organically separated from the herd, he must embrace the forces that undermine it, forces that offer him a last remaining chance for both meaning and survival.

Overcoming the Herd

What are these forces? They are warnings that disturb confidence in the present moment, that remind us of our imprisonment. Although it is true that as Americans we enjoy a high degree of conventional political freedoms, it is also true that we are, in an even larger sense, captives. Bought off by the promises of participation and production, we have exchanged our capacity to act as individuals for the security of centrally directed automata. Enveloped by the comforting fog of representative government, we have become unwilling to question.

The danger was foreseen by Alexis de Tocqueville, who understood that democracy can produce its own forms of tyranny. He envisioned a benignly operating polity that "hinders, restrains, enervates, stifles and stultifies" by imposing "a network of petty complicated rules." Encouraging the citizen to pursue "petty and banal pleasures" and "to exist in and for himself," democratic "inequality" has set the stage for isolation and passivity.[2] Thus, much of our freedom is an illusion. Indeed, we contribute to our unfreedom as individuals because we don't recognize the extent of our captivity. As Jean-Jacques Rousseau writes in *Emile*: "There is no subjugation so perfect as that which keeps the appearance of freedom, for in that way one captures volition itself."

This brings us to the core of the problem. Bereft of volition, we are almost reflexively obedient, ever ready to defer. Captivated by the delusion of potency and autonomy, we have surrendered to impotence and passionless automatism. Overwhelmed by a burlesque chorus of national cheerleaders, we seek shelter in thoughtlessness. And thoughtlessness is rewarded: it is a "virtue" of the "good citizen." We are reminded of Benedetto Croce, who spoke of the strange "duty" not to think. Invoked in the name of "faith," such duty retards personhood and destroys the nation. Today, even many of the best-educated Americans live in intellectual stupor, tolerating the most colossal inner contradictions for the sake of belonging.

But why such a desperate need to belong? The answer lies in our incapacity to find self-worth within ourselves. And this incapacity, in turn, is nurtured by a society that positively despises self-liberation. Offering a cornucopia of "things" to those who maintain the proper faith, this society is determined to cancel the individual.

The shape of this society has been taking form for many years. Sailing to New York from Dublin in 1907, John Butler Yeats, father of the poet, explained (to the critic and scholar Oliver Elton) the problem of America:

> What America needs to rescue it from its unrest and its deleterious collectivism, is poets and solitaries, men who turn aside and live to themselves and enjoy the luxury of their own feelings and thoughts. Poets here are orators—have to be so, since the public is their paymaster and ready to pay them handsomely if only they will desert their caves of solitary personal feeling and come out and work for their generous and affectionate masters.[3]

These caves (not Plato's, of course) are generally empty. We see in America today an unbridled concern for affluence coexistent with growing expressions of pain. The president of the United States has declared war on drugs, but this war ignores the fundamental questions of cause. Why do so many Americans, who have so much, feel such pain? Why has the successful quest for the "good life" produced so much in the way of unhappiness?

The answer to these questions lies in the continuing dispossession of the individual by the collectivity. We are as free as sheep. But, as Max Stirner asked: "Of what use is it to sheep that no one abridges their freedom of speech? They stick to bleating."[4]

We may turn to Kierkegaard and Nietzsche for guidance. Recognizing the "crowd" as "untruth," Kierkegaard warns in *The Point of View* of the dangers that lurk in submission to multitudes:

> A crowd in its very concept is the untruth, by reason of fact that it renders the individual completely impenitent and irresponsible, or at least weakens

his sense of responsibility by reducing it to a fraction. . . . For "crowd" is
an abstraction and has no hands: but each individual has ordinarily two
hands.

And what is the most degrading crowd of all? The answer is found in *Thus
Spoke Zarathustra*: "State is the name of the coldest of all cold monsters.
. . . The state tells lies . . . and whatever it has it has stolen. Everything
about it is false. . . . All-too-many are born: for the superfluous the state
was invented."

In many respects our oppression as Americans is greater than the
oppression of many other peoples throughout history, including several of
those we describe as "enslaved." Never before has a single society been
more vulnerable to instant disappearance. And never before have
individual members of a society been less effectual in producing a change
that could bring survival. Controlled by a popular press and media that
make thinking almost impossible, individual Americans remain quiet in the
world, living in it tentatively, as if it is not theirs. George Orwell's gloomy
prophecy in *1984* described a world of sophisticated surveillance
techniques and the absence of privacy, a world where Big Brother watched
all but was himself invisible. Ironically, the homogenizing and socializing
effect of television and the electronic media now makes such control
unnecessary. Americans do not need to be kept in line by external political
constraints. As we have been baptized into a singular political theology
from earliest childhood, the possibilities for dissent and heresy are
removed in silence.[5]

By its forfeiture of individuality a whole nation now swallows its
breakfast cereals with a hodgepodge of ready-made opinions, a common
store of images that conceals thoughtlessness in a frenzy of mimicry. The
fact that these opinions are often absurd, humiliating, and deformed—and
always the product of an impoverished imagination—is rarely even
considered. The delusions are comforting. They perpetuate themselves
endlessly and effortlessly.

To change all this and to place America inside the world, we must first
return to ourselves. Hope remains, but it must sing in an undertone.
History must be studied but not in an atmosphere of false greatness. To
grasp the lessons of history, false greatness must first be despised. The
ironies abound. Our capitulation to an all-consuming anti-Sovietism is
made possible by the guarantees of a democratic society. At the same time,
these guarantees need not be the source of our debility as a people and as a
nation. Taken as a starting point for a challenge to current foreign

policies—a point for which they were originally intended—they could contribute to our personal and collective liberation.

A renewed awareness of political freedom, however, is not enough. We first must understand that the rewards of compliance are unsatisfactory, that they are erected upon the deception that self-worth flows freely from personal wealth and unceasing consumption. Such an understanding is already under way, animated by wave after wave of dissatisfaction with the trappings of success.

America beyond the Herd

In one of his books, Borges speaks of a time in the future when politics will disappear and politicians will become either comedians or faith healers, because that is what they are most suited to do. For the moment, however, such a time is not yet at hand, and politicians will have to be taken seriously. What do our politicians say? "Our enemy is the Soviet Union. The Soviet Union is always our enemy. This is an axiom of American foreign policy behavior. It remains beyond question. To subject it to scrutiny is inexcusable. It is blasphemy." Yet, if the Soviet Union did not exist our leaders would have to invent it. Otherwise, to whom would we feel superior? To whom would we impute our frustrations, our weaknesses, and our failures?

At the same time, Sovietophobia draws upon more than a general need for projection. It thrives on certain specific features of the Evil Empire. These features concern Godlessness, the official atheism of another society with enormous military forces. Reminding us of our own mortality (because official Soviet doctrine rejects religion, resurrection, and life after death), the USSR offers us a particular reason for hatred. With this offer our adversary becomes irremediable. Moreover, our enemy in world politics must always be beyond redemption. It cannot be vague and shifting, so protean that there is no passionate focal point of hostility. Indeed, this enemy must be opposed passionately, since it is on the plane of passion that anti-Sovietism draws its very meaning.

For Americans, anti-Sovietism is a convenient strategy for public manipulation. Less an ideology than the absence of an ideal, it is exploited by cynical political elites to displace private anguish and to sustain existing patterns of power. A surreal spectrum of clichés masquerading as serious thought, it shamelessly distorts patriotic fervor. The problem has been recognized with unusual insight by George Konrad, one of Eastern Europe's most distinguished writers:

> In point of fact, it is not ideologies that contend today, nor is it systems like capitalism and communism. Anyone who believes that two systems and two ideologies are pitted against each other today has fallen victim to the secularized metaphysics of our civilization, which looks for a duel between God and Satan in what is, after all, only a game. Russians and Americans—their political classes, that is—circle each other in the ring. Each of the two world heavyweight champions would like to show he is the strongest in the world; they are playing a game with each other whose paraphernalia include nuclear missiles. Yet it is impossible to construct from the Soviet-American conflict an ideological dichotomy along whose axis the values of our continent can be ranged. The antitheses which fill our mental horizon—capitalism versus state socialism, democracy versus totalitarianism, market economy versus planned economy—are forced mythologies which the intelligentsias of East and West either confuse with reality or else, being aware that they are not very precise appellations, seek to square with the real facts.[6]

Our contrived hatred of the Soviet Union also points unambiguously toward war. Left unchecked, it will leave only crushed bones as mementoes.

It is time to sit back and ask some truly fundamental questions: Just what is this ideology (some would call it a theology) of anti-Sovietism getting us? Is it really in our best interests to encourage nuclear war? If we wish to create a promising strategy of arms control, can we really proceed under conditions of a steadily hardening dualism of rivalry with another superpower?

The answers are readily apparent. Accepting the vacant syntax of an endless Cold War as a heroic "responsibility," we have permitted the development of a deformed foreign policy. With such development, America supports "authoritarian" regimes and murderous "freedom fighters" in the interests of "democracy." At the same time, betraying both our traditions and our potentialities, we underwrite a frenzied militarization of the world in the interests of "peace." Not surprisingly, therefore, much of the world now looks upon America as an affliction.

For now, it exists outside the world, discarding reason and dignity in a misdirected search for power. Before America can return to the world, we will need to be liberated from Sovietophobia. This is not to suggest that the Soviet Union is a decently governed society (indeed, it is not) or that there are no legitimate points of competition with the USSR (indeed, there are), but that obsession and caricature in global affairs, as Irangate reveals, are invariably self-defeating.

No one can be safe in America until the market for individual meaning is removed from the sweating palms of the herd, until it belongs to the proprietors of awareness. Rejecting the shamans who would deny us our worth apart from the contrived dynamics of endless international belligerence, we must let others know that we were persons only before our disfigurement by politics and that we surrendered our personhood the moment we tolerated the lies of official thought. Once this becomes known, the suffocating and destructive propositions of the new theology will collapse into an incoherent heap, and genuine arms control will become possible. Before this can happen, however, the prophets of a new culture of personal meaning must be willing to speak the truth. Because the power of awareness and the power of the herd are irreconcilable, a price must be paid for honoring the former. In a world where rewards are bestowed upon those who allow themselves to be used as instruments, the price is possible exile from the good life.

Those who would be unwilling to pay this price are, by definition, unsuited for the task. Terrified to offer abilities on their own terms, they remain marionettes of the buyer, content to do useless work, or, even worse, to degrade the dignity of others. More dangerous by far than those who have been fooled by the new theology, because they understand the deception, they are the virtuous lackeys of public authority, the whores of power for whom integrity will always be incomprehensible.

This problem was perhaps best understood by Hermann Hesse. Identifying the characterless philistine who epitomizes mediocrity, compromise, and servility, Hesse described a creature of strong appetites but no taste, of surface confidence but no ideals, of great zeal and even diligence, but no meaningful aspirations. Today, it is to this mass-man that power belongs. Our only hope for serious arms control lies in those who brood and dream at the edges of power, in those *Phantasiemenschen*, or creative dreamers, of Hesse who would reveal the desolation and fragility of a society directed by solid citizens.

There are other problems. The promise of an informed public must depend upon the stature of the intellect. Yet, even as the cerebrum is liberating itself, the intellect falls into disrepute. In the United States, in particular, receptivity to bold, threatening ideas has never been high. But the problems are not insurmountable. If they were, the entire enterprise of seeking a transformation of personal and political life would be a cruel hoax, undermining the remnants of happiness without any purpose. Acknowledging the connections between our current arms control policy and the manipulation of false needs, we can begin to understand the causes of our vulnerability—causes that lie in suppressed individuality and that foreshadow oblivion. Rejecting the hollow rewards of complicity, we can move beyond the transparent pantomime of Soviet-American rivalry to a new world politics of dignity and hope.

The Triumph of Personhood

Speaking of humankind as a whole, the poet Rimbaud once complained that "we are not in the world." So it is with America today. We stand, as a nation, outside the world, drawn to our final rendezvous with extinction because we steadfastly have refused to become persons. How much treasure, how much science, how much labor and planning, how many centuries have we ransacked to make possible the grotesque carnival of nuclear war? Frightened by the stubborn fact of death, how much longer can we extend our self-destructive denials of mortality from individual to collective levels?

The answers cause pain. Our worship of a particular herd, the state, which allows our leaders to maintain a disastrous course, flows from an unwillingness to seek meaning within ourselves. But by transmuting freedom into obedience, we have created a false god before whom millions (or even billions) will be made to pass through fire. In the end, if we are to endure, our sense of self-worth will have to come from the inside. Recognizing that we must die and that our mortality cannot be undone through the acquisition of wealth and influence over others, we could begin to celebrate a new life-affirming ethos of personal value and private meaning—an ethos determined by courage and imagination rather than by Washington and Madison Avenue. Only then could we return to purposeful diplomacy and a safer course as a nation.

Where it is misunderstood, as is the case in America, affluence can be a terrible misfortune. Taken as a payback for loyalty to the herd and for renunciation of self, it crushes individuality and sanctifies the state. In the end, such privilege permits governments to proceed with policies that can bring only humiliation and omnicide.

In our country privilege has always been misunderstood. H. G. Wells, in *The Future in America*, noted that "the typical American has no 'sense of state.' " By this he did not mean that this person is not passionately and vigorously patriotic, but that the connections between private searches for affluence and public authority processes are unknown. Said Wells: "I mean that he has no perception that his business activities, his private employments, are constituents in a large collective process; that they affect other people and the world forever, and cannot, as he imagines, begin and end with him."[7]

As the foundation of U.S. arms control policy, obsessive anti-Sovietism is a prescription for necropolis, time-dishonored, long-beaten, routed from survival by its own history of crimes and errors. But before we can build upon new and more auspicious foundations, Americans will have to cultivate Wells's "sense of state," an awareness that certain forms of personal prosperity are always the result of a bargain and that the costs of this bargain will be both terrible and universal. For now, such cultivation lies beyond the pale of the possible, hindered by the ready availability of wealth to some who keep silent. It will become possible, perhaps, only when economies fail and promises are no longer kept.

What, exactly, must we cultivate today? First, we will have to pay close attention to the *education* of persons. Discarding current emphases on vocationalism and career training, we must aim at the development of human beings rather than citizens. As Rousseau further observes in *Emile*, a masterpiece of educational reform that has yet to be taken seriously:

> The natural man lives for himself; he is the unit, the whole, dependent only on himself and on his like. The citizen is but the numerator of a fraction, whose value depends upon the whole, that is, on the community. Good social institutions are those best fitted to make a man unnatural, to exchange his independence for dependence, to merge the unit in the group.[8]

He does not urge the abandonment of community. Rather, Rousseau understands that true community can never be built upon "numerators," upon people who are afraid to become themselves.

In choosing a path to education, "you must make your choice between the man and the citizen, you cannot train both." Life is the trade Rousseau wishes us all to be taught. When the student leaves his teachers, "he will be neither a magistrate, a soldier, nor a priest; he will be a man." This is the kind of education that must be explored further if America is to be returned to itself and arms control is to become a reality.

Second, we must also look at *work*. "All of his life long," says Rousseau, "man is imprisoned by our institutions," and today there is no place more confining than the workplace. In America, even the more fortunate workers typically are reduced to machine tenders or paper shufflers, and high-status professionals are reminded that their value lies in being members of the team. Not surprisingly, individuals only rarely envision the larger purpose of their work efforts, a condition that splinters all residual sense of self and mandates withdrawal to the herd.

The results, as we have seen, are ominous. Ground down by both education and the workplace, Americans have grown accustomed to belonging. As feelings of self-worth are established according to the standards (reaffirmed by the family) of these primary institutions, the lessons are not treated lightly. When the state demands similar and even greater expressions of loyalty, it is bound not to be disappointed. Prepared in the nonpolitical spheres of home, school, and job for the obligations of citizenship, we quickly learn to understand that without cooperation there is only estrangement and failure. Compared to the distant threat of a nuclear war, such personal losses are much more terrifying.

Americans are "free," if by freedom we mean only a relation to the political sphere. But what is the value of political freedom if our social institutions imprison our *selves* and portend oblivion? This question was raised by the American transcendentalist Henry David Thoreau more than one hundred years ago:

> America is said to be the arena on which the battle of freedom is to be fought; but surely it cannot be freedom in a merely political sense that is meant. Even if we grant that the American has freed himself from a political tyrant, he is still the slave of an economical and moral tyrant. Now that the republic—the *res-publica*—has been settled, it is time to look after the *res-private*—the private state—to see, as the Roman senate charged its consuls, *"ne quid res-PRIVATA detrimenti caperet,"* that the *private* state receive no detriment.[9]

"Do we call this the land of the free?" asked Thoreau. "We quarter our gross bodies on our poor souls, till the former eat up all the latter's substance."[10] Thoreau had ample reason for pessimism, as we still have today, but it is still too early to despair.

To survive for another two hundred years, arms control is imperative. And this means that we the people must aim at a realization of the unique and inquiring self in harmony with all others. Rescued from our captivity in the prison of the majority, we then might accept our emancipation from a disastrous struggle with the Soviet Union. When this happens, we the people will become truly free, displaying the highest forms of patriotism envisioned by the Founding Fathers.

For the members of the Philadelphia Convention, the true patriot was not the smug servant of naked emperors. Rather, it was he who would remain willing to measure his leaders against the immutable standards of reason and a higher law. Challenged by the banal syntax of nuclear mandarins who speak only when there is a pretext for convulsions, we the people now must understand that it was "to form a more perfect Union" that our Constitution was invented. It was not invented to turn this union into a cinder.

The minor party of *The Federalist No. 10* is the irreconcilable enemy, not of the people who seek communion with all other peoples, but of the "overbearing majority" that masquerades as a nation. Indeed, this minor party (Thoreau termed it the "wise minority" in his essay on "Civil Disobedience") is the indispensable condition of every nation that seeks to endure. Without it the herd may call itself "We the people," but the anesthetized minions who feel nothing of importance must inevitably disappear.

To be effective, arms control must rest upon a solid foundation of citizens who have agreed to become persons. Without widespread self-affirmation in America, the inhabitants of our country will continue to draw meaning as a mob, a tragic condition that will sustain false ideologies and accelerate strategic competition. In such a society, leaders can never take thinking seriously, and cooperative international relations must always be weakness. It follows that such a society promises only oblivion.

Today, the false dichotomy of East and West has made both compassion and clear thinking improbable. Yet, it is still not too late to respect the Constitution and to rescue arms control. Tired of a majority that thinks only in clichés, we the people must now leave ideological and strategic warfare to defeated politicians. Recalling humankind's established cycle of rise and fall, we must still learn that America displays the same mortality as an individual life. Only by caring for ourselves as persons can we the people "secure the blessings of Liberty to ourselves and our posterity."

Notes

[1] Jorge Luis Borges, *Seven Nights*, trans. Eliot Weinberger (New York: New Directions, 1984), pp. 12–13.

[2] Alexis de Tocqueville, *Democracy in America*, trans. George Lawrence (Garden City, NY: Doubleday, 1969), p. 692.

[3] See Marc Pachter, ed., *Abroad in America: Visitors to the New Nation, 1776–1914*, pub. in association with the National Portrait Gallery, Smithsonian Institution (Reading, MA: Addison-Wesley, 1976), p. 268.

[4] Max Stirner, *The Ego and His Own: The Case of the Individual against Authority*, trans. Steven T. Byington (New York: Libertarian Book Club, 1963), first published in 1845. A formidable assault on authoritarianism in the middle of the nineteenth century, Stirner's book represented a "third force"—neither a defender of the theological or monarchical state nor a supporter of models offered by liberals and socialists. Conceived as *the* rejoinder to Hegel, it argued that all freedom is essentially self-liberation—an argument that influenced the writing of Henrik Ibsen.

[5] For an interesting work on the homogenizing effects of television and on the manner in which they retard personhood see Joshua Meyrowitz, *No Sense of Place: The Impact of Electronic Media on Social Behavior* (New York: Oxford University Press, 1985). The situational analysis offered by Meyrowitz describes how the electronic media affect social behavior not through the intrinsic power of their messages but by "reorganizing the social settings in which people interact and by weakening the once strong relationship between physical place and social place" (p. ix).

[6] George Konrad, *Antipolitics*, trans. Richard E. Allen (New York: Harcourt Brace Jovanovich, 1984), p. 12.

[7] See Pachter, ed., *Abroad in America*, p. 298.

[8] This and the subsequent citations from Rousseau are taken from Book 1 of *Emile*, trans. Barbara Foxley (London: Dent, 1964). *Emile* was first published in 1762.

[9] Taken from Thoreau's "Life without Principle," which appeared originally in the *Atlantic Monthly* for October 1863. Cited from Perry Miller, ed., *The American Transcendentalists* (Garden City, NY: Doubleday, 1957), pp. 324–25.

[10] Ibid., p. 325.

Morality, Arms Control, and Strategic Defenses

ALVIN M. WEINBERG
JACK N. BARKENBUS

THE INTERMINABLE OUTPOURING of books and articles dealing with the immorality of nuclear deterrence is testimony to the inability of the strategic community to convince others that nuclear deterrence constitutes the best of all possible worlds. Church groups, philosophers, humanists, and others continue to express extreme discomfort at having to ensure national security by holding out the prospect of a nuclear holocaust. That such critics have yet to unite on a distinctly moral, yet feasible, alternative to nuclear deterrence is also evident. Are morality and national security simply irreconcilable in this age? Few of us are content to admit to a deterministic irreconcilability, and hence the search for a better world continues.

It is surprising, in the midst of this virtual avalanche of concern and opinion,[1] that more attention has not been paid to the morality of a defense-dominated world—one in which passive and active defenses combine to ensure national survival in the face of a nuclear attack. One would think that with Ronald Reagan's fervent espousal of such a world, intense scrutiny would follow. Surely the political and the technical aspects of the president's program for achieving such a world—the Strategic Defense Initiative (SDI)—have received sufficient attention. The morality

37

of his program and of alternative means to achieve defense dominance, however, have been neglected save for specious concerns over the "militarization of space."

The moral case for a defense-dominated world deserves further exploration. President Reagan's approach to achieving defense dominance need not, and indeed should not, be the exclusive focus for this exploration. This paper constitutes an attempt to produce a framework for further discussion and investigation of this compelling strategic alternative.

An Explanation of Philosophical Ethics

Joseph Nye, in *Nuclear Ethics*, explains the ethical principles that underlie the debate on nuclear deterrence.[2] According to him, two major and contrasting principles have dominated Western ethical thinking for the past century or more. The first, which goes by the formidable name of deontology, finds its roots in the ethics of Immanuel Kant. This principle holds that an act is moral, right, and acceptable if it conforms to certain prior rules of behavior, quite apart from the consequences that result from the act. Thus, in order not to violate one of God's commandments, a thorough-going deontologist would not kill an assailant even if, by not killing the assailant, he risks losing his own life. A thoroughgoing pacifist is an example of a complete deontologist.

The other, contrasting view is called consequentialism and traces its origin to the utilitarian philosophers Jeremy Bentham and John Stuart Mill. In this view, an act is moral if the consequences of that act are moral, quite apart from whether the act itself is moral as judged by other standards of behavior. Thus, a thoroughgoing consequentialist would condone killing in self-defense, even though this act breaks one of God's commandments. These examples overdraw the distinction between deontological and consequentialist reasoning. In practice, the deontologist always considers consequences, just as the consequentialist considers rules. By and large, the arguments over the morality of nuclear deterrence have been either predominantly deontological or predominantly consequentialist.

Nye introduces a third moral dimension: motives. For him an act that obeys prior rules of behavior and leads to morally acceptable consequences still may be morally unacceptable if it is basely motivated. Of course, the judgment as to whether a motive is base in itself depends upon the prior commitments and values of the judge. Many Americans still regard our involvement in Vietnam to have been motivated by a morally unassailable principle, the defense of freedom. Others, however, might claim that the distinction between Diem's regime and the Communists was not as morally unambiguous as apologists for U.S. intervention claimed it to be, and therefore our motives were suspect.

The Morality of Offensive Deterrence, Disarmament, and Defense

Despite the complexities and endless elaborations that accompany the application of these ethical distinctions to security policies, the case for the morality of alternative security positions can be stated forthrightly. A policy of disarmament is impeccable in terms of deontology and motives. Its failings, however, in consequentialist terms are so severe in this age of superpower rivalry that relatively few groups and individuals seriously advocate this path.

The moral strength of offensive deterrence, built on the assurance of nuclear retaliation, is summarized in the assertion: "Deterrence by fear of massive destruction has prevented, and will prevent, nuclear war; since the threat of a nuclear holocaust prevents the holocaust, the threat is moral. Any posture that undermines deterrence makes nuclear war more likely, and, in consequentialist terms, is immoral." Although an offensive standoff may satisfy one moral criterion (it deters war), the means by which it achieves that end (by a threat to kill millions of innocents) is morally unacceptable.

A policy of defense-dominance, in theory, can resolve the deontological moral dilemmas associated with threatening massive numbers of innocent citizens. A strong defensive standoff deters war by denying an aggressor any hope of achieving his military objectives. Defensive postures, therefore, deter war without threatening immoral acts. Consequently, strategic analysts, no less than philosophers of ethics, might be expected to embrace the defensive posture. That this has not happened—indeed, most discussions of morality and security ignore the defensive posture entirely—can be attributed in large part to the following:

1) Some strategists fear that the defensive posture which deters by denial of aggressive intent is not as powerful a deterrent as is the fear of nuclear retaliation.[3]

2) There is widespread belief that there is not and cannot be an effective defense against nuclear weapons. The image of nuclear weapons as "destroyers of civilization" or "ultimate weapons" is strong. Obviously, moral issues are moot if a defensive posture cannot be achieved technically.[4]

3) The prospect of either superpower willingly substituting defenses for offensive strength is labeled utopian and not worthy of further investigation.[5]

4) The potential application of defenses is frequently derided as a technical fix to a political problem.[6] Certainly, the construction of defenses in addition to increasing offensive weaponry and intense political rivalry is a futile and potentially dangerous initiative; such a policy, however, constitutes just one possible course of action.

5) Many fear that the actual transition from offensive-dominance to defensive-dominance will be fraught with danger and instability.[7] We believe that if such a transition can be structured carefully, either through successive unilateral moves or through a cooperative venture, as discussed at Reykjavik, the transition need not entail great risks.

None of these arguments justifies the omission of a defensive world in discussions of morality in the nuclear world. What we intend to describe is a defensive posture, and a path to it, that meets these objections and retains the moral superiority that so many philosophers find appealing.

Properties of a Defense-Dominated World: The Cheating Threshold

The defense-dominated world that we envisage was first proposed by Herman Kahn in 1967.[8] In this world the offensive warheads on each side have been reduced to what we call the cheating threshold (CT), that is, the number of weapons that can be produced and sequestered clandestinely, given advanced national and multinational verification capabilities. The determination of an acceptable CT would be the subject of intense superpower examination and discussion.

As Jonathan Schell has noted in his contemplation of such a world, the intensiveness of inspection and the capability of defenses are intimately related.[9] If the CT can be kept low through intrusive, yet acceptable, inspection efforts, then defensive capabilities can be built to relatively modest levels. On the other hand, if verification is flawed, either because of inherent difficulties or because of political requirements, then defensive capabilities have to be relatively substantial. In other words, defenses should be constructed to match the challenge posed by a specific CT.

Our belief is that the superpowers would prefer a relatively low CT, thereby reducing the expense of building very complex defenses. This would put a considerable burden on verification capabilities, a burden disproportionately shared given the openness of American society and the closed and secretive nature of the Soviet Union. Assuming intrusive verification methods—such as large-scale investigations carried out by International Atomic Energy Agency (IAEA) inspectors, and real-time satellite reconnaissance—we suspect that an achievable CT level may be as low as a few hundred nuclear warheads. That may be somewhat optimistic given the ongoing miniaturization of nuclear weapons and the growing indistinguishability of nuclear and conventional delivery systems. Yet, the combination of innovative counting methods and a rigorous accounting of fissile material production may place severe limits upon the ability to cheat. Once again, if such optimistic estimates of the CT are not realizable, the capabilities of the defenses will have to be enhanced.

The defense deployed by each side is what might be called "magnificent," that is, a system good enough essentially to neutralize any attack, whether against populations (countervalue) or weapons (counterforce). By definition, this system then can reduce the a priori probability of penetration to, say, 1 percent or less; an attack of 200 warheads therefore would result, a priori, in two warheads landing on target. This number is uncertain; it might be as high as ten warheads or as low as zero.

The term magnificent refers to performance characteristics and not to the technical nature of the defense in isolation. In other words, a sophisticated multilayered defense system employing exotic kill mechanisms (lasers, particle beams, etc.) cannot be considered magnificent if it must contend with an attack of 10,000 warheads and another 90,000 decoys. Conversely, relatively unsophisticated defenses may be termed magnificent in the face of a 200-warhead attack. Because the performance of the defense is fundamentally dependent upon the nature of the challenge posed by the offense, we are surprised that more advocates of defense are not enthusiastic supporters of arms control.

When offenses are set at the CT levels described above, space-based and boost-phase defenses may be superfluous. Midcourse and terminal interceptors that are ground-based and that utilize kinetic-kill vehicles (KKVs) or "smart" rocks then should be able to do the job. The elimination of space-based kill mechanisms would reduce both system vulnerability and system expense as well as have salutary political effects.

We now take up the degree to which magnificent defenses coupled with offense reduced to the CT level meet the moral criteria set forth by Nye: means, motives, and consequences.

Means

The erection of defenses in and of themselves is deontologically neutral; that is, defenses can be erected for opposing reasons, which cannot be distinguished in the absence of other signals. Defenses can be used solely to protect the health and welfare of a nation's citizens— Switzerland's extensive civil defense effort is a prime example. No one would question that Switzerland's efforts are deontologically pure. However, one also can use defenses to enhance one's own offensive capabilities. Defenses can be viewed as a shield behind which one is free to strike with impunity. Some observers in the United States think that the civil defense effort in the Soviet Union is designed to serve this latter purpose (a "damage-limiting" role for defenses to complement offensive purposes). Hence, the very same action—civil defense—can be seen in different lights.

Not surprisingly, President Reagan's SDI has occasioned similar ambiguity. The president stresses that the United States seeks no strategic advantage through the development and deployment of defenses. General Secretary Mikhail Gorbachev claims the opposite and goes even further, accusing the Americans of seeking to deploy new offensive strike weapons in the guise of benign defenses.

The construction of defenses by themselves, therefore, can either be moral or immoral. Obviously, we must probe the motives for the construction to determine inherent morality. On the other hand, a posture in which both sides acquire magnificent defense and in which neither side can threaten the other with nuclear disaster is clearly morally impeccable.

Motives

We must tread carefully in attributing particular motives to policy decisions. Decision makers are all too eager to portray or publicize their conclusions in moral terms even when they are clearly the result of political bargaining, infighting, and ulterior motives. Rhetoric, therefore, is an insufficient guide to the determination of motives. Actions speak louder than words.

In an atmosphere of mistrust, motives are best assessed by the determination of capabilities. We attribute pure motives to the Swiss civil defense effort because, among other reasons, the Swiss have not concurrently developed strong offensive capabilities, as the Soviets have. Similarly, defensive systems that possess dual-use (offensive-defensive) capabilities cannot be judged moral. Even though the motives of the decision maker implementing such systems may be pure, the current decision maker cannot speak for the next generation of leaders who will inherit the system.

While capabilities must be the primary measurement of motives, they need not be the sole measurement. Important policies can be adopted that are consistent with and reinforce the benign nature of capabilities. The declaration of a no-first-use policy, for example, would be consistent with a morally acceptable defensive posture.

The concurrent reduction of offenses to the CT and the construction of magnificent defenses would be a powerful demonstration of pure motives during the transition to defensive strength. A careful and cooperative structuring of the offensive build-down and the defense buildup, in terms of both force structure and timing, can provide the assurance needed for proceeding. We believe such an approach would be clearly moral from a deontological perspective.

Consequences

The moral case for today's offensive deterrence is consequentialist. We have witnessed a peace of unprecedented duration among the major states of the world, and we usually attribute this to the existence of nuclear weapons. The fact that the Soviets and their allies have chosen not to use their superiority in conventional offensive forces to make territorial gains in Western Europe can only be attributed, in the view of many, to the willingness of the United States to threaten the Soviets with nuclear destruction. This point is important. It means that offensive deterrence not only prevents a nuclear collision between the superpowers but also is designed to assist in the containment of Soviet aggression worldwide. Alternatives to offensive deterrence must be judged against both the national security and foreign policy objectives of the United States.

The consequentialist case for offensive deterrence is not unassailable. No one can prove that nuclear weapons are the reason that peace has prevailed over the past forty years. Although the Soviets enjoy conventional superiority in Europe, a very high price for invasion would be exacted and the outcome would be in doubt even if nuclear weapons were not used. And even if we erase such doubts, there is no guarantee, just because nuclear deterrence has worked for forty years, that it can continue to work in the future. The possibility of nuclear war occurring through miscalculation or blundering—the probability of which increases with the extent to which nuclear deterrence is invoked—is finite, and the consequences of the failure of deterrence would be catastrophic. For all of these reasons even proponents of nuclear deterrence are rarely sanguine about the consequences of relying upon offensive deterrence indefinitely. Nevertheless, the burden of proof, in actual policy discussion, is inevitably placed upon those advocating deviation from accepted nuclear policy. It is necessary, therefore, that we present the consequentialist case for magnificent defenses and CT offense as if nuclear deterrence functioned as its true believers claim it does.

The movement from offensive deterrence to magnificent defense and CT offense, as noted earlier, changes the basis for nuclear security from assured retaliation to denial of military objectives. In the CT posture, maintenance of peace still depends to some extent upon fear of retaliation (one cannot guarantee levels of defensive performance),[10] but the mechanism that predominates is uncertainty—that is, uncertainty in the mind of the would-be aggressor as to whether any of his weapons will be effective.

We could argue that even in the relatively undefended world of today uncertainty exists: Will the president really order a retaliatory nuclear strike? Will the missiles actually come close to the intended target? But these uncertainties depend on failures of the system to work as planned, and we generally plan on it working as intended. By contrast, the uncertainty in the CT case as to whether a first strike will succeed only operates if the opponent's system works as planned, not if it fails. Thus, uncertainty dominates the CT posture to a far greater extent than it dominates offensive deterrence.

Would the prospect of launching a futile offense against a magnificent defense actually deter nuclear aggression, in the absence of any credible threat of immediate retaliation? There is no answer. We would think, however, that if defenses clearly overwhelm the offensive threat, the potential aggressor would perceive little advantage in instigating nuclear war. Consequently, a shift to defense dominance should be equally effective in preventing nuclear war.

Nuclear deterrence has been used not only to prevent nuclear war but also to contain Soviet aggression. If the Soviet Union and the United States construct magnificent defenses around their own territories, our ability to threaten retaliation for a Soviet incursion of Western Europe or elsewhere would be seriously compromised. To the extent, then, that our nuclear deterrent supports our foreign policy, a move to strong defenses would have detrimental consequences.

The policy of extended nuclear deterrence is, and has been for some time, fraught with problems. Can we credibly expect U.S. presidents to launch a nuclear attack in defense of Berlin or Hamburg? Is the stationing of nuclear weapons in Europe prudent or an invitation to blunder and disaster? If the threat of nuclear annihilation were the only means available to prevent worldwide Soviet aggression, then we would be forced to remain wedded to extended deterrence. When other means exist for dealing with the Soviet threat, however, we should not prefer to rely indefinitely upon extended nuclear deterrence regardless of its marginal cost savings or the preference of European and other allied governments for the status quo.

These means include both technical and political measures. Technically, advances in conventional weaponry (primarily precision-guided missiles) hold the potential for creating a nonnuclear force able to counter the advantages in manpower and weaponry now held by the Soviets. The deployment of these weapons, combined with the Europeans' greater commitment to their own defense, can provide a viable alternative to a nuclear defense. European states also might seek to develop missile defenses similar to that in the United States. The defense of the Continent may be more technically and economically feasible than that of the United States because of its relatively small area.

Greater insurance could be achieved through political breakthroughs. Negotiations over the defensive transition also might involve demilitarization on both sides of the European front. Such a development could be accompanied by agreements binding each side to no-first-use and no-first-attack policies. In other words, the move to defenses might be directly predicated upon a political thaw in European affairs.

Is the CT Posture Technically Feasible? One cannot argue with the proposition that the smaller the offensive threat, the more effective a given defense will be. Unfortunately, we can hardly give reliable estimates as to the effectiveness of a complex system which is still under development.

A George C. Marshall Institute study has concluded that a three-layer system using only KKVs would be 93 percent effective against a threat of 11,200 warheads accompanied by 90,000 decoys, and 99 percent effective against this threat if midcourse discrimination between decoys and reentry vehicles (RVs) worked.[11] The defensive system envisaged consists of 11,000 space-based KKVs aimed at boost phase; 10,000 exoatmospheric reentry-vehicle interceptor subsystems (ERIS), ground launched and aimed at midcourse; and 3,000 terminal nonnuclear interceptors. According to the Marshall report, the boost-phase interceptors are 76 percent efficient; thus, the bottom two layers of defense must deal with a threat cloud of 2,688 RVs and 21,600 decoys. Since 7 percent of the total threat penetrate, some 784 RVs survive the bottom two layers. This amounts to 29 percent of the threat presented to those layers penetrating.

If we assume a CT of 200 RVs plus 1,607 decoys, the threat cloud presented to the bottom two layers in the CT posture is less than one-tenth of the threat envisioned in the Marshall report, even without boost-phase kill. We therefore would presume that the Marshall defensive system, even without the space-based layer, should be much more efficient than the 93 percent quoted above—possibly ten times better. In that event, instead of 29 percent of the missiles coming through, only 3 percent, or around 6 missiles, would penetrate. This assumes no midcourse decoy discrimination. If this can be achieved, then the two-layer system should be very much better.

The Marshall study estimates the total capital cost of the three-layer systems at 121×10^9, with the cost of the layers being in the ratio of 4:2:1. Thus, the bottom two layers are estimated to cost about 52×10^9, with the operating costs at around $4 to 6×10^9 per year. We are unable to assess the correctness either of the Marshall estimates or of our extrapolations, and we are aware that Dr. R. Garwin, in unpublished notes, has disputed the Marshall results. What we would insist upon is our major point—that by reducing the threat to the bottom two layers of defense tenfold, we have greatly improved the technical feasibility of the two-layer defense. Further work must determine how good a two-layer defense actually can be.

Several important implications follow from this basic consideration. First, the argument offered by C. L. Glaser that defensive postures are more unstable than offensive ones loses force when defense becomes extremely good.[12] Strategists have argued that naked offensive confrontations become more stable as the number of weapons grows. At 10,000 warheads, one hardly worries about 500 clandestine warheads; at a ten-warhead standoff, 500 additional clandestine warheads would be alarming. By like token, a poor defense, even in the CT posture, is less stable than an extremely good defense: a 50 percent defense, which would allow 100 warheads to penetrate, is no match for a 95-percent defense which allows only ten warheads. On the other hand, a 99.9 percent defense, allowing .2 of a warhead to penetrate, is essentially as good as a ten times better defense (99.99 percent effective), which would allow .02 warheads. Thus, there is a symmetry here: overwhelming offense is stable against expansion of offense, and overwhelming defense is stable against expansion of defense. Moreover, overwhelming defense is stable against expansion of offense so long as the expanded offense is not too large. For example, a defense good enough to kill 99.9 percent of a 200-missile attack is still robust against, say, a 400-missile attack, although it may not be robust against 10,000 missiles.

At this very low level of offense and overwhelming defense the difference between area defense and hard-point defense should not be significant. Usually this ambiguity leads to crisis instability: the first striker, with his magnificent defense, is able to thwart his opponents' ragged retaliation. But because our postulated defense on both sides is so good relative to the offense, there is now hardly any difference between a first strike and retaliation. For example, were a 200-warhead force to lose, say, six warheads to an all-out attacker, the retaliation of 194 warheads is hardly less formidable than the initial attack of 200 warheads. The difference between a first and a retaliatory strike is too small to give credible incentive for a first strike.

The defensive CT posture we have outlined is schematic. As described in the Marshall Institute report, it is aimed at neutralizing only ICBMs. This would be a great step forward, but in the final analysis it is insufficient. Eventually we would hope that defenses against cruise missiles, SLBMs, and even tactical nuclear weapons could be achieved. And we would hope as well that adoption of the CT posture by the superpowers eventually would be accompanied by similar reductions in other offensive capabilities, along with employment of compensating defensive systems.

Among these, civil defense must not be neglected. The cost of a system capable of protecting the entire United States in terminal phase clearly would be high. However, not all of the country needs terminal protection; more than 90 percent of the U.S. population live on less than 8 percent of the area. Thus, to protect the remaining 10 percent, civil rather than terminal defense might be deployed, probably at much lower cost than that of a full terminal active defense.

Is the CT Strategy Politically Attainable? We are an enormous distance away from the realization of magnificent defenses and nuclear arsenals at a CT level. The superpower meeting at Reykjavik, however, indicated that the idea of reducing offensive strength to the cheating threshold is not just fanciful illusion. At least we are now talking about very deep cuts, to levels where deployment of defenses becomes not entirely unreasonable.

Skeptics frequently claim that if the superpowers were able politically to negotiate a defensive transition, defenses would be superfluous since the two parties also would be able politically to negotiate a general disarmament.[13] Yet, as we have argued, disarmament is not a preferable alternative to magnificent defenses. The potential for cheating exists, and without the insurance provided by magnificent defenses even the buildup of very small nuclear arsenals would be extremely destabilizing. Moreover, maintaining and rationalizing a state of vulnerability could be very difficult even when both superpowers agree to disarm. In short, defenses are necessary to provide a sufficient degree of assurance; and this measure of assurance would not only function when arms have been reduced to the cheating threshold but also would be crucial in getting the superpowers to agree to deep cuts in the first place. Defenses, therefore, are not an alternative to disarmament but the sine qua non for disarmament.

What would impel the superpowers to move to the defense-dominant world we have described? A fundamental rapprochement between them certainly would be a strong impetus, but we cannot predicate the achievement of a defense-dominated world on this basis. There is a glimmer of evidence, however, that each superpower is beginning to view its own bulging nuclear arsenal as more of a burden than an asset.

Congress has put a hold on the Reagan administration's military buildup, claiming that continued increases in spending are unconscionable in a time of tight budgetary constraints. The Soviets, moreover, have even greater economic incentive to end the arms race.

The increasing accuracy of nonnuclear weaponry means that there are advancing technologies that, in some ways, can substitute for nuclear weapons in deterrent and military applications. As important as economic and technical factors are, perhaps the most significant development has been the devaluation of nuclear weapons as political symbols of prestige and strength. Because of shifting public opinion it now appears that history will judge superpower leaders not on the extent to which they have added to the nuclear stockpiles but rather on how they have reduced such stockpiles. President Reagan, in some manner, must match the "peace offensive" being played very skillfully by General Secretary Gorbachev. There is considerable incentive for each side to move toward reducing its arsenals to CT levels, even in the absence of a fundamental political reconciliation between the superpowers.

What we are suggesting, therefore, is that the path to a defensive-dominant world be established not on the basis of artificial timetables or advanced technology breakthroughs but rather on the pace of offensive arms reductions—the faster the pace of arms reductions, the earlier the deployment of defenses. A number of studies have been completed recently describing theoretical paths to increasing levels of defense that avoid crisis instability.[14]

Assuming a negotiated transition, the superpowers might embark upon an initial arms reduction phase in which defenses would be permitted to ensure the invulnerability of retaliatory forces. During this phase, peace is still maintained through fear of retaliation, although at levels lower than are currently deployed. Area defenses would be permitted only when the superpowers meet carefully negotiated and significant levels of arms reduction. We would argue that this phased process is both arms-control stable and crisis stable since retaliatory forces on both sides are fully defended at every stage. City defense is mutual and symmetric so that a first striker's cities are no less or no more vulnerable to a second strike than are his opponents' cities. Eventually, when the CT has been reached, magnificent defense dominates: both cities and missiles are fully protected.

This phased deployment of point and area defenses responds to the fears expressed by the Soviets over President Reagan's SDI. As noted earlier, if the ultimate CT posture depends only on "smart" rocks and on land-based defense, then space-based, boost-phase technologies are irrelevant and can be sacrificed with little loss. This does not apply to space-based assets required for detection of launch or the discrimination of decoys, but it would apply to the so-called space-strike weapons which seem to be the central concern of the Soviets.

If Gorbachev's plea for nuclear disarmament is to be believed, the Soviets should have little problem with what we have proposed. We should anticipate more political opposition in fact from our own military and from our European allies, as we are asking them to accept a radically different basis upon which to assure national security. Such opposition must be addressed forthrightly and the advantage of such a shift carefully explained.

Conclusion

Polls indicate that the American public strongly supports arms control and the move to strategic defenses.[15] Obviously, the public has not paid attention to conventional strategic thought in this country that claims the United States can have either arms control or strategic defenses, but not both in combination. We believe that the public desires can be satisfied if the movement to defense dominance is not carried out precipitously and if the path described by us is followed.

The proposal just outlined is deontologically sound since our defense is no longer predicated upon the harm we could do to others. Drastically reduced offenses leave little doubt concerning the motives behind the deployment of defenses. Capabilities for mischief are reduced further by the elimination of space-based defenses that could possess potential offensive capabilities. In consequentialist terms our proposal is clearly superior to that advocated by proponents of disarmament. Whether our proposal is superior to offensive deterrence in consequentialist terms is admittedly arguable but, we believe, ultimately persuasive.

Regardless of its consequentialist virtues, we think that the demise of offensive deterrence, at least as we know it today, is inevitable. Its continuation is based upon two unpalatable truths:

1) Stability and security require that each side bares its throat to potential catastrophic harm; and

2)   The actual prevention of harm is dependent not only upon the wisdom, rationality, and capabilities of one side's military and civilian leaders but also upon those of the adversary; mistakes, advertent or inadvertent, simply cannot occur.

Those individuals and groups most disturbed with these truths have correctly questioned their morality, but, unfortunately, they have been far less successful in describing how, in the absence of nuclear weapons, we can devise a moral policy to meet the acknowledged Soviet threat. A strong case can be made that, rather than demonstrating an unflagging and visceral opposition to strategic defense in general, as opposed to President Reagan's SDI in particular, they would be well served by exploring how the deployment of defenses can be combined with arms reduction.

Notes

[1] George H. Quester, "New Challenges to Deterrence: Why Now?" *Arms Control Today* 16, no. 9 (December 1986): 23–25. Quester provides a long list of books, published since 1983, concerning ethics and nuclear deterrence. Although long, the list is incomplete, as authors and publishers continue the outpouring.

[2] Joseph Nye, *Nuclear Ethics* (New York: Free Press, 1986).

[3] Josef Joffe, "Nuclear Weapons, No First Use, and European Order," *Ethics* 95, no. 3 (April 1985): 613.

[4] The following statement is indicative of this belief: "Not only is there no credible defense against nuclear weapons, it is virtually inconceivable that any such defense will ever exist. . . . Offensive force has triumphed definitively over defensive resistance." Robert W. Malcolmson, *Nuclear Fallacies* (Montreal: McGill-Queens University Press, 1985), p. 10. See also Robert Jervis, "MAD Is the Best Possible Deterrence," *Bulletin of the Atomic Scientists* 41, no. 3 (March 1985): 43–46.

[5] Douglas P. Lackey, "Moral Principles and Strategic Defense," *Philosophical Forum* 18, no. 1 (Fall 1986): 1–7.

[6] Gregory S. Kavka, "Space War Ethics," *Ethics* 95, no. 3 (April 1985): 673–91.

[7] Although many strategists will agree that a defense-dominated world is a safer and preferable alternative to our current world, many of these also will claim that there is no way to get from here to there safely. The concern for moving away from the familiar and into the unknown is seen in the following quote: "Until we know of a

path that leads to a safer world, we had best not launch the expedition." Albert Carnesale, "Reactions and Perspectives," in Ashton B. Carter and David N. Schwartz, eds., *Ballistic Missile Defense* (Washington, DC: Brookings Institution, 1984), p. 380.

[8] "[It is] much better to have both countries very strongly defended but with only a limited number of offense missiles ... because the defense is large, even if one side or another cheated by a factor of two in, say, the number of missiles, it would not necessarily make a great deal of difference." Herman Kahn, "The Case for a Thin System," in Johan J. Holst and William Schneider, Jr., eds., *Why ABM? Policy Issues in the Missile Defense Controversy* (New York: Pergamon Press, 1967), p. 67.

[9] Jonathan Schell, *The Abolition* (New York: Alfred A. Knopf, 1984), pp. 112–13.

[10] Colin S. Gray, "Deterrence, Arms Control, and the Defense Transition," *Orbis* 28, no. 2 (Summer 1984): 233–38.

[11] John Gardner et al., *Missile Defense in the 1990s* (Washington, DC: George C. Marshall Institute, 1987).

[12] Charles L. Glaser, "Why Even Good Defenses May Be Bad," *International Security* 9, no. 2 (Fall 1984): 92–123.

[13] Arnold L. Horelick and Edward L. Warner III, "U.S.-Soviet Nuclear Arms Control: The Next Phase," in Arnold Horelick, ed., *U.S. Soviet Relations: The Next Phase* (Ithaca, NY: Cornell University Press, 1986), p. 254.

[14] Roy Radner, "A Model of Defense-Protected Build-Down," in Alvin M. Weinberg and Jack N. Barkenbus, eds., *Strategic Defenses and Arms Control* (New York: Paragon House, 1987); Dean Wilkening et al., "Strategic Defenses and First-Strike Stability," *Survival* 29, no. 2 (March–April 1987): 137–65; Stephen O. Fought, "SDI: A Policy Analysis" (a monograph of the Naval War College), no date; G. C. Reinhardt, "Defense and Stability" (UCRL-53743, Lawrence Livermore National Laboratory, June 27, 1986). Although these studies differ in several respects, all but the Reinhardt article, which deals with city defenses exclusively, claim that one should begin the move to a defensive transformation by protecting one's retaliatory nuclear forces and not through the construction of area or space-based defenses. The Fought and Radner studies go further, stating that crisis stability can be maintained in a defensive transition if there is a concurrent build-down of highly accurate counterforce weapons, particularly of the MIRV variety, with the move to defenses. They also state that while a cooperative, negotiated movement to defenses is desirable, it is possible to envision a series of unilateral steps that can lead us to defensive postures without destabilization.

[15] Public Opinion polling on defense issues is notoriously tricky. Differing phrasing of a question can elicit differing responses. Still, arms control and strategic defenses appear to have a large, faithful following. See Daniel Yankelovich and John Doble, "The Public Mood," *Foreign Affairs* 62, no. 4 (Fall 1984): 30–50; Mitchell Bard, "Strategic Thoughts about SDI," *Public Opinion* 9, no. 6 (March–April 1987): 17–19; and William Schneider, "Congress Openly Defies Public Opinion on SDI," *National Journal* 19, no. 21 (May 23, 1987): 1366.

Offenses and Defenses

Arms Control in a Mixed Environment

Offenses, Defenses, and the Future of Arms Control

DONALD M. SNOW

REGULATION OF THE nuclear arms competition between the United States and the Soviet Union has attained a high level of importance on the public agenda of both superpowers. Highlighted by meetings between General Secretary Mikhail Gorbachev and President Ronald Reagan at Geneva in 1985, Reykjavik in 1986, and Washington in 1987, proposals and counterproposals to reduce or eliminate nuclear arsenals have produced the Intermediate-range Nuclear Forces (INF) Treaty. Meanwhile, substantive talks in the Geneva arms forum, which Secretary of State George Shultz has described as "the most comprehensive and complex of any in history," continue with some apparent progress.[1]

This situation raises two basic questions. First, what has stimulated this newest round of highly visible activities? The structure for three-tiered negotiations involving INF, space-based systems, and strategic offensive forces was certainly not new when talks resumed in Geneva in January 1986, but the bases of discussion had changed. In an unprecedented series of proposals, President Reagan and General Secretary Gorbachev offered their views of how the world could rid itself of the dread of nuclear weapons, and in each leader's vision arms control held a prominent position. For Reagan, the key lay in the transition to a defense-dominant world where the relevance of offensive arms would wither gradually before increasingly impregnable defenses. For Gorbachev, the vision was of a world that would divest itself of nuclear weapons in stages between now and the end of the century. Foremost in his disarmed world was the absence of some of the defense technologies associated with the Strategic Defense Initiative (SDI). From these conflicting images, SDI emerges as "the most important question of nuclear arms competition on the national agenda since 1972."[2] According to the stated Soviet perspective, the militarization of space through SDI "would dramatically increase the threat of a truly global, all-destructive military conflict."[3]

Given this activity and these divergences, the second question is: What are the prospects that the arms control negotiations in Geneva will succeed? This question can be broken down into two parts: whether the sources of disagreement about what kind of world we are trying to create can be overcome, and whether there really is a serious intention on either side to reach a momentous agreement.

SDI is involved in the answer to both subsidiary questions and thus to the overarching one. The existence of SDI-based defenses is the major difference in the worlds envisaged by the two leaders. SDI is central to Reagan's world and missing from Gorbachev's, and it is difficult to imagine the strategic shape of a world that accommodates both visions. This being the case, the willingness of either leader to compromise his position serves as a major indicator of his seriousness about the goal of comprehensive arms control and eventual nuclear disarmament.

Attitudes toward SDI

To hear the Reagan administration and its followers, on the one hand, and the Soviets, on the other, speak of SDI is to gain impressions so radically different that it is difficult to believe they are talking about the same program. For President Reagan, SDI is a benign defensive "space shield" that threatens weapons rather than people, a way to "give us the means of rendering these nuclear weapons impotent and obsolete."[4] For Secretary Gorbachev, the image is not of the shield but of the sword, where SDI is comprised of menacing offensive "space strike weapons" that loom over mankind like the Death Star.

These depictions are diametrically opposed and irreconcilable, and there has been virtually no public attempt to reconcile them. Rather, any dialogue has consisted of accusations back and forth that the other side is lying about its typification, with obdurate refusals to compromise. In his 1987 State of the Union address, President Reagan reinforced this attitude. "In Iceland last October, we had one moment of opportunity that the Soviets dashed because they sought to cripple our . . . SDI. I wouldn't let them do it then, I won't let them do it now or in the future." [5] Particularly in American debate over Soviet opposition, the only position not seriously considered is the stated Soviet view. Because these positions and explanations are central to the impact SDI has and will have on prospective arms control agreements, each merits attention.

Reagan's Vision

Although his acquaintance with and interest in strategic defense can be traced to 1967, when he first became governor of California,[6] the best known commitment by Reagan to SDI dates from his March 23, 1983, speech, dubbed "Star Wars" by the White House press corps. That part of the speech devoted to defense challenged the scientific community to a massive effort comparable to the Manhattan Project or the Apollo space program, to produce a missile defense that would allow us to "save lives [rather] than to avenge them."[7]

In the president's view, the result would be a benign, nonthreatening defense that would allow a different basis for deterrence, a theme that both Reagan and his spokesmen repeat often. General James Abrahamson, head of the Strategic Defense Initiative Organization, for example, suggests that "the overriding importance of SDI . . . is that it offers the possibility of . . . moving to a better, more stable basis of deterrence."[8] Elaborating on this theme, arms control chief negotiator Max Kampelman asserts: "We would all agree that it would be better to base deterrence on an increased ability to deny the aggressor his objectives than to rely solely on our ability to punish him for his aggression. . . . It is this prospect for a more effective deterrence that research on strategic defense offers."[9] The president himself said in early 1987: "This is the most positive and promising defense program that we have undertaken. It's the path, for both sides, to a safer future; a system that defends humanity instead of threatening it. SDI will go forward."[10]

The vehicle for moving toward this altered basis of strategic balance is called the New Strategic Concept."[11] This concept provides both a schedule for implementing SDI, which also could be the framework for an arms control-regulated movement to defense, and the criteria permitting movement toward an SDI world. The schedule calls for three steps to the "ultimate period" when nuclear offensive forces lose their utility: 1) offensive forces are reduced, 2) interim point defenses are deployed, and 3) territorial defenses are erected. The timetable would be determined by the pace of technological availability and would be accompanied by gradual continuing reductions in offensive arms.

Whether the movement to defense is possible and desirable depends on the technologies meeting two criteria. As Richard Perle explains, "defensive technologies . . . must, at a minimum, be able to destroy a sufficient portion of an aggressor's attacking forces so as to deny him either confidence in the outcome of his attack or the ability to destroy a credible portion of the targets he wishes to destroy. . . . Any effective defensive system must be both survivable and cost-effective."[12] The dual criteria are that defenses must not be vulnerable to attack (survivable) and cheaper than offensive countermeasures (cost-effective). The latter, cost-effectiveness, is particularly important if defenses are to avoid spurring a destabilizing measure-countermeasures arms race, as Edward Teller explains: "Defense must be designed so that destroying it is more expensive than deploying it. Defense in itself does not mean progress toward stability. Such progress is only accomplished if defense has sufficiently low price."[13]

Furthermore, Gerold Yonas, former chief scientist for SDI, argues that achieving and maintaining cost-effectiveness is a challenging task because "a defensive system must not only work, it must maintain its effectiveness, at a favorable cost-exchange ratio, against an opponent who attempts to defeat it."[14] Thus, he continues, "capability, survivability, and feasibility—those are the real issues."[15] If these criteria can be met and the transition accomplished, the result would be a defense-dominated world where the space shield would replace the threat of retaliation as the basis for deterrence. Unfortunately, the Soviets do not accept this view.

Gorbachev's Vision

The Soviets have articulated and consistently reiterated a very different view of SDI in statements available in the West. Their position is wholly and relentlessly negative, rejecting the idea that what Gorbachev and other spokesmen have called space-strike weapons are defensive at all.[16]

Rather, they maintain that SDI seeks to create "space strike weapons of purely offensive missions"[17] and that the perception of SDI as a benign defensive environment is a purposeful deceit.

In the Soviet public descriptions, two related goals are ascribed to SDI. The first is to develop "effective weapons for destroying targets in outer space and targets in the atmosphere and on Earth from space."[18] The purpose ascribed by the USSR to the U.S. desire for this capability can be taken straight from a science fiction movie: "To begin with, their range would be global ... they can appear over the territory of any state at practically any time and create a threat to its security."[19] More to the point, the alleged purpose is "to secure military superiority there [in space] so as to threaten the Soviet Union and other nations from outer space."[20]

The second goal, usually mentioned in conjunction with the American strategic offensive force-modernization program, is to achieve first-strike capability against the Soviet Union. As a *Pravda* editorial on May 23, 1985, put it: "What we are dealing with in reality are measures that are part of an overall offensive plan directed at upsetting strategic parity, military superiority, and preparations for delivering a nuclear first strike."[21] An article published in *International Affairs* (Moscow) calls SDI an antiballistic missile—a rare designation—but essentially mirrors the "ragged retaliation" scenario, stating that the intent of SDI is to destroy any Soviet retaliatory forces that might be launched following an American first strike.[22]

The goal of this offensive SDI is clear. A member of the French Communist party describes the ultimate intent: "By coupling space militarization, christened Strategic Defense Initiative, with an upgrading of ballistic and medium-range missiles, Reagan hopes to thereby achieve his goal—world domination."[23] This, of course, is an outcome the Soviet Union refuses to accept, and hence the continuation of SDI only can mean a destabilizing acceleration of the nuclear arms race. To avoid such an unfortunate and avoidable outcome, "any use of force in outer space, from space against Earth and from Earth against targets in space should be banned without delay. There is no other choice."[24]

There is some limited historical basis for the Soviets' position. Stewart Menaul, for instance, traces their belief in the potential military decisiveness of space back to a 1960s pronouncement in *Voyennaya Mysl* (Military thoughts): "As far back as 1965, the USSR defined its doctrine in space. ... The doctrine was said to envisage active hostilities in space and regarding the mastery of space as a prerequisite for achieving victory in war."[25] The Death Star-like allusion to space-based systems looming over the horizon to launch a surprise attack is also imbedded in the apparent Soviet belief system: "Belief that the United States and NATO are plotting a surprise nuclear attack on the Soviet Union and its allies is one of the most basic and (apparently) unshakable Soviet perceptions."[26]

American Reactions to Soviet Views

Virtually nothing emanating publicly from the Reagan administration or in the open-source analytical literature addresses directly the Soviet profession about SDI. Administration statements in particular usually ignore Soviet statements altogether or dismiss them as pernicious, incredible propaganda. Indeed, the basic administration reaction has been to dismiss the Soviet position as little more than deceit. Regarding the USSR's assertion that the American intent is to militarize space, former National Security Adviser Robert McFarlane has said: "The first myth is that the United States is attempting to 'militarize space.' This is a Soviet propaganda line."[27]

Administration denunciations occasionally border on the sarcastic, as in a statement by Kenneth Adelman, director of the Arms Control and Disarmament Agency: "The assault involves disinformation and misinformation. . . . For example, they cast SDI as a dangerous and destabilizing move that will be met by Soviet countermeasures, while at the same time saying it is useless and won't work. It can hardly be both."[28] On those rare occasions when U.S. spokesmen directly respond to Soviet charges, they never refer directly to them. The Kremlin's assertion that the goal of SDI is strategic superiority is denied bluntly by Paul Nitze, for example, who says, "let me be clear that SDI is not an attempt to achieve superiority."[29] In Reagan's 1985 State of the Union address, the president made the same kind of oblique rejoinder to Soviet objections, stating that "some say it will bring war to the heavens, but its purpose is to deter war in the heavens and on Earth."[30]

The administration does have an explanation of what some of its members view as duplicity. Its position is that the Soviets want to scuttle SDI to maintain their monopoly on deployed missile defense and to assure that their own research into exotic defenses remains competitive. The president himself has spoken forcefully to the first point: "Soviet criticism of SDI is more than a little hypocritical. It is quite clear that the Soviets are undermining the U.S. SDI program, while minimizing any constraints on their own ongoing strategic defense activities."[31] In summarizing the administration's position, Secretary Shultz adds: "Rather than asking what will be the Soviet response to SDI, critics ought to be asking, 'given the Soviet Union's major strategic defense effort and its huge offensive forces, what are the consequences for deterrence, stability, and Western security if we do not pursue an adequate research effort?' "[32]

Whether the administration's critique hits or misses the mark depends on whether SDI is viewed as offensive or defensive. That the Kremlin by word and deed is committed to strategic defense is undeniable. The *Galosh* system around Moscow is the world's only operational ABM system, the Soviets have antiaircraft and civil defense programs, and they have devoted considerable efforts into the weapons potential of SDI research areas such as lasers and particle beams. Moreover, "the Soviets . . . have never claimed that a situation in which each superpower's territory is largely invulnerable to strategic attack upsets deterrence."[33] In other words, they do not oppose defense; and if they believe SDI is in fact defensive, they are indeed being hypocritical and the administration's explanation hits its target. On the other hand, if the Soviets oppose SDI but not defenses generally, then those concerns need to be addressed.

Four possibilities come to mind. The first and most obvious is that the Soviets believe what they say—that the SDI is indeed an offensive system or at least part of a complex whose intent is offensive. Gorbachev has stated these positions repeatedly. For instance, he charges that "there is every indication that the U.S. antimissile system is not at all conceived as a 'shield,' but as a part of an integral offensive complex." As a result, "nuclear means of attack will become even more dangerous."[34] Since SDI is not yet concrete, this possibility cannot be dismissed out of hand.

A second possibility is that the Soviets' depictions of SDI mirror their own hopes and aspirations for their own research efforts, but they fear the United States is more likely to succeed in these efforts. Certainly, the vivid imagery they evoke in describing the program suggests that they have given detailed thought to the prospects. As a quasi-official Soviet publication suggests of SDI, its weapons "can appear over the territory of any state at practically any time and create a tangible threat to its security. . . . They may be used not only to knock out ballistic missiles after they are launched, but also to deliver a strike from outer space at earth, air, and sea targets."[35] SDI may be the Soviet dream turned to nightmare.

A third possibility is that the Soviets cannot afford the expenditures that SDI will entail, especially given Gorbachev's well-publicized desire to emphasize domestic economic priorities, but they also cannot afford U.S. success at their expense. The Soviets, in this view, "are equally aware that the costs are going to be monumental,"[6] but they cannot allow the United States a major advantage, which failure to compete technologically might produce. The only way both to save money and to avoid disadvantage simultaneously is to cancel the race by killing SDI. Even if SDI does not produce a significant offensive or defensive breakthrough, the funds it has generated have provided fuel for the American basic research effort—a monster that might not be activated otherwise. In the process this effort has produced unpredictable findings that the Soviets would not want to have to contemplate.

The fourth possible Soviet concern is that SDI is designed to gain U.S. control of all access to space for all purposes. A system capable of destroying nuclear-tipped missiles rising from their silos presumably would be capable of destroying anything else being hoisted into space by a rocket. In that case, the Kremlin's use of space for any reason (say, communications) would require at least tacit American permission. As Gerard Smith summarizes the Soviets' dilemma, "they do not like the prospect of an endless competition with the United States for high cost, high technology defensive systems. They see SDI as a possible way for the United States to regain strategic superiority."[37]

Two points of contrast stand out about the Soviet and American explanations of the Kremlin's position. The first is that they essentially ignore one another. The Soviets acknowledge the Reagan space shield only to the extent of labeling it a deceitful sham, and the administration admits the Soviet position only to the extent of calling it hypocritical propaganda. Neither side offers any detailed critique of the other, and there is little public evidence of any activity seeking either to study or to reconcile the two. Other possible explanations of Soviet objections, such as those detailed above, have not been addressed publicly.

The second point of contrast is even more stark and potentially of greater consequence. If the Soviets truly believe their stated objection to SDI—that it is an offensive weapon intended to assert American military superiority—then their opposition is *fundamental* and unlikely to be changed. If that is the case, they are truly worried about the potential threat to their security that such systems represent. They will resist the program vigorously, as they have consistently to date. American explanations, on the other hand, are more *instrumental*; that is, the opposition is propagandistic (tactical), economic, or technical. Such bases for objection are more easily overcome. If the opposition is indeed fundamental, however, this has strong negative implications for arms control prospects. As Gerard Smith puts it: "It is not wrong to exploit Soviet concerns about the consequences of SDI to improve the likelihood of reaching an equitable arms agreement. . . . But this leverage cannot be translated into Soviet concessions as long as the United States insists it will under no circumstances trade away the Star Wars option."[38]

Arms Control and SDI

Whether resolving the differing conceptions of SDI is important depends upon where continuing disagreement makes a difference. If the consequence of continuing dissension is no more than isolated verbal sparring and name-calling, that outcome is sufficiently inconsequential to be tolerable. Unfortunately, such is not the case. Disagreement over the nature of SDI has emerged as the major philosophical point of difference between the United States and the Soviet Union at the Geneva arms control talks and at the Gorbachev-Reagan encounters at Geneva and Reykjavik. Achieving a mutually acceptable modus vivendi on SDI is essential for achieving a comprehensive agreement on strategic nuclear armaments.

Both General Secretary Gorbachev and President Reagan have put forward bold, even radical, proposals on arms control, each with the avowed purpose of producing a world free of the "reign of nuclear terror." Gorbachev's proposal was made most elaborately in his January 15, 1986, pronouncement,[39] and it was reiterated in essence at Reykjavik. The New Strategic Concept outlines Reagan's intention. Both share the vision of a nuclear-disarmed world and propose a series of steps toward that end. Although the timetables differ in content and in detail, where they differ most fundamentally is on the role of SDI in the disarmed world.

The Gorbachev proposal clearly represents evolutionary Soviet thinking and the consistent need to quash SDI. This position was clearly foreshadowed by the late Konstantin Chernenko in a remarkable statement that appeared in *Pravda* on December 6, 1984:

> If the militarization of space is not reliably blocked, it will erase
> everything that has been achieved in the area of arms limitation . . . and
> [will] dramatically increase the danger of nuclear war. The Soviet Union is
> prepared for the most radical agreements that would make it possible to
> advance along a route to cessation of the arms race, and prohibition and
> eventual and complete scrapping of nuclear weapons.[40]

Gorbachev's proposal, originally put forward in 1986, offers a three-stage
process to create nuclear disarmament by the year 2000. The first stage
would commence in 1986 and continue for five to eight years. During this
stage, each side would reduce those weapons "that can reach each other's
territory" by one half, or down to 6,000 warheads each, whichever is less;
adopt and begin to implement plans to eliminate medium-range missiles
from Europe; freeze (with their compliance) British and French arsenals;
and engage in a moratorium on all nuclear testing.

The second stage of Gorbachev's proposal would begin no later than
1990 and would last for five to seven years. During this second stage, all
other nuclear powers would "begin to join the process of nuclear
disarmament," and reductions in strategic weapons would continue while
medium-range missiles and tactical weapons (ranges less than 1,000 km)
are eliminated. Moreover, there would be a complete and universal test ban
as well as a ban on nonnuclear weapons "based on new physical principles
whose destructive power is close to that of nuclear weapons or other
weapons of mass destruction." In the third and final phase, commencing
no later than 1995 and completed by 1999, nuclear disarmament would be
carried out on the basis of mutually agreed procedures and schedules,
including on-site inspections of disarming activities. As a result, the
statement proposes "that we should enter the third millennium without
nuclear weapons, on the basis of mutually acceptable and strictly verifiable
agreements."[41]

Renunciation of space-strike weapons is the major condition for this
agreement. The first stage proposes that the United States and USSR
renounce these weapons, and all other states join this renunciation in the
second stage. The Soviet view of a nuclear-disarmed world is clear: "To
prevent the arms race from spreading to outer space means to remove the
obstacle barring the way to drastic reduction in nuclear arms. . . . To
block all possibility of resolving the problem of space indicates a lack of
desire to stop the arms race on earth."[42]

The Reagan plan calls for making nuclear weapons obsolete and thus
irrelevant and is tied to movement toward a defense-dominant world. The

timetable is suggested by the New Strategic Concept and also consists of three phases.[43] To reiterate, in the first phase during the next decade or so, offensive arms reductions would occur. Somewhere around the mid-1990s (as technology allows), point defenses would be phased in to constitute the second phase. The third phase then would witness the deployment of territorial defense, culminating in an "ultimate period" where offensive weapons would be rendered obsolete and thus could be eliminated. The nonthreatening defenses would remain in place to enforce nuclear disarmament and to ensure against rearmament. Describing the ultimate period, President Reagan often draws an analogy with the 1925 ban on chemical warfare, where chemical arsenals were disarmed but all parties retained their gas masks. Recent discussions of beginning deployment of interim measures are compatible with this construction.[44]

These two images are critically different in that one is based on SDI and one is not. The reason for this difference is the underlying problem over whether SDI is a destabilizing offensive space-strike weapon or a benign, nonthreatening defensive space shield. Which is it?

The answer, unfortunately, is that it may be either, neither, or both. This ambiguity has two sources. On the one hand, since SDI is still a research program, the characteristics of the weapons it may produce cannot be known but only guessed at. SDI may produce shields, swords, shields and swords, or neither. On the other hand, most weapons are not inherently offensive or defensive; it is the way they are deployed that leads to their description as offensive or defensive.

An example may help. Take, for instance, a cannon. Is it offensive or defensive? The answer lies not in the weapon itself but in the way it is used. If a cannon is placed in a fortification and is bolted securely to the ground, then its use is clearly defensive. If it is placed on a tank, then its use can be both offensive and defensive. By analogy, ground-based missile defenses can be compared to fortifications, while space-based systems are more akin to tanks.

This distinction also may have some value in understanding the disagreement between the Soviets and Americans and in resolving the apparent contradiction between the Kremlin's opposition to SDI and its rigorous support for ballistic missile defense (BMD). The current negotiating impasse can be stated succinctly: "The Soviet Union has made it clear that it regards space weapons, and especially spaced-based BMD, as the most pressing issue for arms control. The United States, on the other hand, regards the reduction of offensive forces—especially the

Soviet ICBM—as a more urgent matter."[45] The matter seems at loggerheads, because "Moscow has been clear in saying that there can be no treaty to reduce strategic weapons without renunciation of the space-based program."[46] At the same time, President Reagan has been equally resolute in his determination to maintain SDI: "I think it's fair to point out that the Soviets' main aim at Geneva was to force us to drop SDI. I think I can say that after Geneva, Mr. Gorbachev understands that we have no intention of doing so."[47]

As long as the discussion remains at this level, progress on arms control or on any other front regarding strategic arms is impossible. The Soviet space-strike weapons conception of SDI research could prove to be correct. Equally, SDI may produce defensive weapons. And there is no reason to doubt the sincerity of President Reagan when, in direct response to a question asking whether SDI has offensive potential, he answered: "That isn't what we are researching or what we are trying to accomplish."[48]

Unfortunately, Washington's reaction to the existence of a problem has been more patronizing than constructive. Edward Rowny, for example, makes the Soviet anti-SDI campaign sound like the work of a petulant, deceitful child: "The Soviets will, by virtue of their highly competitive nature and past successes with their propaganda campaigns, be tempted to continue to tie their offers to demands that the United States give up research on defensive systems."[49] In the long run, however, "with persistence, patience, and constructive ideas, we hope the Soviets will come to see the merits of our position,"[50] and they "should see the advantages of agreed ground rules to ensure that any phasing in of defensive systems will be orderly, predictable, and stabilizing."[51] The end product is to be "a cooperative effort with the Soviet Union, hopefully leading to an agreed transition toward effective nonnuclear defenses that might make possible the elimination of nuclear weapons."[52] With these contradictory positions in mind, we can look at whether offenses and defenses have an arms control future.

Possible Outcomes

Disagreement about the nature of SDI represents a fundamental barrier to progress in U.S.-Soviet strategic arms control negotiations, and the situation is made all the more bleak by the lack of dialogue between the two sides on the subject. As long as each side ignores or ridicules the other, it is difficult to imagine a reconciliation on the SDI controversy. As long as an impasse exists, there is no realistic prospect that a comprehensive arms control agreement between the superpowers is possible.

How will the current impasse be resolved? There are three possibilities: 1) that one side or the other will change its position on SDI, in which case an arms control agreement reflecting either an SDI world or its absence is at least possible; 2) that neither side will compromise, in which case the continuing war of words and absence of agreement are the likely outcomes; and 3) that a compromise will produce a common vision on SDI and break the negotiating logjam.

In the first possibility, either the United States will admit that SDI technologies could yield offensive space-strike weapons that should be abolished, or the Soviets will admit that their opposition has been misinformed and that SDI really is the space shield portrayed by the president. How likely is such a conversion?

President Reagan clearly has made SDI the major priority in his defense program, as witnessed by his frequent and impassioned advocacy of its defensive nature. The constancy and consistency of his support leave no doubt about either his belief that SDI seeks to create a benign defense or his unshakable commitment to the program. The U.S. government is likely to change direction on SDI only through the election of a candidate hostile to it in the 1988 presidential campaign.

Whether the Soviet government will undergo a metamorphosis depends on which interpretation of its opposition is correct—if the space-strike weapon argument is crucial to the Kremlin's ability or inability to compromise or reverse policy. Gorbachev has remained obdurate in his assertion that offensive force limitation and reductions could be tied only to an agreement on SDI. This frames the concern over whether the Soviets can compromise their position. If their fear of space-strike weapons is genuine, then their opposition is fundamental and they are unlikely to renounce their position. And the more often and explicitly they state it, the more difficult it will be for them to reverse course. As the *glasnost* campaign increasingly informs the Soviet public of this position, the ability to recant becomes even more politically problematical for a regime unwilling to admit its mistakes.

That both sides steadfastly hold to the positions they have espoused represents the second possible outcome in the SDI arms control controversy. Certainly, the harsh and repeated depictions of one another's point of view do not suggest a high likelihood of compromise. Thus, "to justify their policy of militarizing outer space, the U.S. leaders resort to outright deceit, portraying their 'star wars' plan as 'defensive'. . . . The U.S. portraying its highly dangerous space plans as defensive cannot fool the Soviet Union."[53] In an equally harsh response, Secretary Shultz reiterates that "they have devoted their greatest effort to propaganda against SDI and held everything hostage to getting their way on SDI."[54]

These statements represent entirely divergent views that, if actually believed by both sides, make the prospects of compromise very difficult. We must at least consider that this is the case: the United States firmly believes that SDI is purely defensive and that Soviet opposition is disingenuous, while the Soviets really believe that SDI defenses are a Trojan horse from whose belly will emerge offensive space-strike weapons. If that is the case, then meaningful progress in space arms and strategic offensive arms control is virtually impossible. Instead, "this combination of circumstances is more likely to lead to political jockeying and propaganda exercises in Geneva than to arms control agreements."[55] From a Soviet viewpoint, compromise between now and 1989 makes little sense, because "the next incumbent of the White House is very unlikely to have the 'born-again' commitment toward [SDI] evinced by Ronald Reagan."[56]

Although current rhetoric obscures it, compromise also may be possible. Part of the rhetorical problem is that the space-strike weapons/SDI dichotomy may be depicting two different concepts. The complex of technical possibilities encompassed within the SDI research program contains both defensive and offensive potentials. The possibilities with the greatest potential offensive applications are space-based systems, and it is that part of SDI seized upon by the Soviets in describing the offensive aspects of the program. Clearly, however, there is more to SDI, including some applications that are probably limited to defensive tasks.

Herein may lie the key to compromise. "The Soviet Union is not unfriendly to the idea of homeland defense,"[57] as their impressive efforts across the spectrum of defenses attest. Rather, they appear to oppose defenses that are not unambiguously defensive and thus the space-based applications of SDI: "Unlike old-fashioned, ground based missile defense systems, which have no potential for making a first strike more feasible, space-based beam weapons could easily be transformed from shield to arrow."[58] Whatever the basis of its motivation, the Kremlin's opposition to SDI "reflects simply a conviction that deploying the kinds of defenses envisioned by the SDI would not serve its interests in the strategic environment Moscow sees existing today and continuing for the future."[59]

This combination suggests a compromise, the third possibility. Simply put, the Americans could renounce those aspects of SDI that are not unambiguously defensive (those based in space above or near Soviet territory for boost-phase intercept), in return for an allowance to continue the program in unambiguously defensive technologies (those that are ground-based or based in space at places where they could not possibly be used to attack the Soviet Union). Since the Soviets actively are engaged in work on such systems themselves, they could hardly use such a proposal as the continuing base for opposition. Both sides would get what they say they want: the Soviets are rid of space-strike weapons, and the United States continues to work on strategic defense. In the process, the floodgate is opened for progress in reducing offensive arms which, in turn, makes the prospects brighter for effective ground-based defenses.

Such a proposal may not be instantly acceptable. It changes the calculus and requires investigation into whether it meets the criteria for eventual deployments, which are described by Kampelman: "If in the future we decide favorably on SDI, deterrence and stability would be the strategic concepts by which we would measure the value of strategic defenses."[60] Part of the problem is that limiting the possible "architectures" for defenses probably dilutes their effectiveness. As General Abrahamson puts it, "experience with strategic defenses has taught us that layered defense offers the best chance of achieving the required effectiveness against a broad range of existing and potential future threats and attacks."[61]

Unambiguously defensive defenses necessarily eschew part of the layered-defense concept (boost-phase interception by space-based defenses over Soviet territory) and thus cut the system's effectiveness. Such a compromise, however, may allow offensive reductions otherwise impossible to attain but equally necessary for highly effective defenses. The inability to limit offenses leaves the alternative possibility that "the more capable that U.S. systems are assumed to be, the more they motivate responsive Soviet deployments that may leave us worse off."[62]

There are, thus, some reasons to believe that a compromise may be possible and beneficial. The basis for this assertion comes from the rather well-agreed assumption that no defense against offensive missile attack can succeed against the kind of unconstrained offense threatened by the Soviets if the United States does not renounce SDI, or at least those parts of it that they find threatening.[63] This places the pro-SDI faction in a difficult position. The most effective outcome of SDI is the layered system that includes boost-phase interception in space, but this is unacceptable to the Soviets, who will act to overcome it rather than cooperate and limit the offenses. The only way that constraint can occur is through arms control agreements, but these are also the only way to attain at least part of what is desired.[64]

Conclusion

Tying SDI to the Geneva arms control process greatly complicates the prospects for those talks. The Soviets, however, have done so, and there seems to be no way to disentangle the two issues. Up to this point, nothing in the public record indicates that the Reagan administration has given serious attention to Soviet depictions of SDI and why those conceptualizations lead to the strident rejections of the program that they do. It may be that such serious consideration has occurred within confidential administration counsels. If this is the case, deliberations have not resulted in considered, articulated public explanations of why the U.S. government rejects the Gorbachev position. If the problem of SDI and arms control is as important as has been suggested here, such an explanation is warranted.

There seem to be only two ways to break the impasse. One is for either the Soviets or the Americans to renounce their current stand. The United States could simply abandon SDI, or the Kremlin could admit that its position to this point indeed has been the propaganda sham described by the Reagan administration. Neither of these possibilities appears likely, particularly given the frequency and consistency with which the positions are stated.

A second way to break the impasse is to find common ground on which compromise can be reached. The two positions may not be as fundamentally in conflict as the rhetoric suggests. If there are parts of SDI to which the Soviets do not object, then concentrating on those parts while renouncing the others may represent the most reasonable U.S. position. Agreement on movement in the area of unambiguously defensive defenses, employing SDI technologies that are not seen as "space strike weapons," should be possible if Soviet grounds for objecting to SDI are genuine expressions of their discontent. Until that occurs, progress in arms control is impossible.

Notes

[1] George Shultz, "Arms Control: Objectives and Prospects," *Department of State Bulletin* 85, no. 2098 (May 1985): 24.

[2] McGeorge Bundy, George F. Kennan, Robert S. McNamara, and Gerard Smith, "The President's Choice: Star Wars or Arms Control," *Foreign Affairs* 63, no. 15 (1985): 16.

[3] Mikhail Gorbachev, "Speech Welcoming Willy Brandt," *Information Bulletin* 23, no. 15 (1985): 16.

[4] Ronald W. Reagan, "Speech to the Nation, March 23, 1983," *Weekly Compilation of Presidential Documents* 19, no. 12 (1983): 448.

[5] Ronald W. Reagan, "Text of President's Message to the Nation on the State of the Union," *New York Times*, January 28, 1987.

[6] Edward Teller, "Better a Shield than a Sword," *Defense Science 2003+* 4, no. 5 (October–November 1985): 12.

[7] Reagan, "Speech to the Nation," p. 447.

[8] Lt. Gen. James A. Abrahamson, Statement on the Strategic Defense Initiative, Statement to Committee on Armed Services, U.S. Senate, 99th Cong., 1st sess., February 21, 1985, p. 5.

[9] Max M. Kampelman, "SDI and the Arms Control Process," *Atlantic Community Quarterly* 23, no. 3 (Fall 1985): 224.

[10] Reagan, "Text of President's Message," p. 6.

[11] For a summary see Gary L. Guertner and Donald M. Snow, *The Last Frontier: An Analysis of the Strategic Defense Initiative* (Lexington, MA: Lexington Books, 1986), pp. 103–5, 132–33.

[12] Richard N. Perle, "The Strategic Defense Initiative: Addressing Some Misconceptions," *Journal of International Affairs* 39, no. 1 (Summer 1985): 23–24.

[13] Teller, "Better a Shield," p. 20.

[14] Gerold Yonas, "The Strategic Defense Initiative," *Daedalus* 114, no. 2 (Spring 1985): 87.

[15] Quoted by David E. Sanger in "Many Doubtful of Early Move on 'Star Wars,'" *New York Times*, February 11, 1987.

[16] Mikhail Gorbachev, "Outer Space Should Serve Peace," reprinted from *Pravda*, July 6, 1985, in *Information Bulletin* 23, no. 18 (1985): 4.

[17] *Star Wars: Delusions and Dangers* (Moscow: Military Publishing House, 1984), p. 37.

[18] *Whence the Threat to Peace* (Moscow: Military Publishing House, 1984), p. 37.

[19] *Star Wars*, p. 9.

[20] *Whence the Threat to Peace*, p. 40.

[21] "Geneva: What Has the First Round of Talks Shown?" *Information Bulletin* 23, no. 14 (1985): 46. The same depiction can be found in *Whence the Threat to Peace*, p. 40.

[22] Yu Tomilin, "To Stop the Arms Race: Imperative Task of Our Day," *International Affairs* (Moscow), no. 10 (October 1985): 92–94.

[23] Louis Baillot, "Not One Step Forward in the Escalation of the Star Wars," *Information Bulletin* 23, no. 20 (1985): 57.

[24] Andrei Gromyko, "Along a Leninist Course in Foreign Policy," *World Marxist Review* 28, no. 2 (1985): 57.

[25] Stewart Menaul, "Military Uses of Space—Ballistic Missile Defence," *Space Policy* 1, no. 2 (May 1985): 122. The same sort of statement is made in V. D. Sokolovskii, *Soviet Military Strategy* (Englewood Cliffs, NJ: Prentice-Hall, 1963), p. 424.

[26] William T. Lee, "Soviet Perceptions of the Threat and Soviet Military Capabilities," in Graham D. Vernon, ed., *Soviet Perceptions of War and Peace* (Washington, DC: National Defense University Press, 1981), p. 70.

[27] Robert C. McFarlane, "Strategic Defense Initiative," *Department of State Bulletin* 85, no. 2099 (June 1985): 19.

[28] Kenneth L. Adelman, "SDI: Setting the Record Straight," ibid., no. 2103 (October 1985): 42–43.

[29] Paul H. Nitze, "The Objectives of Arms Control," *Department of State Bulletin* 85, no. 2098 (May 1985): 62.

[30] Ronald W. Reagan, "State of the Union Address," *Department of State Bulletin* 85, no. 2097 (April 1985): 9.

[31] Ronald W. Reagan, "Interview with J. N. Parimoo," *Weekly Compilation of Presidential Documents* 21, no. 43 (October 28, 1985): 1285–86.

[32] Shultz, "Arms Control," p. 27.

[33] David B. Rivkin, "What Does Moscow Think?" *Foreign Policy* 59 (Summer 1985): 89.

[34] Mikhail Gorbachev, "Our Policy Is Clear: It Is a Policy of Peace and Cooperation," *Information Bulletin* 24, no. 2 (1986): 17, 13.

[35] *Star Wars*, pp. 9, 27.

36 Dmitri Simes, "Are the Soviets Interested in Arms Control?" *Washington Quarterly* 8, no. 2 (Spring 1985): 155.

37 Gerard Smith, "Star Wars Is Still the Problem," *Arms Control Today* 16, no. 2 (1986): 3.

38 Ibid.

39 Reprinted as an advertisement, as "Nuclear Disarmament by the Year 2000," *New York Times,* February 5, 1986.

40 Reprinted as "Reply to an Appeal from the Fourth World Congress of 'International Physicians for the Prevention of Nuclear War,'" *Information Bulletin* 23, no. 3 (1985): 4.

41 All quotations are from "Nuclear Disarmament by the Year 2000."

42 Ibid.

43 Guertner and Snow, *The Last Frontier,* pp. 103–5.

44 See Sanger, "Many Doubtful of Early Move on 'Star Wars,'" pp. 1, 11, for details.

45 David Holloway, "The Strategic Defense Initiative and the Soviet Union," *Daedalus* 114, no. 3 (Summer 1985): 276.

46 Michael R. Gordon, "U.S. Not Sure if Soviet Links Missile Accord to 'Star Wars,' "*New York Times*, February 6, 1986.

47 Ronald W. Reagan, "United States-Soviet Relations," *Weekly Compilation of Presidential Documents* 21, no. 48 (December 2, 1985): 1435.

48 Ronald W. Reagan, "The President's News Conference of September 17, 1985," *Weekly Compilation of Presidential Documents* 21, no. 38 (September 23, 1985): 1106.

49 Edward L. Rowny, "Gorbachev's Next 100 Days," *Department of State Bulletin* 85, no. 2103 (October 1985): 18.

50 Paul H. Nitze, "On the Road to a More Stable Peace," *Department of State Bulletin* 85, no. 2097 (April 1985): 29.

51 Shultz, "Arms Control," pp. 26–27.

52 Nitze, "On the Road," p. 27.

53 *Star Wars*, pp. 7, 34.

54 George Shultz, "Arms Control, Strategic Stability, and Global Security," *Department of State Bulletin* 85, no. 2105 (December 1985): 23.

55 Arnold Kanter, "Thinking about the Strategic Defence Initiative: An Alliance Perspective," *International Affairs* (London) 61, no. 3 (Summer 1985): 460.

56 Neville Brown, "SDI: The Cardinal Questions," *The World Today* 42, no. 5 (May 1986): 83.

57 Colin S. Gray, "Space Arms Control: A Skeptical View," *Air University Review* 37, no. 1 (November–December 1985): 85.

58 Paul Barrett, "Star Wars: Return of the Nerds," *Washington Monthly* 17, no. 12 (January 1986): 51.

[59] Rivkin, "What Does Moscow Think?" p. 86.

[60] Kampelman, "SDI and the Arms Control Process," p. 226.

[61] Abrahamson, Statement, p. 7.

[62] Stephen J. Cimbala, "The Strategic Defense Initiative: Political Risks," *Air University Review* 37, no. 1 (November–December 1985): 35.

[63] For a representative sample of this view see David Holloway, "The Strategic Defense Initiative and the Soviet Union," *Daedalus* 114, no. 3 (Summer 1985): 227; Joseph Kruzel, "What's Wrong with the Traditional Approach?" *Washington Quarterly* 8, no. 2 (Spring 1985): 130; and James R. Schlesinger, "Rhetoric and Realities in the Star Wars Debate," *International Security* 10, no. 1 (Summer 1985): 7.

[64] This argument is made in considerably greater detail in Donald M. Snow, *The Necessary Peace: Nuclear Weapons and Superpower Relations* (Lexington, MA: Lexington Books, 1987), pp. 85–104.

Turning Back the Clock: SDI and the Restoration of MAD

MICHAEL F. ALTFELD*
STEPHEN J. CIMBALA

THE REAGAN ADMINISTRATION has articulated a strategic concept that intends to move deterrence from total dependence on offensive forces to reliance upon a mixture of offensive and defensive forces. The president's Strategic Defense Initiative (SDI) is a research program to provide a basis for development and deployment decisions during the 1990s and beyond. While candidate technologies for ballistic missile defense (BMD) have received much attention from the press, academia, and contractors, the search for defense has been opposed by some analysts whose minds appear closed to the idea that defenses could be functional for deterrence stability.[1]

This study considers one of the important conceptual issues in the strategic defense debate: whether U.S. defenses would contribute to or undermine strategic stability. It will be argued that advocates of mutual assured destruction (MAD) who have opposed strategic defenses have not followed consistently their own arguments about desirable outcomes of U.S.-Soviet strategic force deployments: that each side's forces should be survivable while its cities remain vulnerable to the other's strategic forces.

*The views and characterizations of U.S. policy expressed in this article are those of the authors and do not reflect the official policy or position of the Department of the Army, the Department of Defense, or the U.S. government.

We argue that, far from precluding this eventuality, strategic defenses may make it more plausible. Thus, the opposition of proponents of MAD to America's BMD cannot be based on a consistent interpretation of their own reasoning and must be assumed to rest on other grounds.

The Status of MAD: Fact of Life or Strategy?

Whether MAD is a fact of life in the nuclear age or merely a strategy depends on the level of casualties and societal destruction attendant to a large-scale counterforce first strike. This destruction can be interpreted narrowly and technically or in the broader context of its political significance. If it is large enough to make the results of counterforce operations largely indistinguishable from those expected to result from large-scale countervalue attacks, then MAD is certainly unavoidable. Furthermore, if the levels of destruction are noticeably different from a technical standpoint, but the absolute amount of societal damage done by the counterforce attack is expected to be large enough so that the difference is not noticeable from a political standpoint, then MAD is still a strong candidate for the status of fact of life.

If neither of these conditions is met, we must treat MAD as a strategy, subject to the willingness of leaders to execute it. One can make the argument that whether damage levels from these two types of attacks are noticeably different does not matter, since "it does not seem possible . . . to envisage any situation where escalation to general war would probably not occur given the dynamics of the situation and the limits of the control mechanisms . . . to manage a limited nuclear war."[2] However, "control mechanisms" are subject to improvements in their capability and survivability such as those envisaged by the Carter and Reagan administrations. Moreover, if planners are fatalistic about escalation control, they have no basis for credible deterrent threats that can be matched to the degree of the opponent's provocation.

Additionally, whether the "dynamics of the situation" will result in escalation is very uncertain. So long as leaders are faced with a counterforce attack in which the level of damage is noticeably less than that suffered in a countervalue attack, the question of whether they will respond with a countervalue retaliation is one on which the leaders will be open to influence.[3] Only if the counterforce attack can be expected to produce a degree of damage which itself justifies a countervalue response can MAD be a fact of life. If not, it must be viewed as a strategy in competition with other strategies, like counterforce or damage limitation.[4]

MAD and the Advance of Technology

MAD probably came closest to being a fact of life, as opposed to a strategy, when ICBMs were far too inaccurate and numbers of weapons far too few to contemplate serious attacks on a large system of military targets (hardened or not). It may even have been the case that likely levels of collateral damage from large-scale counterforce operations made MAD a plausible outcome when it was enshrined in the form of the ABM Treaty in 1972. At that time, the average U.S. ICBM warhead yielded over 1 megaton, while the average Soviet ICBM warhead yielded over 3 megatons. Total megatonnage for the U.S. ICBM force was said to be 1,656, while for the Soviet force it was said to be 6,430.[5] It is quite possible that the use of such large weapons in counterforce attacks (especially in ground bursts on silos and other hard targets) were expected to result in very high levels of collateral damage, perhaps even high enough to justify a countervalue retaliation.

This situation, if it existed at all, did not last very long. By 1974, even before the deployment of the SS-18, Secretary of Defense James Schlesinger reported that, assuming maximum use of what little fallout shelter protection was available, a Soviet attack launched in March (worst winds for fallout) and comprised of two warheads on each U.S. missile silo and one warhead on each U.S. bomber and SSBN support base would produce 6.7 million killed and 5.1 million injured. In addition, it would destroy less than 2 percent of America's industrial potential.[6] These estimates did not go unchallenged. By 1979 the Congressional Office of Technology Assessment (OTA) issued its report on *The Effects of Nuclear War*, which stated that the "range of uncertainty" for U.S. casualties from a counterforce attack was 1 to 20 million, with the most likely total being 8 to 10 million for an attack "preceded by a crisis period during which civilians are educated about fallout protection."[7] While these figures were higher than those of Secretary Schlesinger, they hardly begin to approximate the 138 to over 200 million people who would likely die in an all-out attack on U.S. military forces, economic assets, and population.[8]

Despite the fact that 10 million deaths would be unprecedented, an American president might not want to respond in a manner which caused an additional 100 to 200 million deaths. That is, it seems to us that, after deterrence failed, national leaders could see a clear difference between 10 million and 100 million deaths. Furthermore, the expected casualty levels attendant to a counterforce attack probably were obtained by OTA under the assumption that the individual warheads used in at least the countersilo portion yielded about 1.5 megatons.[9] However, by the early 1980s, the Soviets were replacing these warheads with ones yielding one-half megaton.[10] Unfortunately, extensive estimates of the difference in the casualties attendant to attacks with one-half megaton weapons as opposed to the larger ones that OTA used for its assessments were unavailable. OTA did note the existence of an executive branch study to the effect that an attack on the U.S. ICBM force with weapons yielding .55 megatons (one ground burst, one air burst per silo) would produce about 6.9 million deaths, as opposed to 18.4 million for an identical attack with warheads yielding 3 megatons.[11] Of course, all of this calculation is hypothetical. The point here is that policy planners cannot simply assume only the worst case and design war plans without options for other circumstances.

If the present looks bad for those advocating the notion that MAD is an automatic consequence of war with nuclear weapons, the future looks even worse. For example, William Perry, the Carter administration's undersecretary of defense for Research and Engineering, noted in 1982 that "in the course of the next decade, improvements will be made in inertial systems which will reduce delivery error to about half of what it is now."[12] Indeed, utilizing a "smart" warhead as well as high-quality inertial guidance, the Pershing II already reportedly has achieved an extremely small circular error probable (CEP). Once this degree of accuracy is achieved by ICBM, it will result in higher estimated kill probabilities against Soviet silos with lower yield warheads than have thus far been achieved with Minuteman III MK-12A warheads. This development will lower even further the expected degree of civilian damage done collaterally by countermilitary strikes and make a massive countervalue response to even large-scale countermilitary attacks less automatic than it was previously thought to be.

Responses to the Weakening of MAD

The result of these advances in missile accuracy may cause policy planners to doubt whether countermilitary attacks, even on a large scale, will inevitably be accompanied by levels of societal damage indistinguishable from those associated with large-scale countervalue attacks. Apparently, nearly total societal destruction will not necessarily happen unless it is emphasized exclusively in targeting plans while more selective options are ignored. Some authors appear to advocate precisely this response to the problem. Spurgeon Keeny and Wolfgang Panofsky, for example, speak with apparent equanimity about ground-bursting our retaliatory strike to increase Soviet civilian casualties due to fallout and of specifically targeting evacuated Soviet civilians in order to overcome their civil defense measures and successfully commit the "assured destruction" of the population.[13] Obviously, they do not really expect to carry out the threat, but they suggest that it is more deterring than the capability for graduated escalation.

Fortunately, this approach has not appealed to most American policymakers. Instead of endorsing only blunt strategic options fatalistically, they have attempted to restructure the U.S. strategic force for warfighting and credible deterrence within the restraints of the ABM Treaty and SALT I interim agreement. This approach was endorsed in the doctrine of Countervailing Strategy articulated by the Carter administration.[14] This strategy called for weapons such as the MX/Peacekeeper, which could achieve reasonably high kill probabilities on hard targets, as well as a revitalized civil defense program designed to minimize casualties from a countermilitary strike.

The fate of this approach is well known. It was opposed both by citizens' groups and a Congress imbued with a misperception of MAD doctrine that confused necessary expedients with eternal verities. As a result, the MX/Peacekeeper deployment has been limited to fifty by Congress (pending further study of survivable basing modes), despite the fact that both the Carter and Reagan administrations agreed with the view of former Secretary of Defense Harold Brown that silo basing "is a minimally acceptable fallback."[15]

In addition, the Carter and Reagan civil defense programs suffered an even worse fate. Although the Carter administration requested funds for an upgraded program in 1978 and the Reagan administration came into office with ambitious plans for civil defense, both of these efforts were quickly shown to be politically infeasible. Congress apparently banked exclusively on a MAD deterrent and on the hypothesis that any nuclear war, no matter how begun, would escalate almost instantly to all-out strikes against populations. Thus, despite some small improvement in U.S. counterforce capability stemming from the deployment of the MK-12A reentry vehicle on 300 of the 550 Minuteman IIIs, the net result of the political battles fought by both administrations was to leave the United States with a declaratory policy on nuclear war with the Soviet Union that probably could not be carried out with the weapons and defenses at hand. Despite talk in Washington of "countervailing" or even "prevailing" in a countermilitary war, it was the Soviets who possessed the advantage in this arena.[16]

This was the situation when President Ronald Reagan made his "Star Wars" speech on March 23, 1983. This speech and the resulting SDI have been roundly condemned by some supporters of arms control. They have argued that defenses would be destabilizing and that they would undermine MAD, increase the probability of war, reduce crisis stability, and fuel the arms race. Yet, if the preceeding discussion is even close to the truth, all of these effects already have occurred to some degree and are continuing to intensify as the result of ongoing improvements in missile accuracy and the concomitant reductions in warhead yield that have followed. Furthermore, as we hope to show below, the result of moderately effective defenses will not undermine MAD still further but rather help restore it to its previous position of primacy in the field of strategic theory.

How to Think about Strategic Defense

Before we can move to an assessment of how strategic defenses will affect MAD, we must discuss how to conceptualize the effectiveness of strategic defenses. In particular, unless we assume that defenses will work perfectly or that they will work not at all, we must assume that the defense will be, to a greater or lesser extent, "leaky." The question, then, is how to characterize the process by which these leaks occur. One simple way is to assume that the defense can stop some specified number of warheads, after which it collapses and all subsequent warheads are unopposed. This is sometimes called a "pure price-of-entry" system and has been employed to one extent or another by, among others, Patrick Friel, Glenn Kent, and OTA.[17]

Unfortunately, this approach appears to be unrealistic. While there may be a price-of-entry effect for very small attacks, once the attack size becomes reasonably large, the defense, instead of collapsing, likely will possess some specified probability (p) of destroying any given missile or warhead that comes its way (with p greater than 0 and less than 1) and a probability q = (1-p) of letting that missile or warhead through. If this view is correct, any attack of reasonable size can be viewed as something akin to a Bernoulli process. When an attacker fires N warheads into the defense, the probability of getting R warheads through is given by the Bernoulli process as:

$$\frac{N!}{R!(N-R)!} * p^{(N-R)} * q^R$$

If the probability with which penetration to a specific target is required is known in advance, the above formula can determine the number of warheads needed to fire.[18]

In this way of looking at leakage, the parameters which must be identified are the effectiveness of the defense, the number of warheads that the attacker wishes to place on a gi. en target, and the confidence that he needs that the required number will get through. For example, suppose that there is a ground-based defense of 50 percent effectiveness and that the attacker wishes to be at least 90 percent sure of placing at least one warhead on the target. Given a defense effectiveness of 50 percent and a requirement of at least one warhead on target, the probability of success when firing, say, three warheads is equal to one minus the probability that the defense intercepts all three warheads. Furthermore, this probability that the defense intercepts all three is given by the Bernoulli formula as:

$$\frac{3!}{0!(3-0)!} * .5^{(3-0)} * .5^0 = \frac{6}{6} * .125 * 1 = .125$$

Thus, there is a 12.5 percent probability that no warhead will get through the defense. Again, the probability that *at least* one warhead will get through is equal to one minus .125, or .875. In this case, four warheads are required to produce at least a 90 percent probability of at least one warhead penetrating the defense. Thus, in order to be confident of penetrating a defense, a disproportionate number of warheads is needed. Moreover, although it is not clear from this example, it turns out that the greater the confidence required, the more disproportionate this number will be. It is in part on this conclusion that our argument rests.

A Scenario for Defense

In order to show how the method of characterizing leakage affects the calculation of the number of warheads required to attack different target systems, we first must make some assumptions about what the defense will be like and how effective it will be. We also must make some assumptions regarding the nature of the attacking force and the degree of confidence required by an attacker. And we must finally make an assumption about the nature of the target systems being considered for attack.

For analytical purposes, we may divide the defense into three functional layers. The first layer, or "boost-phase" defense, attacks missiles and buses before they release their warheads and decoys. The second layer, or "postboost" defense, attacks the warheads from the time they are released by their buses until their flight brings them to a point low enough to threaten soft area targets such as cities. The third layer, or "hard-point" defense, attacks the warheads at altitudes too low to be of use in city defense but high enough to prevent destruction of hardened military targets such as missile silos and command bunkers.[19]

Finally, we assume that there is no theoretical limit to the number of shots that the defender may take at an attacker's boosters or warheads. Limits that exist due to factors such as flight times are incorporated, along with possible countermeasures to the defense, into the various intercept probabilities that we will postulate later.

With regard to the attacker, we assume for convenience that all boosters carry ten warheads. We also assume that, regardless of which target system the attacker is attempting to eliminate, he requires a 95 percent chance of putting at least two warheads on each target. That is, we assume that, whether an attacker is attempting to destroy silos or cities, he is very risk avoidant and will not strike unless his probability of success is very high. To the extent that an actor interested only in countercity attacks can be satisfied with a lower probability of success than that postulated, we will understate the difference in warheads required for the two options and make for a more conservative analysis.

With regard to target systems, we assume that there are two which can be aimed at. The first is the defender's 100-largest urban/industrial areas. This would constitute an "assured destruction" strike. The second is 1,000 ICBM silos. This constitutes a "large-scale countermilitary attack." In reality there would be far more targets to be destroyed in a counterforce, let alone countermilitary, attack. However, this comparison should give the rough magnitude of the differences in the two attacks.[20]

Since we cannot postulate accurately just how effective the defense will be against attacking missiles and warheads, our analysis will postulate a number of possible levels of effectiveness for the boost, postboost, and hard-point defenses and determine the number of warheads necessary to breach the defense with the required level of confidence. The defense can be considered marginally successful if it requires the Soviet Union to employ at least as many warheads as it has currently available to perform the postulated mission. And it can be considered very successful if it requires the Soviets to employ at least as many warheads as they could have for the mission in the post–1990 period.

Currently, the Soviet strategic force possesses around 9,000 SALT-accountable ICBM and SLBM warheads. Of these, only the 3,080 SS-18 warheads are said to be capable of serious prompt counterforce attacks.[21] It is difficult to determine just how many warheads the Soviets will have available in the mid-1990s, given their divergent doctrines and different geopolitical environment. In his 1981 work on this problem, Colonel Raymond Starsman, then of the National Defense University, estimated a maximum threat to U.S. ICBM forces of 22,988 warheads. This would imply an overall Soviet strength of over 30,000 warheads.[22] These are the figures which we will use in judging the effectiveness of the defense.[23]

The Attacks

Urban/Industrial (Assured Destruction) Strike

Given the scenario, the attacker must be 95 percent confident of placing at least two warheads on each of 100 targets. Table 1 gives various values for boost and postboost phase intercept probabilities and the number of warheads required by the attacker in each case. Values of effectiveness between .2 and .9 are given for each of the two portions of the defense.

Note that the defense does not become marginally successful until at least one of its elements achieves an intercept probability of at least 70 percent. Furthermore, the defense cannot be termed very successful until one of its elements achieves an intercept probability of 80 percent and the other achieves 70 percent, or until one of its elements achieves a 90 percent intercept probability and the other achieves 60 percent. Thus, assuming that defenses are likely to be of moderate effectiveness (achieving kill probabilities, say, of between 40 and 60 percent), it is unlikely that they could foreclose a countervalue strike by a Soviet Union determined to have the forces for one.

Table 1. Warheads Required for Countervalue Strike for Various Levels of Boost and Postboost Defense Effectiveness*

		Postboost Effectiveness							
		.2	.3	.4	.5	.6	.7	.8	.9
	.2	800	1,200	1,600	2,000	2,400	3,600	5,600	11,600
	.3		1,800	2,400	3,000	3,600	5,400	8,400	17,400
Boost-	.4			3,200	4,000	4,800	7,200	11,800	32,200
Phase	.5				5,000	6,000	9,000	14,000	29,000
Effective-	.6					7,200	10,800	16,800	34,800
ness	.7						16,200	35,200	52,200
	.8							39,200	81,200
	.9								168,200

*Because each attacking misile is assumed to carry the same number of warheads, this matrix is symmetric.

Countersilo Strike

Table 2 shows the number of warheads necessary for an attacker to launch a high-confidence counterforce strike against 1,000 missile silos for values of boost and postboost intercept probabilities between .2 and .5 and values for the intercept probability of a hard-point defense ranging between .2 and .8. Note that, in this case, even very low intercept probabilities for all components of the system result in at least marginal success, while very modest intercept probabilities (around 30 percent) for all components foreclose large-scale counterforce attacks not only with the postulated Soviet force but also with a force over one third larger than that postulated. These provide a large margin for error in Starsman's assessment of the number of Soviet warheads with counterforce capability. In short, a very high-confidence, large-scale counterforce attack would appear to be totally precluded by the additional layer of defense, combined with the large number of targets which would have to be attacked successfully.

Table 2. **Warheads Required for Counterforce Strike for Various Levels of Postboost, Boost, and Point-Defense Effectiveness**

Post-Boost	Boost	*Point-Defense Effectiveness*						
		.2	.3	.4	.5	.6	.7	.8
.2	.2	12,000	16,000	20,000	24,000	32,000	44,000	72,000
.2	.3	16,000	20,000	24,000	28,000	40,000	52,000	80,000
.2	.4	20,000	24,000	28,000	36,000	44,000	64,000	96,000
.2	.5	24,000	28,000	36,000	44,000	56,000	76,000	116,000
.3	.3	24,000	30,000	36,000	42,000	60,000	78,000	120,000
.3	.4	30,000	36,000	42,000	54,000	66,000	96,000	144,000
.3	.5	36,000	42,000	54,000	66,000	84,000	114,000	174,000
.4	.4	40,000	48,000	56,000	72,000	88,000	128,000	192,000

These results immediately beg the question of cost-exchange ratios between the offense and defense. Specifically, how costly will it be for the offense to penetrate a given level of defense, relative to the cost of mounting it? Clearly, it is far too soon to make good judgments about this. One conclusion that can be drawn with reasonable certainty, however, is that penetrating a defense of a given level of effectiveness for a large-scale countermilitary attack appears to be far more costly for the attacker than penetrating for purposes of a countervalue strike. This is not only because of the larger number of warheads that must be employed but also because the warheads themselves must be counterforce-capable and therefore must be far more accurate than those meant for a countervalue strike. This level of accuracy, in turn, requires an advanced and expensive guidance system.

An additional conclusion appears obvious from the results: defenses designed to exact a given warhead cost to the attacker must possess far higher kill probabilities per layer in the countervalue case. Constructing a three-layer system, each of whose layers must have an intercept probability of at least .4, and maintaining that probability in the face of enemy countermeasures may prove far easier technically and far less costly than the construction of a two-layer system, one of whose layers must possess at least a kill probability of .7 and the other of .8, and maintaining those probabilities in the face of enemy countermeasures.

To summarize, if the defense is to obtain a cost advantage over the offense sufficient to foreclose an option, the most likely option is that of a large-scale countermilitary attack. Furthermore, it seems almost impossible to foreclose the option of a large-scale countervalue attack, short of highly effective defenses such as those that the SDI program is seeking.[24] However, the *point* of any large-scale, countervalue first strike, against a comparably armed superpower opponent, escapes convincing justification.

Even if the Soviets could build the large striking force required by a moderately effective defense, there is yet another problem for them. The use of the estimated number of warheads needed for a high-confidence attack on silos may produce many more detonations than desired. For instance, in our earlier example, four warheads were necessary to obtain a 90 percent probability of getting at least one on target. However, the most likely number of warheads to penetrate in that case was 2 (37.5 percent). Thus, although 24,000 warheads might ensure a 95 percent probability of placing two on each silo, the most likely number to actually fall on the United States would be on the order of 8,000, unless the Soviets could count on fratricide effects to prevent all but the first two penetrators from detonating. Even if the yields of these warheads were quite small by current standards, say, 100 kilotons, this would mean subjecting the United States to a total weight of attack of 800 megatons, or about what it would receive now from a countersilo attack with two .5-megaton warheads on each silo.

Furthermore, since all of these warheads would have to be ground burst (since the Soviets could not know which would get through and which would not), this attack might produce much more fallout than one in which one ground burst and one air burst were employed—assuming fratricide did not eliminate all those beyond the first two to detonate. As a result, such an attack might involve a greater risk of producing sufficient collateral damage to justify a countervalue response than would a countersilo attack now. This, in itself, might have a significant deterrent effect.

This discussion marks off an important point frequently disregarded during strategic debates. Soviet counterforce attacks that require the expenditure of more than a small proportion of their prompt counterforce arsenal, *or* those that would attack U.S. forces with more than a small number of warheads per target, are self-defeating if they are intended to intimidate us by reciprocal targeting restraint. Critics of moderately effective defenses somehow imagine that defenses are not credible unless they can defeat even worst-case attacks that would exhaust Soviet postattack countermilitary potential. But the effectiveness of U.S. defenses is related to the capabilities of the offensive forces which would survive and penetrate Soviet defenses. Unless the Soviet Union deploys active defenses superior to their U.S. counterparts and the United States foregoes a competitive strategic offensive modernization program, "nonsurgical" Soviet attacks will result indirectly in their societal destruction.

This is the ironic and paradoxical sense in which defenses for retaliatory forces and countersocietal capabilities are mutually supportive. As a result, defenses that can raise the marginal cost (in warheads) of attacking U.S. silos beyond the threshold of either a small proportion of all Soviet prompt RVs or a restricted number of detonations on American soil, such that societal destruction is minimized, will be cost-effective deterrents to counterforce attacks. Certainly, the role of defenses in deterring countervalue attacks is less easy to specify and may not even be amenable to definition since the rationale for a Soviet first strike against U.S. cities, as noted earlier, is both militarily and politically unclear to us.

MAD, Defenses, and Arms Control

Thus far, we hope to have shown two points to be true. First, MAD as a fact of life has only a conditional validity—the condition being mutual superpower incapacity to plan for nuclear exchanges below thresholds that must invite virtually unlimited retaliation. Such incapacity, if it ever existed, has been undermined by the advancing technology of missile accuracy. Second, far from undermining MAD still further, moderately effective defenses are likely to preserve a situation in which "victory is impossible"—a situation in which (a) large-scale countermilitary attacks must be ruled out because of the mass of warheads that must be dedicated to the attack in order to achieve a high probability of success and the risk of collateral damage sufficient to justify countervalue retaliation, but (b) each side can retain a capacity to launch a devastating countervalue strike. How do these facts impact on the prospects for offensive arms control?

Without defenses but with continued improvements in guidance technology and concomitant reductions in warhead yield, estimated levels of societal destruction due to nuclear countermilitary strikes are likely to become ever lower. As a result, the prospect of "prevailing" at reasonable cost in a nuclear war is likely to become increasingly attractive to policy planners. This, in turn, could cause deterrence to be based on nuclear warfighting concepts like Countervailing Strategy. Such concepts require very large nuclear forces with a potential for waging counterforce wars of attrition. In this circumstance, and given the conservatism of defense planners in assessing enemy capabilities, it is hard to see how the control of offensive arms could prove successful.

However, with defenses that ruled out the possibility of "victory at reasonable cost," each side might conclude that it can afford to agree to reductions in offensive forces to at least a level significantly below that required to undertake a serious countermilitary campaign.

One further point should be noted here. The results obtained in this study depend primarily on two differences between the counterforce and countervalue target sets. First, the counterforce targets are protected by an additional layer of defense that cannot protect cities.[25] Second, the number of counterforce targets that must be successfully attacked is much larger than the number of cities that would have to be destroyed in a countervalue attack. Two lessons can be drawn from these facts. First, terminal defense is critical to an effective overall defense and should not be eschewed unless the higher layers are extremely effective (say, above 90 percent each). Second, whether a defensive system can achieve a favorable cost-exchange ratio over an attacker depends not only on the relative costs of attackers and defenders but also on how many targets need to be attacked. A nation-wide defense system may not be effective in a cost-exchange sense (or any other sense) if the attacker needs to destroy only a small number of targets.

The same defensive system, however, might prove very efficient indeed if the attacker has to destroy a very large number of targets. This implies that lower defense intercept probabilities could be compensated for, at least in part, by increasing the number of aim points for Soviet targeteers or by combining mobile forces with active defenses. This, in turn, means that basing systems like the Carter administration's multiple protective shelters might prove especially troublesome to an attacker in a defense-emphasis environment. Therefore, they might be worthy of new consideration in the event either of Soviet advances in offensive technology or an arms control agreement which significantly lowers the number of missiles which either side could possess.

MAD, Defenses, and Current Policy

Defenses also are important for implementing some of the requirements of U.S. declaratory policy which cannot now be guaranteed. Among these requirements are flexible targeting of survivable strategic forces, escalation control during nuclear exchanges, and war termination on terms as favorable as circumstances permit.[26] Although considered desirable evolutions in policy by many analysts and officials in several recent administrations, these declaratory objectives struggle against the limitations imposed by our inability to defend U.S. strategic forces and command centers after war begins. Soviet ICBMs threaten the survivability of our ICBMs, which some think soon may have to be placed on a launch-under-attack status.[27] Plausible Soviet counterforce attacks also would destroy the bulk of our strategic bomber force and the one third to one half of the fleet ballistic missile submarines usually in port.[28] We believe that U.S. forces of dubious survivability have virtually no capability for protracted warfighting, although endurance in wartime was called for in both the Carter and Reagan declaratory policies.[29] Active defenses of these forces are corequisites for their survivability against those kinds of attacks that the USSR might make during the 1980s or in later decades.

Even more problematical than U.S. force survivability (without defense) is command survivability: transattack and postattack connectivity among the National Command Authorities (NCA), retaliatory force commanders, and warning and attack assessment sensors and fusion centers. In the judgment of professional assessors of U.S. command vulnerability, current strategic command, control, and communications (C^3) systems, despite plans for their improvement, would not survive very long after strategic war began.[30] Some analysts have posited that the system might fail catastrophically within hours after deterrence failed. Bruce Blair, for example, notes that half of our 400 primary and secondary strategic C^3 targets could be attacked by launches from Soviet ballistic missile submarines on routine patrol.[31] He also notes that, from 1973 to 1985, the "vulnerability of command aircraft has not been remedied, although the U.S. has become totally dependent upon airborne command channels to execute a retaliatory strike."[32]

The present condition of command vulnerability extends to the warning sensors, attack assessment, and postattack response capability of

U.S. fixed and mobile command facilities. We believe that destruction of NCA or its isolation from retaliatory forces might not prevent retaliation in the form of assured-destruction city attacks; more calibrated and protracted command responsiveness, however, is improbable today.[33] The current vulnerability of C^3, along with that of nonalert bombers and in-port SSBNs, could lead Soviet leaders to conclude that a surprise attack using both counterforce and countercommand targets would result in a successful outcome.[34] Such a conclusion, in turn, could make war more likely.

The relationship between SDI and MAD is thus many sided. Feasible defenses could protect forces and strategic C^3 against plausible attacks with present and near-term Soviet forces. Only defenses very much beyond anything now foreseeable might preclude large-scale Soviet countervalue attacks. For these reasons of technological capability and policy congruity, SDI could rescue MAD from its present precarious state. Forces and commanders might have credible defenses against the earliest and most precise counterforce and countercommand attacks the USSR could make. Cities, however, would remain vulnerable to comparatively small attacks. The post-SDI gap between protected forces and vulnerable cities could be much wider than it was pre-SDI. This would be MAD with a vengeance but also with a more credible policy and technology story.

Conclusion

SDI, as currently structured, seeks eventually to develop defenses competent enough to provide protection to the U.S. civilian population as well as possibly to fulfill intermediate goals including strategic force defense. However, the requirements of population defense are very stringent and may not be capable of satisfaction at a cost we are willing to pay. Further, such defenses that are economically feasible may well prove to be of only moderate effectiveness. Yet, the fact that defenses might not provide comprehensive population protection against a determined attack should not lead us to discard them. Deployment of modestly effective defenses likely would guarantee that no attacker could reasonably expect to be able to destroy his opponent's capacity to wage war in a single, decisive strike which produces low collateral damage. As a result, the forces on both sides now kept in being (as well as those under development) to conduct such attacks might become a burden rather than an asset. If that happens, genuine offensive arms control may become a possibility.

Notes

[1] McGeorge Bundy et al., "The President's Choice: Star Wars or Arms Control," *Foreign Affairs* 63, no. 2 (1985).

[2] Spurgeon Keeny and Wolfgang Panofsky, "MAD versus Nuts," ibid. 60, no. 2 (1982): 290–91.

[3] Not the least of such efforts to influence a defender not to launch a countervalue retaliation will come from the initial attacker. These could take the form of passive and active defenses that will blunt the effect of the retaliation as well as a threat by the attacker to launch a third strike directly against the defender's cities, which, thus far, presumably had not been specifically targeted. For more on this see Paul Nitze, "Deterring Our Deterrent," *Foreign Policy* 25 (Winter 1976): 195–210; Richard Pipes, "Why the Soviet Union Thinks It Could Fight and Win a Nuclear War," *Commentary* (July 1977): 21-39; and Colin S. Gray, "Nuclear Strategy: The Case for a Theory of Victory," *International Security* 4, no. 1 (Summer 1979): 1154–87.

[4] For a discussion of alternative nuclear strategies see Colin A. Gray, *Nuclear Strategy and Strategic Planning* (Philadelphia: Foreign Policy Research Institute, 1984).

[5] These figures were computed using data provided by the International Institute for Strategic Studies (IISS), *The Military Balance, 1972–73* (London: IISS, 1972), p. 65.

[6] James Schlesinger, "Briefing on Counterforce Attacks," before the Subcommittee on International Law and Organization, Committee on Foreign Relations, U.S. Congress, Senate, September 11, 1974 (made public January 10, 1975).

[7] U.S. Congress, Office of Technology Assessment (OTA), *The Effects of Nuclear War* (Washington, DC: Government Printing Office, 1979), p. 86.

[8] Ibid., app. D.

[9] Ibid., app. B, assumes this yield for the SS-18.

[10] IISS, *The Strategic Balance, 1983–84* (London: IISS, 1984).

[11] U.S. Congress, OTA, p. 141.

[12] William Perry, "Technological Prospects," in *Rethinking the U.S. Strategic Posture*, ed. Barry M. Blechman (Cambridge: Ballinger, 1982), p. 130.

[13] Keeny and Panofsky, "MAD versus Nuts," p. 303.

[14] Walter J. Slocombe, "The Countervailing Strategy," *International Security* 5, no. 4 (Spring 1981): 18–27.

[15] Harold Brown, *Thinking about National Security* (Boulder, CO: Westview Press, 1983), p. 70.

[16] For a more detailed discussion of the recent state of the strategic balance see Colin S. Gray and Jeffrey Barlow, "Inexcusable Restraint: The Decline of American Military Power in the 1970s," *International Security* 10, no. 2 (1985): 27–69.

[17] Patrick J. Friel, "Communication," *Comparative Strategy* 5, no. 2:212–19; Glenn Kent's interview in *Wall Street Journal*, October 15, 1985; and Congressional OTA, *Ballistic Missile Defense Technologies* (September 1985), pp. 103–7.

[18] For a discussion of Bernoulli trials see William L. Hays and Robert L. Winkler, *Statistics* (New York: Holt, 1971), pp. 178–85. A Bernoulli process requires each trial to be independent of all others. This may not be entirely true in the case of ballistic missile defense: the probability of whether a given missile or warhead is attacked or destroyed may influence the probability with which a succeeding missile or warhead is attacked or destroyed. However, the extent to which independence is compromised when looking at a large system of defenses consisting of several integrated layers is not clear. Nor is it clear to what extent, if any, such departures from independence that occur in real life will affect our conclusions, since we are making comparative rather than absolute judgments.

[19] Two points should be noted here. First, the analytical division of the defense into three functional "layers" does not imply that the defense consists of only three layers of systems. Indeed, the postboost/midcourse layer actually may consist of several different systems designed to attack warheads at different points in the midcourse phase. The function of all these systems, however, is midcourse defense, and for analytical purposes and also for simplicity we treat them as a single layer. Second, it should be noted that, should the Soviets be interested not in destroying cities per se but rather in destroying specific targets that happen to be located in cities, they may choose to employ ground-bursts. Their purpose would be to maximize the likelihood of destroying the target or to minimize the collateral blast damage associated with the target's destruction, or both. If the Soviets followed such a strategy, so-called point-defense systems would be capable of defending the targets in question. However, if the city itself is the target and weapons are burst so as to maximize the area covered by, say, 5 psi, it is very unlikely that point defenses could be used to much effect.

[20] These two scenarios represent ideal types. In reality, there may be many military targets located within cities, and whether these would be attacked or not is an open question. However, such attacks would leave the attacker's cities open to destruction as well. Furthermore, even a "pure" countervalue strike would

inadvertently destroy many militarily relevant targets, while even a "city avoidance" attack would produce fallout endangering civilians. Thus, the two scenarios should be seen as illustrative rather than descriptive. Beyond certain levels of destruction, neither national leaders nor citizens in general would be concerned with relative damage levels. For recent estimates see William Daugherty, Barbara Levi, and Frank von Hippel, "The Consequences of 'Limited' Nuclear Attacks on the United States," *International Security* 10, no. 4 (Spring 1986): 3–45. These authors estimate deaths from large attacks on U.S. strategic targets at 13 to 34 million, depending on whether an "overpressure" or "conflagration" model is used (p. 35).

21 Committee on the Present Danger (CPD), *Can America Catch Up?* (Washington, DC: CPD, 1984), pp. A3, A6.

22 Raymond E. Starsman, *Ballistic Missile Defense and Deceptive Basing* (Washington, DC: National Defense University, 1981), p. 19.

23 The specific numbers of warheads required for each attack were computed first by determining the number required to obtain a 95 percent probability of getting one warhead through the defense and then by multiplying that number by 2. The resulting number then was multiplied by the total number of targets to be destroyed in the attack (200 or 1,000). This method slightly overestimates the total number of warheads required. It was used because computer algorithms designed to iterate to the exact number were unavailable. This overestimation was offset somewhat by ignoring the additional boosters and warheads required by the lack of 100 percent mechanical reliability of these offensive systems.

24 It might be argued here that the possibility of preferential defense in the midcourse phase vitiates this conclusion. Since the attacker cannot know which corridors have been most heavily defended, he would have to program warheads as if all corridors were very heavily defended. And since the attacker likely would have insufficient numbers of warheads to accomplish this, he would be deterred from attacking at all. However, this sounds like the flip side of Douhet's argument that defense (against bombers) would be impossible because the defender has to protect all targets while the attacker can pick and choose. As Brodie noted, "It turned out that the military worth of a target could be appreciated by the defender as well as the attacker, and that anti-aircraft guns could be distributed accordingly." *Strategy in the Missile Age* (Princeton: Princeton University Press, 1964), pp. 104–5.

There seems to be no reason why the same would not hold true for the attacker and the distribution of warheads. Thus, what appears to be most important with regard to our conclusion is not the maximum probability of interception, which can be enforced in any given corridor, but the average probability across all corridors. Since increasing this probability in one corridor would reduce it in others, the situation created by preferential defense is much more like the one we have postulated than it might appear at first glance.

[25] SDI proposes a multilayered defense of all classes of targets. However, as we noted earlier in note 19, those capable of protecting cities are all subsumed in the two analytical layers which we have called boost phase and postboost/midcourse.

[26] Desmond Ball, "Counterforce Targeting: How New? How Viable?" *Arms Control Today* 11, no. 2 (February 1981): 1.

[27] William R. Van Cleave, "U.S. Defense Strategy: A Debate," in *American Defense Annual, 1985–86*, ed. George E. Hudson and Joseph Kruzel (Lexington, MA: D. C. Heath, 1985), p. 21; John D. Steinbruner, "Launch under Attack," *Scientific American* 250, no. 1 (January 1984): 37–47.

[28] Congressional Budget Office, *Modernizing U.S. Strategic Offensive Forces: The Administration's Program and Alternatives* (Washington, DC: Government Printing Office, 1983).

[29] Leon Sloss and Marc Dean Millot, "U.S. Nuclear Strategy in Evolution," *Strategic Review* 12, no. 1 (Winter 1984): 19–28.

[30] Desmond Ball, "Can Nuclear War Be Controlled?" *Adelphi Papers* 169 (London: IISS, 1981).

[31] Bruce G. Blair, *Strategic Command and Control: Redefining the Nuclear Threat* (Washington, DC: Brookings Institution, 1985), p. 189.

[32] Ibid., p. 191.

[33] Ibid.; and Paul Bracken, *The Command and Control of Nuclear Forces* (New Haven: Yale University Press, 1983).

[34] John D. Steinbruner, "Nuclear Decapitation," *Foreign Policy* 45 (Winter 1981–82): 16–28.

Arms Control and New Weapons Technology: The Case of the Advanced Cruise Missile

DAVID S. SORENSON

IN THE ONGOING relationship between the Soviet Union and the United States, arms control issues are a kind of permanent feature on the landscape. From the Baruch Plan on, the superpowers have jousted over how to control arms in ways that are consistent with their national security objectives. But along this road, which has led to a number of agreements, obstacles continue to appear that complicate and, in some cases, prevent arms control altogether. These obstacles include agreement on exactly how to define the weapons systems considered as candidates for arms control and how to verify compliance with agreements once they are in force. They also include what might be termed "asymmetrical valuation," where a weapon poses a greater threat or serves as a greater asset more to one nation than to the other, and so the two nations value the weapon differently. Agreement on mutual conditions for controlling the weapons thus becomes difficult.

We will consider how the advanced cruise missile (ACM), scheduled to enter the arsenals of the two superpowers shortly, may affect future arms control efforts—both because it may create ambiguity with respect to its mission and because it promises to complicate verification and monitoring arrangements believed necessary for successful arms control. The focus will be on U.S. and Soviet arms control policies, but the impact of other nations who might either develop their own cruise missiles or have an interest in superpower missiles also will be considered.

The debate on strategic modernization has been dominated by new ballistic missiles and bomber aircraft, while modernization of the presently deployed generation of cruise missiles has proceeded with little notice. But these new systems are scheduled to come on line in the United States in the next few years, and the Soviet systems are expected to follow soon after. In considering their impact on future arms control negotiations, it is important to attempt some explanation of what they will be capable of doing and what their characteristics will be.

The coming ACMs are expected to be spinoffs of presently deployed cruise missiles, a factor that will help us to understand what they will be like, since the program now is masked in great secrecy in both nations. Therefore, information on their capability can be gleaned in part by some understanding of the deficiencies of the present models that the ACM is designed to solve as well as by hints about them in official government records.

The cruise missile itself dates back to the first days of flight, when remotely controlled "flying bombs" were tried in several nations. The concept was furthered by the V-1 buzz bombs used by Nazi Germany during World War II, and the first American cruise missiles were variants of this design.[1] Interest in these missiles waned in this country, however, due to the persistent failures of some early models and to opposition from bomber crews who did not want to be replaced by "smart" weapons.[2] In the early 1970s new technology was developed that made the weapons smaller and easier to carry in a variety of delivery systems, and the system won support in part because the very pilots who had initially opposed it saw it as a means of extending the life of the manned bomber. The new advances included a miniaturized turbojet engine, lightweight construction techniques, and a sophisticated guidance known as terrain-contour matching (TERCOM), which combines an altimeter with a computerized map of the altitudes the missile is to travel from launch to target. TERCOM locates the missile in relation to its planned target track by using altitude variations, and it can correct for any deviation from that path.

The present cruise missile generation has been touted as a weapon with many virtues. It is flexible in its launch requirements, which allow it to be launched from submarines, bombers, and even from the back of trucks. It is relatively slow in its flight times compared to the ballistic missile and thus allows some measure of warning time for its intended victims. Consequently, it is incapable of a preemptive strike that could paralyze the target nation's ability to retaliate; in short, it does not threaten the assumption that superpower deterrence is preserved by each side's ability to respond with massive punishing damage after an initial attack. But, as we will note below, the cruise missile also has had problems, and these have become the instigation for the ACM likely to be deployed by the United States and the USSR in the next decade.

Probable Features of the ACM

The ACM is officially "black," to use the language of the Defense Department. It is shrouded in secrecy for a number of reasons, but it is possible to derive some information about it from select sources in order to establish some general parameters. Also, because the ACM is proposed largely as a remedy for the shortcomings of the present generation of cruise missiles, we can learn something about it by knowing what their deficiencies are. The ACM, in all likelihood, will incorporate the following features.

Low-Observable Technology

The present-generation cruise missile was designed to be relatively invisible to enemy detection through its small size, low power (reduced infrared signature), and low-flight profile. A small object flying very close to the ground gets lost in the ground-clutter effects of the surrounding terrain, but the advent of "look down/shoot down" capacity currently featured in modern Soviet interceptor aircraft has threatened to nullify this advantage. Therefore, the ACM will carry low observable technology (LOT) features that will assist it in evading discovery by either radar or infrared sensing. A substantial portion of its construction likely will be of radar-absorbing material such as carbon-fiber matrix, and the aerodynamics will be designed to minimize radar signature. This would mean, for example, that engine air inlets will be flush to the fuselage and extended only for supersonic speed. Other improvements can mask or reduce the infrared signature given off by the engine.

Increased Power

Another limiting factor of the present cruise missile is its lack of power. Its engine was designed as a cheap throwaway, and the system is not capable of exceeding the speed of sound (Mach 1). Moreover, the missile cannot "power down" after rising to crest an incline and thus skips off the top, gains altitude, and exposes itself to radar and visual detection. With additional power the ACM is expected to be capable of speeds of better than Mach 1 and in short dashes of achieving speeds of much greater than Mach 1, aided by an add-on rocket or ramjet propulsion unit. Its ability to hug the terrain also will be improved with more power. Such performance increases will come as a result of improved aerodynamics, turbine engine improvements, and better fuel management. These improvements also will enhance the missile's range, another problem inherent in current models.

Enhanced Range

The range is difficult to determine, since the cruise missile is designed to fly an evasive course. However, it is not presently capable of a range greater than 1,500 nautical miles. It does not have the intercontinental range of an ICBM and therefore must be carried to its target by a delivery system. But intercontinental ranges were demonstrated by an earlier generation of cruise missiles, including the Snark, which had a planned range of over 6,000 nautical miles. Given present technology, it is conceivable that the ACM may be able to reach intercontinental distances (6,000 nautical miles), perhaps by incorporating expendable fuel tanks, and at the same time retain the size of the present generation. And even if it were not possible (or desirable) to provide such range, the ACM surely will have potential in excess of 3,000 nautical miles—enough to provide deep standoff delivery by its launch platform and to permit long flights that might be very difficult to detect, given the LOT design.

Improved Guidance

A presently deployed cruise missile is guided by computer maps of the terrain over which it must fly to its target. The map and the actual flight path are compared by a matching system, and the missile is guided by altitude differences over its path. The system is limited, however, by uniform contours like plains or oceans. It may not be reliable over the longer distances the ACM will be required to fly because even a small error can be compounded as distance increases. Therefore, the ACM is likely to incorporate additional guidance from satellites like the NAVSTAR or the Soviet GLONASS. Such guidance can allow accuracies in the hundreds or tens of feet, which gives the ACM counterforce capability in terms of its accuracy if not its surprise factor.

What Are the Strategic Implications of the ACM?

At present, cruise missiles are considered "stabilizing" weapons because they lack the range, surprise capacity, and/or flight time to be considered preemption capable. This is one reason why they have not dominated the arms control agenda as has, for example, the ICBM. Cruise missiles have fallen into a second-order category in this area, a system to be resolved only after the truly threatening weapons are negotiated. They came under some control in SALT II (although in very nonspecific ways— they were not placed under some numerical limit, for example), and they have hardly been mentioned as an issue during the Reagan years.

The ACM, however, gives the capacity for surprise and thus becomes a potential "destabilizing" weapon. Its high speed and LOT characteristics would allow it to be fired from the tubes of a submarine close to enemy territory and penetrate air space before any meaningful warning and response can take place. It also could be launched from a bomber deep over the northern territories of an adversary and fly so close to the surface of the sea that detection would be almost impossible. Penetration is also possible across the barren areas of Canada and the northern Soviet Union, and again detection would be very difficult, given the expected characteristics of the ACM. And ground-launched cruise missiles (GLCMs), even those considered theater or INF weapons, are capable of striking targets in the USSR from launch points in Western Europe.

Even with a range restriction of 600 kilometers they still can reach Soviet military targets in Eastern Europe, but with the restriction lifted a range of 2,000 kilometers would put in reach Moscow, Leningrad, and a sizable portion of Soviet military assets, including many ICBMs and their associated hardware. The ACM, like the Poseidon SSBNs now committed to NATO, would be capable of dual roles, serving as both a theater weapon (and, unlike the Poseidons, a proportedly visible link to U.S. strategic systems) and as a strategic system itself capable of participating in the Single Integrated Operational Plan (SIOP).

A whole range of targets now considered "safe" because of the warning time from ballistic missiles is now in jeopardy. This list of targets includes bomber bases; command, control, communications, and intelligence (C^3I) sites; submarine bases; power sources supplying warning and communications systems; and, particularly in the case of the United States, national leadership itself, considering the proximity of Washington, DC, to the coast.

ICBM silos might be more difficult to target, given their hardness and distance from ACM penetration points, but ACMs theoretically can provide the accuracy for silo attacks given their expected upgrades in guidance technology. A 1983 report concluded that "the high accuracy of the ALCM will increase the air-breathing forces' retaliatory capabilities against a broad spectrum of targets, *including hard targets*."[3] A potentially more useful role for the ACM might be to couple with surveillance satellites to seek out and attack the coming generation of mobile ICBMs.

In a sense, the ACM becomes more destabilizing than the ICBM. It substitutes stealth for speed, and in the end it could provide even less warning and response time than does the ICBM, which presently gives about thirty minutes response time to its intended target nation. As William Bajusz notes: "By the mid-1990s the survivability of the bomber and the ICBM legs of the triad could be at risk if the technologies for short-warning attack offset existing surveillance and warning."[4]

From all this it would appear that technology shortly will alter not only the performance of cruise missiles but also their strategic impact upon superpower security assumptions. They cannot remain a peripheral issue in any future arms control talks.

What Should ACM Limits Be?

SALT II set somewhat of a pattern in its efforts to place the strictest limits on those weapons considered most destabilizing. While the total number of strategic launchers was limited to 2,400, the ballistic missile was limited to 1,200 and the ICBM to 820.[5] The cruise missile was not limited at all in terms of specific numbers of weapons (counted as warheads on bombers under SALT). The platforms, in fact, were limited, but the cruise missiles themselves were not. This represents a view held in 1979 that cruise missiles were more stable than were ICBMs due to their longer flight times, which allowed their victims some time to escape and retaliate. But the ACM, as we know, is now capable of surprise—dangerously capable, because it threatens those systems that the superpowers rely upon to be survivable: their bombers, C^3I, possibly their ICBMs, and whatever portion of SSBNs might be in port during an attack. Such a capacity makes preemption under crisis conditions a more likely response for those fearing the ACM, and surprise attack with ACMs may be seen by its holders as more successful as its capacity to paralyze retaliation becomes greater. As Thomas Schelling and Morton Halperin noted in their classic *Strategy and Arms Control*, "whatever reduces the ability of weapons to achieve advantage by going quickly, and to suffer a great disadvantage by responding slowly, may reduce the likelihood of war."[6]

This is clearly a strong argument for placing the ACM under some kinds of limits. But what should such limits be? Ideally, they should be low enough that, when added to the other threats to second-strike capability, such capability will still survive with sufficient C^3I to retaliate. The inevitable contradiction between arms control and targeting doctrine begins to emerge more clearly. Why develop the ACM if not to threaten retaliatory assets? Why would nations which do develop the ACM suddenly be willing to limit its capacity to levels that would negate the very task it is designed for? While it is likely that strict limits on the ACM may be demanded by a rival against the nation that develops it first, those demands are likely to be resisted by the ACM developer. This is the asymmetry of interests identified earlier. As Patrick Morgan says, "where governments rely on the same kinds of weapons, hold parallel views about how wars should be fought, and use similar indexes of national military strength, this facilitates communication about restrictions on arms."[7]

The first aspect of the problem is asymmetrical *development*, where one side, probably the United States, develops the ACM first. Washington officials will be no more eager for unilateral restraints than they were in 1969 when the Soviets proposed a MIRV ban, or the Soviets were in 1982 when Ronald Reagan proposed the "zero option" for INF. The second part of the problem is the asymmetry of *risk* from the weapon. There are some attack scenarios where the United States might be more at risk and thus more willing in theory to limit the ACM. We have more bombers (particularly vulnerable to the ACM) than does the USSR, and more of them are close to coastal areas despite efforts in recent years to relocate them. The U.S. leadership locations also are much more exposed to surprise attack than are the Soviets'. Finally, should air defenses be erected against the ACM, the Soviets may have some advantage; they have the huge PVO air defense organization that such a defense could be built upon, while we do not have a defensive organization (NORAD aside) that can match the PVO in power or experience. Even NORAD is small by comparison. These two asymmetries may in the end cancel each other out, but the point here of raising them is to indicate that ACM interests are unlikely to be mutual, particularly once the weapon is developed.

This suggests that if arms control limits that mean anything strategically are to be set on the ACM, they must be done soon, before the weapon reaches that stage of its life where it has established a constituency. The subject of limits also confronts the perpetual problem between strategic and theater weapons that has bedeviled arms control for so long. Given the enhanced capacity of European-based ACMs, the distinction will make less sense to the USSR than ever before, and Soviet pressure will be high to include the European-based ACMs within some *strategic* weapons ceiling.

This would be complicated enough if it just involved GLCMs, but since submarine-launched cruise missiles (SLCMs) also are counted as theater weapons, both the United States and the Soviets may demand that these weapons and their launch platforms count as strategic weapons since both nations are vulnerable to advanced SLCMs. On the other hand, as Michael Higgins and Christopher Makins have noted, "the Soviets should be delighted with the prospect of limiting the numbers and improvements in allied systems capable of striking the Soviet Union (and also targets deep in Eastern Europe)—a capability for which the West needs the greatest improvements, while exposing a small fraction of their forces to negotiation and retaining the ability to target all of Western Europe."[8]

Who Should Be Parties to the ACM Agreements?

By the 1990s the United States and the USSR may not be the only nations to possess ACMs. Both Britain and France have been studying cruise missile technology for some time, and there is no reason why they could not build some in the near future.[9] British and French ACMs would not require the range expected for U.S. and Soviet models, but in many other ways they would resemble them. Should either Britain or France adopt their own ACMs, the Soviets might well demand compensation if the two countries choose not to participate in some arms control limit on cruise missiles. On the other hand, should Britain and France agree to participate in some multilateral or general arms control framework on cruise missiles, their particular demands may only complicate the path to agreement.

Other nations also could develop ACMs by the 1990s. The Federal Republic of Germany, for example, might develop one for a conventional force role that would be almost indistinguishable from ACMs intended for nuclear roles. Should some agreement limit American or other Western ACMs, the Soviets could point to the ease by which Americans could circumvent the limits by placing their warheads on German missiles.

Verification Problems

The strategic cruise missile itself receives little attention in recent arms control efforts in terms of definition because the only precise wording refers to the range. This missile is defined as having a range of 600 kilometers or more, in order to distinguish it from the shorter-range SLCM and GLCM that were considered intermediate-range forces, or INF, and thus not covered by the SALT II accords. Verification might become complicated on this score, since the physical characteristics of the INF cruise missiles and the air-launched cruise missile (ALCM) counted as a strategic missile are nearly identical and, indeed, could become identical without any change in performance. The ACM also could appear similar to INF cruise missiles, and ACM versions also could be delivered in several ranges like the present generation of cruise missiles. The problem involves actually verifying that a cruise missile is *strategic* and therefore counted within a strategic weapons count. Range is impossible to verify except with on-site inspection, and even that might be imprecise.

This was not a problem earlier because cruise missiles themselves have not been limited by arms control agreements. Only their launch vehicle capacity has been limited with respect to bombers. The number of bombers that can carry cruise missiles is restricted under the MIRV ceiling to 120 (1,320 MIRV carriers are allowed, with no more than 1,200 MIRVed missiles) and thus 120 bombers if the side in question chooses to MIRV its missiles to the permissible limits. Moreover, bombers carrying cruise missiles must be equipped with functionally related observable differences (FROD) to distinguish them from bombers not so equipped. Finally, bombers equipped with cruise missiles can carry no more than twenty if they are included specifically in the SALT agreement.[10] Because the present generation of cruise missiles needed a carrier to reach homeland targets due to range limits, both the United States and USSR seemed satisfied to count the carriers and limit them rather than try to count individual cruise missiles.

The ACM will likely change this state of affairs. Because its ranges may allow for intercontinental flights, or launches from relatively unsophisticated platforms far away from their targets (like surface ships, for example), the launch vehicles will no longer serve as a means to limit cruise missiles. Range could be verified through telemetry of test results or by national technical means (NTM) observations of test flights. But because the ACM is expected to fly very low to the ground, the telemetry will be transmitted over very short distances in comparison to a ballistic missile test, and thus it will be difficult to detect from NTM.[11]

Visual inspection of actual flight tests would be undependable for several reasons. First, for purposes of deception, the flights could be sandbagged or restricted in ways that would not reflect real operating conditions. Second, satellite coverage of a test flight would be extremely difficult; sequential overflights would be necessary to cover the full flight, which would probably last for a number of hours and exceed the brief minutes an orbiting satellite takes to overfly a test site. Furthermore, specific test ranges would have to be identified for such monitoring, as satellites are not very useful in discovering sites in areas where they are not expected to be—it reportedly took eighteen months for U.S. satellite reconnaissance to discover the Krasnyarsk radar site in southern Siberia. If such difficulty is encountered in finding a very large fixed site, we can imagine how hard it would be to discover the flight of a very small missile in the vast territory that makes up the Soviet Union.

On-site inspection might address some of these concerns, but it is hardly a panacea. Both the United States and the USSR have demonstrated real apprehension about the espionage possibilities available to the other side that could come from on-site inspection. The Soviets have been portrayed as the more sensitive of the two adversaries, perhaps because Washington has more often presented them with on-site inspection proposals. But when the Soviets themselves have proposed on-site inspection, as they have done recently as a means of limiting Eurotheater weapons, the United States has drawn away, citing a fear that commercial secrets would be compromised.[12] And the small size of the ACM means that it could be assembled covertly after subcomponents are manufactured separately.[13]

Can the Problems Be Solved?

It should be clear by now that the ACM is likely to cause considerable complications for arms control. What can be done to address the problems? A number of alternatives exist, including banning production or tests, imposing specific limits on the missiles or their launch platforms, and banning certain versions of the ACM.

Ban Production

Production bans are one of the most difficult arms control objectives to accomplish. They must define specifically what is and is not allowable (for example, should they include short-range attack missiles?), and verification problems can be staggering. Without on-site inspection, indirect reconnaissance measures would have to scan vast areas in search of buildings in the hope that some phase of the manufacturing process would be revealed outside an assembly building, either as parts going in or finished weapons stored outside before shipment. If violations indeed are being carried out by either side, the offending party is not likely to place completed weapons in the parking lot outside the factory. Moreover, production is not liable to be concentrated in one place but rather spread out through subprocesses such as the engine, avionics, and subassemblies; all of these processes involve small packages, presumably fabricated in small assembly areas over a wide geographic area, and thus are very difficult to find and monitor. Finally, a prohibited ACM probably would contain at least some components common to other weapons systems not so constrained by arms control (such as avionics, engines, warheads), and it would not be difficult to construct clandestinely an illegal ACM.

Ban Testing

This sort of ban could be less encompassing; a test limit could be reached only on certain ACM features seen as especially destabilizing. This step might be somewhat easier than a total ban on production, however, because testing is easier to monitor. But problems still exist. For example, if the ACM incorporates LOT, then monitoring it clearly becomes more difficult. It probably would not be impervious to high-resolution photography ("stealth," after all, does not really mean "invisible"), but night tests might be difficult to discover if the LOT package includes masking the engine's infrared signature. Furthermore, testing of the ACM probably will not occur at once but rather in parts, say, with the engine tested initially on an earlier airframe. Some tests can be simulated, and some conducted statistically; the reliability of the engine and other components can be demonstrated on a fixed test stand with no flight at all.[14] Testing, in other words, is likely to be segmented. There would have to be a ban on the testing of each component of the ACM—very difficult to define and monitor—and not just on the ACM itself.

Impose Specific Limits on the ACM

Supersonic speed as well as range, two factors that render the ACM potentially destabilizing, could be limited, but verification problems quickly emerge that render such limits impractical. Problems also occur with guidance limits; if satellite guidance systems are developed, the satellites deployed for verification have a number of other tasks that they are designed to perform, and it is highly unlikely that other aspects of satellite enhancement could be prohibited altogether.

Impose Specific Limits on ACM Launch Platforms

As we noted earlier, the present generation of cruise missiles is limited by range, and they all require a delivery vehicle to reach enemy territory. Limits were placed on the bombers designated as cruise missile carriers, and such constraints could be continued for the ACM. Again, problems emerge. The limits in SALT II specified the B-52, then the only bomber capable of carrying cruise missiles. Now, additional specifications would be required for the B-1B and the advanced technology bomber (ATB), and in these systems it might be difficult to find specific functional aircraft components unique to the ACM, as was the case of the FROD. The B-1B was designed as cruise missile capable, unlike the B-52 which required specific aerodynamic additions to carry the missile externally, and it probably would be difficult to find specifics on the aircraft to distinguish it from a B-1B not so equipped.

One way around this problem would be to designate all B-1Bs as cruise missile capable and cover them in some overall MIRV category. But some B-1s may be refitted for a conventional role,[15] and clearly Washington would not want them counted as strategic vehicles. Some kind of basing arrangement might suffice here: B-1Bs configured for a conventional role and based only in certain locations outside of the United States so as not to be counted as strategic weapons. But one of the advantages of the B-1B as a conventional platform would be lost—its capability to be flown long distances to perform missions, which makes it more difficult to destroy by some short-range weapon. The ATB presents even more serious problems, as it remains a "black" project so highly secret that the U.S. Air Force barely recognizes its existence. It would be impossible to negotiate specific limits under such conditions, and so negotiations would have to await its public unveiling.

An alternative is simply to assume that all strategic bombers are capable of carrying, and indeed are likely to carry, cruise missiles and place them in their own sublimit. In fact, the SALT limits on the number of cruise missiles carried by bombers could be continued, while the bombers themselves are limited numerically to no more than 100.

Even if limits can be reached on the kinds of cruise missile platforms covered in SALT II, substantial problems still remain. The long range expected in the ACM means that it would not need a launch platform, say, a sophisticated submarine or bomber aircraft, capable of surviving near defended territory. It could be launched from a variety of platforms such as trucks, surface vessels, fighter/attack aircraft, and even cargo planes. A specific limit on launchers, therefore, could be easily circumvented by a shift to some other uncounted alternative. And the ACM could be designed ultimately as an intercontinental-range weapon with no launch platform required. After all, the early American versions were deployed in the 1950s as intercontinental missiles, and this again could be accomplished by enlarging the ACM's fuel capacity.

Ban All INF Cruise Missiles

Given the difficulty of distinguishing INF from strategic cruise missiles, a total ban on the INF missiles could be entertained. This might include a total ban on deployment of any GLCMs. This already has occurred in the European theater, since U.S. GLCMs in Europe will be dismantled as soon as the INF Treaty goes into force. Those of a range of less than 500 kilometers are not covered by the treaty and still can be produced and deployed. GLCMs also can be used in a conventional role to deliver deep-strike munitions, fuel-air explosives, or chemical weapons. A total ban might be seen as stabilizing because these missions are sometimes defined as objectionable for strategic or ethical reasons even if they lie under the nuclear threshold. Certainly, manned aircraft also can perform these other missions if GLCMs are banned.

SLCMs pose more problems, however, since they are easier to hide than GLCMs. They could be banned from surface vessels (where verification would be easier) and limited to submarines carrying SLCMs to a "keep-out zone." Such a zone would have to encompass many thousands of square miles because of the long ranges of the ACM, and immense patrol time would be required to monitor the area. Moreover, all submarines would not be subject to such restrictions. Specific identifying signals would have to be developed unique only to SLCM boats in order to distinguish them from SSBNs or subs gathering intelligence.

Can an ACM Agreement Be Reached?

The arms control literature is replete with references to the need to employ arms control as a means of reaching or preserving strategic stability. Richard Burt, however, puts it well when he claims that a central fallacy of the existing approach to arms control is the belief that the primary function of negotiations is to alleviate sources of military instability. Probably the most conspicuous aspect of the SALT enterprise is the absence of any shared consensus between the two sides over the role and utility of long-range nuclear weapons—in particular the meaning of "strategic stability."[16]

Indeed, strategic stability is often defined in self-serving ways. The United States has stressed for years the particular instability of the heavy ICBM, a weapon in which the Soviets maintain an impressive lead, while the USSR complains about the destabilizing effect of the Strategic Defense Initiative (SDI), where the United States probably has a technical lead. Therefore, it is not surprising that the Soviets have led their recent arms control proposals with a demand that the Americans give up SDI research as a precondition for further reductions, while the Reagan administration would have severely constricted Soviet ICBMs under its strategic arms reduction talks (START) proposals of 1981.

This only serves as a reminder that arms control is, in the end, political, something that is on the one hand obvious and yet often lost in the flurry of proposals for limiting military technology in the arms control forums. Nations are quite willing to demand that the other side give up weapons that are considered destabilizing to the first party's interest, but they are unwilling to give up weapons that gain them an advantage over the other side. In other words, arms control contains a built-in contradiction. The more valuable a weapon is to one side, the more that side will demand that it be reduced by arms control, while its very value makes it out of bounds for arms control by its developer.

The ACM very likely will take on this character. This does not necessarily mean that arms control prospects are rendered impossible by the ACM; indeed, weapons similar to it in technical advantage have appeared before, and yet arms control limits have been negotiated in the end. But the asymmetrical value of weapons systems may mean that reductions beyond the marginal type seen, for example, in SALT II are extremely difficult, and expectations should be adjusted downward.

Likewise, the verification problems noted above do not mean that future arms control is impossible. They may mean in the long run, however, that compromises will have to be reached that relax the type of verification requirements of SALT II demanded by the United States. In fact, SALT II may provide an example pertinent to the ACM case— GLCMs and SLCMs were restricted to ranges no greater than 600 kilometers, yet the Soviets did not demand the kinds of strict verification procedures required in order to guarantee that all GLCMs and SLCMs did not exceed that range.[17] This is not to suggest that all verification requirements be relaxed for the sake of obtaining an agreement, but verification should not be the final reason to reject arms control altogether or to limit it to what can be verified with certainty. As George Quester has noted: "It might be good to entertain a little skepticism about whether difficulties in monitoring the cruise missile would really be such a direct problem."

He further argues that other weapons also are pushing the verification limits.[18] At the time of Quester's observation, multiple aim-point ICBM basing was threatening verification; today, mobile ICBMs pose similar challenges to verification counting rules. Given that nuclear delivery platforms have become increasingly accurate, both superpowers have more incentive than ever before to hide potential targets like the very weapons which must be seen to be counted under an arms control agreement. So the choice finally may be either to compromise on arms control verification or to give up hope that any results may come from arms control from this point on.

Conclusion

Technology has a way of complicating the political life of the superpowers, and the coming ACM promises to be no exception. In a sense it does not pose so many new problems as to make old ones even more intractable. It makes the already difficult task of separating weapons into functional categories for purposes of controlling them even more cumbersome. It further takes the cruise missile out of the category of a less serious weapons problem and demands that it be dealt with on a par with ballistic missiles in an arms control framework. And it complicates the already complex world of verification for purposes of assuring compliance.

For the past several decades, arms control has brought rather sparse results, even to its defenders. There are many reasons for this that go far beyond the scope of this article, but the technical hurdles posed by the weapons themselves, including past versions of the cruise missile, are likely to make future arms control agreements even more difficult to reach.

Notes

[1] Good histories of the development of the cruise missile can be found in Kenneth P. Werrell, *The Evolution of the Cruise Missile* (Maxwell Air Force Base: Air University Press, 1985); and Ronald Huisken, *The Origins of the Strategic Cruise Missile* (New York: Praeger, 1981).

[2] Werrell, *The Evolution of the Cruise Missile*, pp. 102–3.

[3] *Fiscal Year 1983 Arms Control Impact Statements*, Statements Submitted to the Congress by the President Pursuant to Section 36 of the Arms Control and Disarmament Act, 97th Cong., 2d sess., March 1982, p. 68. (Emphasis supplied.)

[4] William Bajusz, "Deterrence, Technology, and Strategic Arms Control," *Adelphi Papers*, no. 215 (London: International Institute for Strategic Studies, Winter 1986–87), p. 18.

[5] *The SALT II Treaty*, Hearings before the Committee on Foreign Relations, U.S. Senate, 96th Cong., 1st sess., pt. 1, pp. 46–48.

[6] Thomas C. Schelling and Morton H. Halperin, *Strategy and Arms Control* (Washington, DC: Pergamon-Brassey's, 1985), p. 10.

[7] Patrick J. Morgan, "Arms Control: A Theoretical Perspective," in Robert Harkavy and Edward A. Kolodziej, eds., *American Security Policy and Policy-Making* (Lexington, MA: Lexington Books, 1980), p. 214.

[8] Michael Higgins and Christopher J. Makins, "Nuclear Forces and 'Gray Area' Arms Control," in Richard Burt, ed., *Arms Control and Defense Postures in the 1980s* (Boulder, CO: Westview Press, 1982), p. 84.

[9] Joseph I. Coffey, "Arms, Arms Control, and Alliance Relationship: The Case of the Cruise Missile," in Harkavy and Kolodziej, *American Security Policy*, p. 76.

[10] The accords specify the B-52 and B-1 types for the United States and the TU-95 and Myasischev-4 for the USSR.

[11] Dean A. Wilkening, "Monitoring Bombers and Cruise Missiles," in William C. Potter, ed., *Verification and Arms Control* (Lexington, MA: Lexington Books, 1985), p. 116.

[12] *New York Times*, June 7, 1987.

[13] Wilkening, "Monitoring Bombers," p. 118.

[14] Christoph Bertram, "Arms Control and Technological Change: Elements of a New Approach," in Christoph Bertram, ed., *Arms Control and Military Force* (London: Gower Publishing Co., for the International Institute for Strategic Studies, 1980), p. 163.

[15] "OTA Claims Bombers Could Raise Interdiction Ordnance Delivery," *Aviation Week and Space Technology* (September 1, 1986): 183.

[16] Richard Burt, "Defense Policy and Arms Control: Defining the Problem," in Burt, *Arms Control*, p. 5.

17 Missile ranges are not easy to define, in part because of uncertainties in the systems. The errant flight of a U.S. Pershing I from Utah to New Mexico that instead landed in Mexico demonstrates the point.

18 George H. Quester, "Arms Control: Towards Informal Solutions," in Richard K. Betts, ed., *Cruise Missiles: Technology, Strategy, Politics* (Washington, DC: Brookings Institution, 1981), p. 287.

Linkages

*Arms Control and
Politico-Military
Strategies*

The Dilemmas of Deterrence, Defense, and Disarmament

KEITH B. PAYNE

THE U.S. DEFENSE COMMUNITY tends to consider its subject in bite-sized pieces. Arms control often is considered and pursued with little regard for deterrence requirements, strategic force needs are posited with little reference to U.S. alliance commitments, and congressional funding for strategic weapons typically is only remotely related to strategy-derived requirements. These subjects, all interrelated, tend to be assessed in isolation for analytical convenience. This article will examine some of the linkages among issues confronting the United States and NATO-Europe. These issues include: arms control, the Strategic Defense Initiative (SDI), nuclear deterrence, conventional force requirements, and Washington's nuclear guarantee to NATO. Recent developments in the areas of arms control and active defense are compelling a holistic reexamination of these issues, and the outcome will have profound implications for U.S. strategic policy and NATO strategy.

Deep Offensive Reductions and SDI

The relationship between SDI and arms control has come under intense scrutiny since the Reykjavik Summit of October 11–12; 1986. At

Reykjavik the United States and the Soviet Union achieved a near miss on a package of sweeping arms reductions. During these negotiations both sides attempted to couple offensive reductions with SDI and future prospects for the deployment of ballistic missile defense (BMD), albeit in contrary directions. The Soviets sought to link offensive reductions to tighter restrictions on BMD testing and development than now exist under the ABM Treaty; the Americans sought to tie offensive reductions to Soviet concurrence on BMD testing, development, and, eventually, the possibility of deployment. As part of the tentative package deal, President Ronald Reagan endorsed a ten-year commitment to the ABM Treaty if the offensive force reductions proceeded apace. If the Soviets were negotiating in earnest, it appears that differences concerning the elimination of nuclear weapons, testing under SDI, and the future of BMD precluded agreement.

Criticism of the U.S. position during the Reykjavik Summit arose from many quarters: proponents of SDI were critical of Washington's willingness to affirm a conditional ban on BMD deployment for ten years; SDI opponents were critical of the president for forgoing offensive reductions in favor of maintaining SDI. Our allies publicly were cautious of the reductions envisaged at Reykjavik. Privately, they appear to have been pleased that SDI stood in the way of an agreement that would have eliminated much of NATO's nuclear deterrent—the perspective being that Reagan's commitment to SDI saved the alliance from a potentially dangerous undermining of nuclear deterrence. Such a situation clearly does not represent "business as usual" in arms control policy.

Following Reykjavik, General Secretary Mikhail Gorbachev made the surprising offer to decouple considerations of SDI from progress toward an agreement on intermediate-range nuclear forces (INF). Specifically, he endorsed a double-zero solution to the INF question. The subsequent double-zero INF agreement, signed by Reagan and Gorbachev at the December 1987 summit in Washington, built on the long-standing U.S. zero-solution proposal vis-à-vis long-range INF (LRINF) by including short-range INF (SRINF) in a comprehensive agreement.

As might have been expected, given the critical European response to Reykjavik, many voices in Western Europe have declared their opposition to the comprehensive elimination of INF on their continent. Their fear is that the U.S.-NATO nuclear deterrent would be severely undermined by such a reduction in nuclear potential and that Western Europe—and particularly West Germany—would become "safe" for conventional war. As NATO Secretary General Lord Carrington observed in regard to INF elimination, the West Europeans have "for the first time ever come against the real possibility of a Soviet proposal likely to lead to denuclearization, and they do not like it at all."[1]

Reykjavik

According to the U.S. interpretation of the Reykjavik Summit, the two sides reached a tentative agreement with the following key features:[2]

Strategic Nuclear Forces

Phase I (1986–1991)

1) The reduction of strategic nuclear delivery vehicles to 1,600 each.

2) The reduction of counted strategic warheads to 6,000 each.
    Bombers count as one warhead if not armed with ALCMs.
    Each ALCM counts as one warhead.
    Bombers with gravity bombs, SRAMs, and ALCMs count as one warhead plus the number of ALCMs.

3) Significant cuts in heavy ICBMs.

Intermediate Nuclear Forces

1) The elimination of LRINF in Europe, a ceiling of 100 systems in the Asian portion of the USSR, and an equal number on U.S. territory.

2) The maximum number of SRINF to be frozen at current levels; reduction would be addressed at subsequent negotiations.

During the negotiations the United States sought a second five-year phase (1991–1996) of offensive reductions. By the end of that period, offensive ballistic missiles of all ranges will have been eliminated. Washington also apparently sought Moscow's agreement on testing and developing BMD components according to the broad interpretation of the ABM Treaty and, following the ten-year period of reductions, the freedom to deploy BMD unless both sides agreed not to do so. The quid pro quo for Soviet agreement was a U.S. commitment not to exercise its right to withdraw from the ABM Treaty during the ten-year period of reductions.

The Soviet position in the key area of SDI research would have limited development and testing to the four walls of the laboratory, and BMD deployment following the second five-year period would have required mutual agreement; that is, the Soviet Union would have a veto over U.S. BMD deployment at the end of ten years. During the final hours of the weekend at Reykjavik the Soviets appear to have made the issue of BMD testing the key to an agreement leading to no agreement. President Reagan's parting words to General Secretary Gorbachev were: "I don't think you really wanted a deal. I don't know when we'll see each other again."[3]

There are elements of promise and peril in the U.S. pursuit of deep-force level reductions as reflected at Reykjavik and the subsequent U.S.-Soviet agreement to a double-zero elimination of INF in Europe. The discussion below will outline the benefits and pitfalls of such offensive reductions and illustrate the relevance of SDI and BMD.

The Promise of Deep Offensive Reductions

The promise of Reykjavik is the promise of a new approach to arms control that embraces, rather than rejects, strategic defense. This approach should not come as a complete surprise. It is quite consistent with discussions by Reagan administration officials of the role of arms control in a "cooperative defensive transition." Such a transition, as discussed officially, would be characterized by 1) deep negotiated reductions in offensive forces, particularly ballistic missiles, that would ease requirements for reliable and effective strategic defenses and be stabilizing (defined as reducing the warhead-to-launcher ratio so as to reduce first-strike incentives); and 2) the agreed and possibly regulated development, testing, and deployment of advanced BMD systems.[4] The U.S. position at the Reykjavik Summit and subsequent acceptance of a comprehensive INF agreement certainly follow the outline of the desired cooperative defensive transition as described officially for over two years.

The approach to arms control under a defensive transition represents a radical departure from past U.S. policy because it envisages the coordination of BMD deployment with deep offensive reductions. This contrasts sharply with the "traditional" approach to arms control pursued throughout SALT, the basic assumption of which was that offensive arms control would be possible only in the absence of serious BMD. As John Rhinelander, general counsel for the SALT I delegation, has observed: "The SALT I and II negotiations were premised on the assumption that limitations on strategic offensive forces would not be possible without extensive constraints on strategic defense."[5]

The importance of a new approach to arms control only can be appreciated if the relative failure of traditional strategic arms control is acknowledged. The traditional approach has not come close to achieving its intended objectives. Indeed, Soviet strategic force deployments since the 1972 SALT I agreements have been the reverse of what U.S. arms control policy was expected to achieve. This is not a politically partisan viewpoint. As Brent Scowcroft, John Deutch, and James Woolsey have observed:

> Our major effort over 17 years of arms control negotiations on strategic offensive systems has been dedicated to preserving the survivability of our own silo-based ICBMs. To this end we have used, and wasted, much negotiating leverage in trying to get the Soviets to agree to restrictions on their large MIRVed ICBMs. They have noted our concern about survivability and have cheerfully made it worse with their massive investments in the programs we most want to restrict.[6]

Leslie Gelb, one of President Jimmy Carter's SALT II architects, has been even more frank: "Arms control has essentially failed. Three decades of U.S.-Soviet negotiations to limit arms competition have done little more than to codify the arms race."[7]

The problem is that the United States traditionally has approached strategic arms control as a means of supporting deterrence by threat of mutual retaliation. In particular, this country attempted throughout SALT to achieve reductions in those Soviet strategic forces that were thought to pose the greatest counterforce threat to the U.S. retaliatory capability: heavy ICBMs. Unfortunately, neither SALT I nor SALT II led to the expected limitation and reduction of Soviet countersilo capabilities. Indeed, since 1972 the number of Soviet heavy ICBM warheads has increased by over 1600 percent; and, as a consequence, U.S. ICBMs and other fixed hardened targets have become highly vulnerable to a first strike. This is precisely the situation that SALT I and subsequent negotiations on offensive forces were supposed to preclude.

At SALT I the Safeguard BMD system was, in large part, the U.S. bargaining tool to achieve control of Soviet heavy ICBMs. The logic at the time was clear: Moscow wanted BMD limitations, while Washington wanted offensive limitations; thus the two were linked in a quid pro quo. The result was twofold: 1) an enduring ABM Treaty that effectively eliminated BMD and that was followed by a decline in U.S. BMD research and development; and 2) the five-year Interim Offensive Agreement that was presented officially as having capped the Soviet offensive buildup. In addition, there was the official expectation of a subsequent and more complete offensive agreement that would control and reduce on a long-term basis the offensive threat to U.S. retaliatory forces.

Unfortunately, SALT I did not cap the Soviet buildup of destabilizing ICBM capabilities, and SALT II codified the increase in such capabilities deployed after 1972. The result has been a U.S. ICBM force vulnerable to the now-matured Soviet ICBM threat together with a decade-long search for a means of defending U.S. retaliatory assets other than through BMD. So important was the linkage between the ABM Treaty and expected offensive reductions that Ambassador Gerard Smith stated at the time that the United States could consider withdrawal from the ABM Treaty if SALT I was not followed within five years by a "more complete" offensive agreement, which would "constrain and reduce on a long-term basis threats to the survivability of our respective strategic retaliatory forces."[8] That standard of success has not been achieved; rather, Soviet capabilities have moved in the opposite direction.

In short, the traditional U.S. approach to arms control, by this internal standard, has failed. Arms control has been unable to stabilize the offensive balance by facilitating the security of retaliatory forces. Washington was unable to persuade Moscow to sign on for the notion that stable deterrence requires survivable retaliatory forces for both sides. The Soviets saw great value in amassing counterforce firepower, and, as noted by Scowcroft, Deutch, and Woolsey, proceeded to place much of the U.S. retaliatory force at first-strike risk. Consequently, when considering a cooperative defensive transition and the new approach to arms control reflected at Reykjavik, it is important to recall the demonstrated inability of the traditional arms control path to achieve its stated objectives. The next important questions are: What was new about the U.S. arms control position at Reykjavik, and how was it a step forward from traditional arms control policy?

First, and most importantly, the U.S. proposal at Reykjavik appears to have been based on an expanded definition of the goals of arms control. Rather than pursuing arms control primarily as a means of stabilizing deterrence through threats of mutual retaliation, the United States sought the combination of offensive reductions and defensive deployment options that could lead to a stable defensive transition. This transition, if successful, would reduce the vulnerability to nuclear attack of the United States and its allies through a combination of deep offensive reductions and defensive deployments—that is, instead of simply using arms control to perpetuate mutual offensive deterrence, Reykjavik reflected a new arms control agenda intended ultimately to reduce vulnerability to nuclear attack and to do so through a stable defensive transition. This approach to arms control attempts to provide both stability and the potential for limiting the level of nuclear destruction in the event deterrence ever fails. Clearly, there is, at least in principle, a strong linkage between an arms control goal of deep offensive reductions and the long-term SDI goal of rendering nuclear weapons impotent and obsolete.

Second, at Reykjavik the United States finally moved away from the notion that arms control and strategic defense are incompatible. This recognition is important, because any future deep reductions in offensive forces almost certainly will require BMD. The contrary notion that these reductions can be obtained on the basis of a BMD ban has been undermined by history since 1972. The compatibility between BMD and deep offensive reductions is derived from two factors:

1) In the absence of BMD, the strategic balance following these reductions would be vulnerable to even modest levels of cheating, levels that almost certainly could not be detected; consequently, verification requirements make BMD "insurance" vital for deep offensive reductions. It is important to note that BMD as an insurance policy is not an American invention. It was the basis of the Gromyko Plan presented by the Soviet Union to the United Nations in 1962.[9]

2) The Soviet Union places great value on its offensive counterforce capabilities as a means of destroying U.S. retaliatory forces preemptively and thereby limiting the damage it would sustain in the event of war. Soviet counterforce systems serve an important damage-limiting role. How to achieve reductions in these forces when Moscow has few damage-limiting alternatives is the question

SALT was unable to answer. It sought to reduce Soviet counterforce capabilities while simultaneously banning the alternative means of defense, that is, BMD. The evidence of the past decade and one half confirms that this approach did not work. Combining BMD options with deep offensive reductions would provide the Soviet Union with an alternative route to damage limitation that is not dependent on the accumulation of offensive counterforce firepower.

The new approach to arms control presented at Reykjavik thus addresses some of the critical roadblocks to deep offensive reductions that have undermined the prospects for arms control success in the past. It also expands the goals of arms control to include reducing the vulnerability of the United States and its allies to nuclear attack—an objective that was part of the U.S. arms control approach until the mid-1960s. The wisdom of having abandoned that goal is questionable. If no alternative to unrestricted vulnerability exists, then perhaps arms control ought to remain the handmaiden of deterrence through mutual vulnerability. However, Reykjavik illustrates how a combination of deep offensive reductions and prospective strategic defenses could reduce vulnerability to nuclear attack and help stabilize the strategic relationship.

The Perils of Deep Offensive Reductions

There have been two main criticisms of the U.S. position at Reykjavik and the corresponding new approach to arms control intended to facilitate a cooperative defensive transition. The first, based on the traditional view, argues that President Reagan cannot pursue both arms control and BMD (or SDI) because the two are incompatible. BMD systems are thought to increase the need for offensive capabilities—specifically, countermeasures to BMD.[10] At Reykjavik, the president demonstrated that he would not give up SDI and the prospect for BMD deployment. Consequently, it is suggested that a historic opportunity at the summit was missed and that arms control will continue to elude us if the president maintains his commitment to SDI.

The traditional and new approaches to arms control, however, have much in common regarding the expected incentives for arms competition and arms control. Those attempting to breathe intellectual life once again into the traditional approach posit that unilateral U.S. offensive force survivability measures, especially the mobile small ICBM (SICBM), can undercut the counterforce value of Soviet ICBMs and thereby provide the basis for reducing those systems through negotiation.[11]

Interestingly, the traditional and new approaches focus on precisely the same lever to achieve reductions: undercutting the military value of Soviet ballistic missiles. And both are vulnerable to the charge of being a catalyst to the arms race. The only difference is that the traditionalists seek to devalue Soviet ballistic missiles by using *passive* measures (such as mobility, deception) to increase the survivability of U.S. forces, while the pursuit of a defensive transition focuses on *active* defense (that is, BMD) as the primary means of devaluing Soviet missiles. Moreover, the traditionalists rely on a continuation of an offensive strategic deterrent for stability, while those endorsing a defensive transition seek a fundamental restructuring of the strategic order.[12] Thus, the arms-control lever in both approaches is the same; only the specific means of implementation are different. And both approaches are subject to precisely the same critical presumption: that the Soviet Union will be motivated to overcome defenses, whether active or passive, and therefore increase its offensive capabilities in response. This question confronts both approaches to arms control, and the answer in either case is not entirely clear.

However, the decade-long failure of SALT to achieve offensive reductions after BMD had been abandoned renders less than compelling the proposition that real arms reductions can be achieved if only SDI is curtailed. The avenue of banning BMD in order to facilitate offensive reductions already was attempted under SALT, and history demonstrates its failure. Indeed, only incomplete ceilings permitting significant offensive increases have occurred. With such a record to inform us, it is hardly incumbent on those endorsing a cooperative defensive transition and a new approach to arms control to demonstrate immediate success.

The Soviet stance at Reykjavik appeared to support the thesis that arms control and BMD are incompatible. Gorbachev and his colleagues forcefully maintained that any progress in offensive arms control would be tied to strict restrictions on SDI. Many of those claiming that Reagan must choose between "Star Wars" and arms control pointed to the results of Reykjavik as confirmation of their position.

By late February 1987 the Soviet stance had changed dramatically. Moscow decoupled progress in INF negotiations from SDI and BMD. And soon thereafter, Gorbachev proposed even more far-reaching INF reductions than those contained in the U.S. position at Reykjavik. In addition to the reduction of LRINF systems, the general secretary endorsed the elimination of SRINF in Europe (that is, 142 Soviet SS-12/22s and SS-23s), a category of weapons in which the Soviet Union has a preponderant advantage. Significantly, Gorbachev made this proposal at a time when serious consideration was being given to BMD systems within NATO (and by the West Germans in particular),[13] and highly visible SDI demonstrations included prospective antitheater ballistic missiles (ATBMs). The Reagan commitment to SDI and the prospect of BMD for North America and NATO-Europe did not obstruct Soviet enthusiasm for an agreement which actually would reduce a large number of theater nuclear weapons and entire categories of launchers. Whether the Soviet Union ultimately will decouple the prospect for reductions in strategic offensive systems from SDI is unknown. However, that country's actions in 1987 demonstrated the fallacy of continuing to claim that offensive arms reductions and active defense are inherently incompatible.

The second criticism of Reykjavik involves the U.S. extended-deterrence commitment to its allies, particularly to NATO. This criticism is based on the fact that NATO relies on the threat of nuclear escalation to deter Soviet exploitation of its conventional force advantage on the Continent. It is suggested that the nuclear reductions envisaged at Reykjavik, and particularly an ultimate ban on ballistic missiles, would undercut this nuclear threat. Unless NATO could increase significantly its conventional force capabilities in relation to those of the Warsaw Pact, Europe would become "safe" for a Soviet conventional offensive. However, there is general and deep skepticism within NATO concerning the prospects for, and wisdom of, relying on conventional defenses and moving away from the existing security regime of nuclear deterrence.

More recently, the same fear of Soviet conventional force advantages and the potential of that advantage for undercutting NATO's nuclear deterrent have led to anxiety regarding the double-zero INF agreement. For this reason, political leaders and military analysts in the United States and Europe, including Dr. Henry Kissinger, French Prime Minister Jacques Chirac, and members of the West German governing coalition such as Chancellor Helmut Kohl and Defense Minister Manfred Woerner, were reluctant to endorse Reykjavik-type reductions or the double-zero elimination of INF in Europe.[14] The general concern is that a nuclear deterrent is necessary for European security because it is unlikely that NATO could achieve a level of conventional force capability sufficient to compensate for Soviet advantages. The fear is that the former NATO commander, General Bernard Rogers, is correct in his argument against a double-zero agreement:

> There is no way that nations in Western Europe can find the resources for sufficient conventional forces [to offset Soviet conventional superiority]. The resources aren't there. And so as a consequence it's that nuclear umbrella tied to the U.S. that is the basis of our deterrent. . . . The Soviet Union has to continue to be faced with the prospect that if she aggresses against us that we will use nuclear weapons as we believe necessary and appropriate.[15]

There are close connections among Reykjavik-type deep offensive reductions, the double-zero INF agreement, and the SDI notion that active defense makes nuclear weapons "impotent and obsolete." They present the same potential problem to NATO-Europe: they could undermine offensive nuclear deterrence. This is one of the primary reasons why there has been a largely frigid response from the Europeans to the proposal, endorsed by some in the Reagan administration and Congress, for near-term BMD deployment (as opposed to continuation of a strict program of research). The actual deployment of multitiered layers of BMD by the United States and the Soviet Union eventually could eliminate the potency of NATO's nuclear deterrent and the independent nuclear threat of the French and British.[16] Consequently, SDI portends the same shake-up of the existing nuclear deterrent that could be caused by deep reductions in nuclear forces; both SDI and deep offensive force reductions thus have been labeled as potentially destabilizing.

While the SDI threat to offensive deterrence may appear too far into the future to be of immediate concern, there appears to have been a consensus within NATO that a comprehensive INF agreement was either useful or unavoidable and likely to occur in the not-too-distant future. Consequently, the negative response to double zero was more immediate and less diplomatic than the response to notions of defense dominance. Many in NATO-Europe expressed strong opposition to the elimination of INF, yet they grudgingly recognize that any political party wishing to remain in power must not be seen as obstructing the reduction of nuclear weapons.

This acceptance of a double-zero agreement has been accompanied by a striking recognition of the resultant increased importance of improvements in NATO's conventional forces. The reasoning is logical: if the current nuclear deterrent capability is to be reduced, then NATO must redress the imbalance in conventional forces. Europe, as a result of nuclear force reductions, must not become "safe" for conventional attack. And improving NATO's conventional force posture is seen as a means of responding to the Soviet conventional threat.[17] This conventional force solution to the problem of denuclearization is now highly visible because of the INF Treaty. As David Abshire, the former U.S. ambassador to NATO, observed with regard to a double-zero agreement:

> A [conventional] threat cannot be deterred with the threat of nuclear weapons when we are significantly less than equal at lower nuclear levels. Meeting this new task of deterrence—deterrence at the conventional level—should be at the top of NATO's agenda for the 1990s.
> Plainly, the heart of deterrence in the 1990s will depend more and more on NATO's conventional forces. Dramatically improving conventional forces is the way to regain the flexibility of flexible response. [18]

There is a clear connection between this general response to the INF Treaty and SDI. The response to INF elimination unintentionally illustrates how a defensive transition could be pursued without undermining European security. A comprehensive INF agreement and such a transition pose a similar potential threat to NATO's nuclear deterrent. The same conventional force improvement also is the key to stability for NATO-Europe in a defensive transition.

The inevitability of a comprehensive INF agreement highlighted the need for conventional force improvements in a way that SDI has not. A robust conventional defense improvement (CDI) program would help preserve NATO security whether the weakening of the existing nuclear deterrent were the result of negotiated reductions or the deployment of BMD and ATBMs. In short, if NATO can see to the maintenance of its security in the context of denuclearization, it also can deal with the weakening of offensive nuclear deterrence resulting from the Soviet deployment of active defenses. The connection between offensive reductions and active defenses is not only that they pose a similar threat to nuclear deterrence that may be ameliorated by a common solution (that is, a CDI), but also that the deployment of active defenses could contribute directly to that CDI made necessary by offensive reductions. Indeed, the deployment of ATBMs would provide an important element in any CDI program.[19]

The point is that denuclearization, with its effect on NATO's nuclear deterrent, can occur through negotiated reductions and/or the deployment of active defenses. And it appears that the alliance will be compelled to confront the problem sooner rather than later as a result of the INF agreement. Consequently, a typical question regarding defenses—what about extended deterrence?—is answered by the discussion of necessary conventional force improvements following the elimination of INF.

This discussion illustrates the consistency between deep offensive force reductions (at theater and strategic levels) and a cooperative defensive transition. A comprehensive INF agreement has focused attention on the need for conventional force improvements that also would be a key to stability following a defensive transition. And the deployment of ATBMs may well be critical in this regard for two reasons: 1) to protect NATO conventional forces against attack from ballistic missiles that are not included in the agreement (such as the SS-21s), and 2) to provide a means of safeguarding against the threat of covert or rapid Soviet deployment of prohibited offensive systems. Indeed, another key linkage is that deep offensive reductions simplify the defensive mission that must be borne by active defense systems.

There are, to be sure, additional problems in the triangular relationship among arms control, deterrence, and the deployment of active defense systems. The outline of some of these already is visible; others are on the horizon. A problem now perceptible but yet to boil involves the U.S. response to NATO-European concerns that a double-zero INF agreement will undermine nuclear deterrence. This response, in part, has been to point to the large number of tactical, theater, and strategic nuclear forces that will remain to provide nuclear deterrence coverage for Western Europe following the elimination of INF. Yet, it should be recalled that the rationale for SDI is to render nuclear weapons, particularly strategic nuclear weapons, impotent and obsolete and to replace an "immoral" offensive nuclear deterrence regime with defensive capabilities. And the cooperative defensive transition is discussed in terms of significantly reducing both American and Soviet vulnerability to nuclear attack, that is the Soviet "carrot" to cooperate. It may be difficult to coordinate U.S. reassurances to its NATO allies not to worry about the elimination of INF because the nuclear deterrent will remain, while simultaneously pursuing strategic arms reductions and active defenses as a means of transcending offensive nuclear deterrence.

Another problem involves Chancellor Kohl's call for negotiations on offensive systems of less than SRINF range (fewer than 300 miles). Kohl hoped that such negotiations would be related in an undefined fashion to a comprehensive INF agreement.[20] Yet, it is difficult to imagine how any government in Bonn could muster sufficient political support to deploy ATBMs as long as negotiations were taking place that might eliminate the SS-21 threat. These negotiations could continue indefinitely while the integrity of NATO's conventional force improvement program could be undermined by the absence of ATBMs and the presence of SS-21s and follow-on tactical ballistic missiles.

A final concern is that U.S. support of the double-zero INF agreement and a transition away from nuclear deterrence will severely test relations between NATO-Europe and the United States. As discussed above, NATO-Europe (and again, West Germany) places great value on the coupling of the U.S. nuclear deterrent to Western Europe. NATO's doctrine of Flexible Response is built on the premise that the alliance must be willing to use nuclear weapons first in order to deter Soviet conventional or nuclear attack. Yet, for two decades Washington in various ways has encouraged NATO-Europe to become less reliant on the U.S. nuclear deterrent. The reasoning for this push has been clear: Soviet attainment of significant strategic nuclear capabilities in the mid-1960s meant that any American nuclear threat would have to be made with the realization that Soviet nuclear retaliation would destroy much of the United States. In many ways the U.S. nuclear deterrent for NATO-Europe had become suicidal.

Only France openly has discussed doubt about the credibility of the U.S. nuclear commitment to NATO. The issue generally has been too sensitive to broach. Only occasionally has this simmering question been presented publicly, as when, in 1979, Kissinger frankly stated:

> We must face the fact that it is absurd in the 1980s to base the strategy of the West on the credibility of the threat of mutual suicide. . . .
> And therefore I would say—what I might not say in office—that our European allies should not keep asking us to multiply strategic assurances that we cannot possibly mean or if we do mean, we should not want to execute because if we execute, we risk the destruction of civilization.[21]

However, reliance on nuclear deterrence has become the norm, and it is comfortable for NATO-Europe. Nuclear deterrence is viewed as considerably more economical and effective than attempting to provide the resources necessary to stop a Soviet offensive on the ground. In the past, the general U.S. goal of moving away from overreliance on nuclear threats came into conflict with this European appreciation for nuclear deterrence. And now, the U.S. goal of a defensive transition away from nuclear deterrence through a combination of offensive reductions and defense is sure to be suspect in NATO-Europe.

The credibility of Washington's commitment to NATO, and the extended deterrent in particular, has become an open question in the minds of many conservative West Germans as a result of U.S. enthusiasm for the double-zero INF agreement. The political right in West Germany has joined the left in expressing its skepticism concerning this commitment. For example, Franz Josef Strauss, head of the Christian Social Union, responded to the double-zero initiative by saying that "the whole thing naturally means a decoupling of America from Europe."[22] This new world of doubt about the United States as an ally can only increase as a result of Washington's push for a more defensive-oriented approach to deterrence in general: the maintenance of a strategic nuclear deterrent on behalf of NATO-Europe is altogether incompatible with the long-term goals of a cooperative defensive transition.

How the United States might pursue deep offensive force reductions as part of a defensive transition away from offensive nuclear deterrence without further aggravating feelings of *Verrat* (betrayal) is not clear. As discussed above, a renewed emphasis on NATO conventional force improvements is an obvious key. But it is clear that many Europeans share General Rogers's view that nuclear deterrence is a necessity for NATO-Europe, and that radical offensive reductions (as reflected in Reykjavik, the double-zero initiative, and discussions of a cooperative defensive transition) are a threat to deterrence.

Conclusion

The concept of a cooperative defensive transition will involve a fundamental change in traditional U.S. thinking about arms control, deterrence, and active defense—that is, SDI, BMD, and ATBMs. It will involve a new defensive-oriented approach to arms control and deterrence. Such a mental transition will be difficult because, in the past, active defense generally has been considered incompatible both with arms control and deterrence stability.

The first casualty of a defensive transition will be traditional notions of strategic arms control. However, the history of arms control since SALT I was signed in 1972 does not provide fertile ground for claims that a new defense-oriented approach will lead to the ruination of an otherwise hopeful arms control process. The traditional approach to arms control has largely been a failure according to the rather modest stability goals set for it. The hue and cry surrounding Reykjavik, coming from those who continue to argue that Reagan must choose between "Star Wars" or arms control, demonstrates that accepted wisdom is questionable.

However, the recent Soviet decoupling of some offensive reductions from restrictions on SDI demonstrates that traditional wisdom may be faulty. General Secretary Gorbachev has concurred in the first agreement to achieve real reductions in nuclear weapons—that is, the elimination of INF. Significantly, this occurred after ATBMs had become a highly visible element in SDI and after several U.S. allies had voiced a strong interest in the possibility of ATBM deployment.

There undoubtedly will be great difficulty in coordinating the triangular relationship among deep offensive force reductions, the eventual deployment of active defenses, and the maintenance of deterrence stability. The American defense community tends to think and analyze its subject in a segmented fashion, assessing interrelated factors in isolation. In our thinking about deterrence, arms control, strategic nuclear forces, theater nuclear forces, conventional forces, and NATO requirements, more often than not we separate these inherently interrelated factors for the sake of analytical convenience. However, when assessing or planning for a defensive transition—whether cooperative or not—the linkages among all of these factors must be held firmly in mind.

The Reykjavik Summit and the double-zero INF Treaty foreshadow the type of deep offensive reductions consistent with a cooperative defensive transition. The debate surrounding those arms control initiatives illustrates how important are the linkages among the factors we tend to treat in isolation. For example, U.S. enthusiasm for deep offensive reductions has offended allied (especially West German) views of their unique security requirements, and the INF agreement has resulted in increased concern for NATO conventional capabilities.

The greatest danger in any potential defense transition is that we will disaggregate interrelated topics and pursue them as separate streams of thought and activity. If so, it will not be surprising if U.S. policy toward the deployment of active defenses and the reduction of offensive forces has an unintended and challenging ripple effect on deterrence requirements, allied security concerns, or conventional force needs. Proper planning and integration of our thinking in the direction of broad strategy will be the first step toward avoiding discontinuities and initiating a stable transition.

Notes

[1] Quoted in "NATO Chief Assails Offer on Short-Range Missiles," *Washington Times*, May 7, 1987. Official German comments also have reflected caution concerning a comprehensive INF agreement. See, for example, "Angst vor der Courage" (Fear of boldness), *Der Spiegel*, April 27, 1987; and Herbert Winkler, "Verhandlungen von heute stellen Fragen nach der Strategie von morgen" (Negotiations of today present questions concerning tomorrow's strategy), Deutsche Press Agentur, *Washington Journal*, May 1, 1987.

[2] See the summaries of Reykjavik in White House, Office of the Press Secretary, *Statement by the Deputy Press Secretary*, December 2, 1986, p. 1; and *The Reykjavik Talks: Promise or Peril?* Report Prepared by the Staff of the Subcommittee on Arms Control, International Security, and Science, Committee on Foreign Affairs, House of Representatives, 100th Cong., 1st sess., January 1987, pp. 4–5, 15.

[3] Quoted in *The Reykjavik Process: Preparations for and Conduct of the Iceland Summit and Its Implications for Arms Control*, Report of the Defense Policy Panel, U.S. House of Representatives, Committee on Armed Services, December 15, 1986, p. 14.

[4] For discussions of arms control and the potential defensive transition see, for example, Paul Nitze, "The Objectives of Arms Control," *Survival* 27, no. 3 (May–June 1985): 99, 103, 105; Nitze, *On the Road to a More Stable Peace*, Speech to the Philadelphia World Affairs Council, February 20, 1985, pp. 2–7; Nitze, "SDI: Its Nature and Rationale," in *Current Policy*, no. 751 (Washington, DC: U.S. Department of State, Bureau of Public Affairs, October 1985), pp. 1–2; Nitze, "U.S. Strategic Force Structure: The Challenge Ahead," *Current Policy*, no. 794 (February 1986), p. 2; General James Abrahamson, "The Strategic Defense Initiative," *Defense 84* (August 1984): 3; George Keyworth, *Strategic Defense: A Catalyst for Arms Reductions*, Presentation to the Center for Law and National Security, University of Virginia, Charlottesville, June 23, 1984, p. 8; Fred Ikle, "Nuclear Strategy: Can There Be a Happy Ending?" *Foreign Affairs* 63, no. 4 (Spring 1985): 810–26; and Louis Marquet, "SDI Is a Catalyst to Devalue Soviet Offensive Capabilities," *ROA National Security Report* (May 1987), pp. 13–16.

5 Quoted from Thomas Longstreth, John Pike, and John Rhinelander, *The Impact of U.S. and Soviet Ballistic Missile Defense Programs on the ABM Treaty* (Washington, DC: National Campaign to Save the ABM Treaty, March 1985), p. 4.

6 Brent Scowcroft, John Deutch, and R. James Woolsey, "A Small, Survivable, Mobile ICBM," *Washington Post*, December 26, 1986.

7 "A Glass Half Full," *Foreign Policy* 36 (Fall 1979): 21.

8 This phrase is from U.S. Unilateral Statement A, attached to the ABM Treaty.

9 For the text of Soviet Minister Andrei Gromyko's statement to the United Nations see U.S. Arms Control and Disarmament Agency, *Documents on Disarmament, 1962*, vol. 2, July-December (Washington, DC: U.S. Government Printing Office, November 1963), pp. 904–5, 916–17.

10 This thesis is perhaps best presented in McGeorge Bundy, George Kennan, Robert McNamara, and Gerard Smith, "The President's Choice: Star Wars or Arms Control?" *Foreign Affairs* 63, no. 2 (Winter 1984–85): 266–67.

11 See, for example, "A Small, Survivable, Mobile ICBM"; and Brent Scowcroft, John Deutch, and R. James Woolsey, "A Way Out of Reykjavik," *New York Times Magazine*, January 25, 1987.

12 See Ikle, "Nuclear Strategy," p. 825.

13 See, for example, the discussions in Thomas Enders, "Gedanken zu einer europäischen Raketenabwehr" (Thoughts on a European missile defense), in *SDI oder "Krieg der Sterne"* (SDI or "war of the stars") (Bonn: Bonner Friedensforum, 1986), pp. 87–107; and "Raketenabwehr als Teil einer erweiterten NATO-Luftverteidigung" (Missile defense as a part of an extended NATO air defense), *Interne Studien* 2 (Sankt Augustin: Sozialwissenschaftliches Forschungsinstitut der Konrad-Adenauer-Stiftung, 1986).

14 See the discussions in Scowcroft et al., "A Way Out of Reykjavik," p. 42. West German Defense Minister Manfred Woerner reportedly denies that NATO could make up the conventional gap. Quoted in Lou Marano, "German Hopeful on SDI, Arms Talks," *Washington Times*, November 19, 1986. See also Thomas Hirschfeld, "Tactical Nuclear Weapons in Europe," *Washington Quarterly* 10, no. 1 (Winter 1987): 108–11; Richard Nixon and Henry Kissinger, "An Arms Agreement—on Two Conditions," *Washington Post*, April 26, 1987; Rene Hermann, "Missile Deal Strains German Coalition," *Wall Street Journal*, May 4, 1987; Wolfgang Wagner, "Europe's Credibility Is on the Line over Missiles," *Hannoverliche Allgemeine*, May 2, 1987; and "Konventionelle Uberlegenheit des Ostens nicht vergessen" (Don't forget the conventional superiority of the East), Deutsche Press Agentur, *Washington Journal*, May 6, 1987.

15 Quoted in Elizabeth Pond, "A Nuclear-Free Europe? Outgoing NATO Chief Warns against It," *Christian Science Monitor*, April 23, 1987.

[16] See the discussion in Keith B. Payne, *Strategic Defense: "Star Wars" in Perspective* (Lanham, MD: Hamilton Press, 1986), pp. 193–223.

[17] This appears to have been the consensus view at the May 1987 meeting of NATO defense ministers in Brussels. See in particular the statements by General Wolfgang von Altenburg, chairman of NATO's Military Committee, quoted in James Dorsey, "Offset Cuts in Missiles, W. German Tells NATO," *Washington Times*, May 27, 1987. See also Dorsey, "NATO Defense Unit Calls for Buildup of Conventional Forces," ibid., May 28, 1987.

[18] From an address by Ambassador Abshire at Georgetown University, April 30, 1987. Quoted in *Washington Post*, May 6, 1987.

[19] See Manfred Woerner, "A Missile Defense for NATO Europe," *Strategic Review* 14, no. 1 (Winter 1986): 13–20; and Pete Wilson, "A Missile Defense for NATO: We Must Respond to the Challenge," ibid. 14, no. 2 (Spring 1986): 9–15.

[20] For statements by Kohl see "Kohl bleibt trotz CDU-Verlus ten bei seinem Abrüstungskonzept" (Despite CDU losses Kohl remains in support of his disarmament concept); and "Kohls radikaler Vorschlag zur Abrüstung sorgt für Verwirrung" (Kohl's radical proposal for disarmament causes confusion), *Washington Journal*, May 29, 1987. See also German Information Center, *The Week in Germany*, May 29, 1987.

[21] "The Future of NATO," in Kenneth Myers, ed., *NATO, The Next Thirty Years: The Changing Political, Economic, and Military Setting* (Boulder, CO: Westview Press, 1980), pp. 7–8.

[22] Quoted in Robert McCartney, "Soviet Missile Offer Wins Bonn Accord," *Washington Post*, June 2, 1987. Perhaps more surprising is a discussion among German conservatives that has followed from the double-zero initiative: the notion of negotiating with the Soviet Union on the issue of German reunification. See, for example, "Union berät geheim Abrüstungs-Antwort" (Union secretly considers disarmament answer), *Washington Journal*, June 5, 1987.

The North American Dyad: U.S.-Canadian Relations and the Prospects for Arms Control

CYNTHIA A. CANNIZZO

CANADA AND THE United States form a single, indivisible strategic entity. For the former, this is both a blessing and a curse—a blessing in that Canada can count on U.S. protection, and a curse in that Canada therefore is inextricably linked to U.S. strategic policy. For the latter, it is largely a nuisance, in having to deal with an independent country that comprises its strategic forefield. In this paper are explored the complications posed by these primary facts for Ottawa's current arms control policy and thus for Washington's strategic and arms control policy.

The indivisibility of the two countries stems from a variety of factors. Let us begin with geography. Canada would be on the flight path of ballistic missiles and long-range bombers, should a strategic nuclear exchange occur between the superpowers. This passage provides the United States with increased warning time in the event of war, with defensive depth as enemy bombers (and potentially cruise missiles and ballistic missiles) can be engaged and intercepted before they reach U.S. territory, and with additional dispersal or refueling areas that increase operating ranges and decrease vulnerability for U.S. fighters and

bombers.[1] Those radar stations and air bases on Canadian territory that contribute to U.S. deterrent and warfighting capacities
probably are targeted by the USSR. Moreover, even in a conventional war, the targeting of Canadian ports, oil centers, and other
facilities important to the allied war effort would be logical.[2] Due
to its geostrategic position and the power differential from its
neighbor, which would allow Washington to use these facilities even
without Ottawa's consent, Canada is at risk should a major East-West war
occur.

Not only does geography place Canada in harm's way, but its
economic relationship with the United States also figures prominently in
this equation. The two countries form the single largest trading partnership
in the world. Twenty-two percent of U.S. trade is with Canada, while 77
percent of Canada's exports go to the United States, and 69 percent of its
imports come from the south. In 1986 the total volume of this two-way
trade was U.S. $120 billion.[3] One of the best ways to drag a reluctant ally
into a war is to threaten its economic interests.[4] In the case of Canada, it is
almost inconceivable that the U.S. economy could go to a war footing
without affecting that country. This is due to general interdependence as
well as to the relatively high degree of integration in defense economics.
The defense trade alone in 1985 was worth Can. $3,634 million, covering
such items as aircraft, electronics, parts, shipbuilding, vehicles, and
armaments.[5]

In addition to geography and economics, the two countries share close
political, social, and cultural ties, including the same dominant language.
Basic principles of democracy and the rule of law are the foundations of
both governments. Most Canadians can tune in U.S. television and radio
stations, and American programming is so prevalent that Canadian stations
are under federal restrictions to have a majority of domestic broadcasts.
The transborder tourist trade totaled Can. $8,948 million in 1986.[6] Such
linkages reinforce the geostrategic and trade commonality: regardless of
any legal or technical protestation of neutrality, Canada is clearly aligned
with the United States.

This alignment is formalized in two basic contracts: NATO and
NORAD. Both may pose problems due to the strategic direction of U.S.
policy and Canadian sensitivity to arms control. While it may seem trivial
and peevish to argue that Washington needs to pay attention to Ottawa's
voice, there are sound reasons to do so. In a recent survey, 96 percent of
U.S. "leaders" and 78 percent of the public rated Canada as very important

to their interests.[7] The trade statistics noted above confirm that opinion. Moreover, geostrategic unity cannot be overlooked; the United States needs its neighbor for its own security. In addition, Canada often acts as a bellwether for allied and world reaction to U.S. actions. If Ottawa disagrees with Washington on an issue, it is likely that the latter has gone on one of its "binges" and that world reaction will be critical; in this respect, Canada often speaks with a wisdom that the United States would do well to heed. Thus, while the issues discussed below are from a Canadian perspective, they implicitly may raise questions about the soundness of U.S. arms control policy and strategic doctrine.

Canadian Arms Control Priorities

The current Conservative government has established six priorities for its arms control agenda,[8] most clearly elaborated by the Secretary of State for External Affairs in the UN 39th General Assembly and reiterated in 1986:

1) deep and verifiable reductions in the existing arsenals of nuclear weapons;
2) the achievement of a comprehensive test ban treaty;
3) the conclusion of a chemical weapons treaty;
4) the prevention of an arms race in outer space;
5) successful review of the Non-Proliferation Treaty; and
6) an agreement on a mutual and balanced reduction of conventional forces in Europe.

These and other arms control initiatives are pursued unilaterally through numerous bilateral and multilateral channels, but here we focus on U.S.-Canadian issues that can be organized in terms of NATO, NORAD, and other forums.

Negotiations and Problems Related to NATO

Through its participation in NATO, Canada is involved directly in mutual and balanced force reductions (MBFR) talks and in the Conference on Security and Cooperation in Europe (CSCE), and indirectly in the nuclear space talks (NST) in Geneva. On the conventional side, Canada supports the move to enfold MBFR in phase two of the Committee on Disarmament in Europe (CDE) of the CSCE. Two basic reasons lie behind this position. After thirteen years, MBFR has made little progress, while the CSCE-CDE process produces agreements fairly regularly (in 1975, 1983, and 1986). It is a compromise bureaucratic position between those in the Department of External Affairs who push the human rights aspect and those who champion the militarily significant measures. As a country with a relatively small population and a foreign service of only 4,031 persons,[9] Canada is not able to pursue all the negotiations in which it has interests or at the level of representation which may be desired. A reduction in the number of forums, therefore, is generally desirable. Moreover, the number of Canadian troops involved in MBFR is not large (6,500), and the size of the contingent is mainly dictated by national concerns. Thus, particular U.S. negotiating positions, as long as they are reasonable, are unlikely to generate much controversy.

Certain elements within the government do see the enfolding as a mistake and base their opposition on three premises. First, treaty principles and language usually are more difficult to work out in a large, diverse group than in a small, relatively cohesive one. Second, the inclusion of the neutral and nonaligned countries provides them entrée to meddle in NATO defense politics, which tend to be unwieldy and tortured enough without additional actors. Third, while the neutral and nonaligned countries might propose interesting ideas, they cannot possibly be given full and unrestricted access to NATO and Warsaw Treaty Organization classified material, thus diminishing their ability to make concrete input; moreover, they currently are free to make suggestions through normal diplomatic channels. These arguments have been answered to some extent by the creation of a working group of original MBFR participants, thus gaining fairly widespread bureaucratic support for the enfolding principle.

One caveat must accompany these arguments. Some sentiment exists among the Canadian public, spurred on in no small measure by Gwynn Dyer's *War* and *Defence of Canada* movie series, for withdrawal of Canadian troops from the Central Front and, less strongly, for neutrality and nonalignment. Overall support for NATO remains fairly high, around 60 percent, basically the same as a decade ago,[10] but opponents are quite vocal today. Very few people actually follow MBFR, CSCE, or CDE negotiations, yet any publicized proposals for demilitarized or nuclear-free zones would rally the other 30 to 40 percent. This could create a certain amount of additional pressure on the Ottawa government to continue its pursuit of the reduction of tension in Europe, including diplomatic entreaties to Washington to bargain in good faith. Moreover, the New Democratic Party (NDP), which advocates withdrawal of Canadian troops from Europe, is at an all-time high in the public opinion polls. While the NDP is unlikely to embark immediately on such a course, were it elected, the threat to do so could generate tension within the NATO caucus over MBFR.

Nuclear armaments are the most problematic. Canadian governments have repeatedly stressed the importance of mutual assured destruction (MAD) as a doctrine that has brought (albeit uneasy) stability and prevented war. If MAD is in danger of being undermined either by a growing Soviet counterforce arsenal or by increased escalation linkage (such as intermediate-range nuclear forces, or INF), the way to mitigate those problems is through arms control, not through an accelerated U.S. arms acquisition under warfighting or denial doctrines or through a massive shift to defensive panaceas (such as the Strategic Defense Initiative, or SDI). The reasoning here rests on several points. First, the only major military threat to Canadian territorial integrity is a general war between the United States and the USSR: the higher the level of escalation, the greater the threat. Thus, Ottawa shares a Janus-like interest with Washington in publicly stressing the threat of escalation for the sake of deterrence while privately hoping that a war could be limited if it should occur. Such duality can be maintained under MAD, linked to the smoke-and-mirrors ambiguity of flexible response. If the United States were to change its strategic doctrine, NATO would relive the horrific coupling-decoupling debates of the mid-1960s, opening a Pandora's box full of right- and left-wing interest groups. These would not be conducive to the conduct of a sound and rational defense policy in any NATO country and could seriously weaken alliance solidarity. Since NATO is the centerpiece of Ottawa's security policy, the instability engendered by a major shift in U.S. doctrine would be resisted strongly by any Canadian government.

Second, even assuming that the alliance could muddle through doctrinally, the proponents of SDI cannot guarantee that the program would work as well as MAD is presumed to have worked. A number of noted analysts have conceded that the transition years could be dangerous.[11] It is one thing to embark on a perilous journey when you yourself are in command but quite another to be taken along as an unwilling passenger. Canada has no influence over the selection of U.S.

leaders; the American electoral process does not necessarily inspire confidence abroad, nor do the recent products of that process.[12] Having no say and little confidence in who is at the helm of the ship of state makes acceptance of Washington's policy dictates difficult.

Third, the Canadian government has linked the testing of ALCMs with general, unspecified NATO commitments and with the specific NATO two-track decision.[13] This testing, begun under an agreement signed by the Liberals in February 1983 and then continued under the Conservatives,[14] is opposed by a significant proportion of the Canadian public, and some polls even register majority opposition.[15] ALCM testing is believed by many to run counter to Pierre Trudeau's suffocation policy and, more broadly, to the claims of the current government that the reversal of the arms race is one of its top priorities. The Liberal party is now badly split on the issue, and the NDP is strongly opposed to further testing. While supporting cruise missile testing, the current government's response to the deployment of the 131st bomber was couched in fairly harsh language: "The Government viewed with serious concern the Administration's announced intention in the spring and deplores the implementation of that decision today."[16] If the SALT II restraints on ALCMs continue to be violated by the United States and if ALCMs are not placed under constraints elsewhere (that is, INF), public pressure to halt cruise missile testing may provoke governmental action.

The Canadian government has consistently supported the U.S. negotiating position on INF since talks opened in 1981, and it hailed the U.S.-USSR treaty signed in December 1987 as a significant step in the reduction of tension and in arms control. While the treaty eased the minds of many, the more radical elements of the Canadian disarmament movement argue that now, more than ever, cruise missile testing must stop.

Negotiations and Problems Related to NORAD

The ALCM issue is closer to NORAD concerns, since one of the side benefits of the testing is practice for US F-15s/16s and Canadian F-18 teams in tracking and intercepting cruise missiles. With the new Bear-Hs and Blackjacks configured for missile carrying and the September 1986 interception of the former off the coast of Alaska,[17] Soviet ALCMs pose a new threat to North America. The new North Warning System (NWS) will have only a limited capacity for cruise missile detection, the primary responsibility falling to the AWACS with the first line of defense the CF-18s. The training is thus fairly critical to the defensive capabilities of NORAD.[18] Should the public outcry on ALCM arms control limits gather intensity and should cruise missile testing be suspended, the United States will have to face the loss of the training experience gained thereby. More importantly, if public perception regards U.S. actions and arms control violations as the main reasons why Canada must increase defense spending to counter a Soviet ALCM threat, that money may not be forthcoming. Washington then would have to decide either to pay the money (with Canadian sovereignty concerns still determining how to spend it) or to live with somewhat reduced security.

The submarine-launched cruise missile (SLCM) threat is beginning to receive public attention.[19] LRSLCMs would pose the same type of strategic threat as ALCMs, with the same concerns about NORAD/NWS sufficiency. However, they also touch the sovereignty nerve on two counts. First, just as it would be preferable to attack the bomber before it could launch its missiles, so too would it be preferable to attack the cruise missile submarine (SSGN). Current technology does not provide an exploitable full-scale surveillance capacity for the Arctic to enable such a mission, and, even were that possible, Canada currently has no attack submarines (SSNs) by which it could mount a defense. Thus, Canada must be prepared to allow in its waters U.S., British, or French submarines capable of under-ice operations until the late 1990s, when deployment of its own ice-capable SSNs is scheduled.[20] In war this would pose few difficulties, but peacetime planning could and has engendered serious and acrimonious debates concerning the sovereignty of those waters. Arctic sovereignty is an issue that could bring down a government in Canada.

Second, one of the images held by Canadians about their defense is that it is nonnuclear.[21] As hypocritical as that may seem, since Canada is part of NORAD and NATO, it is nevertheless true that Ottawa's participation in those arrangements is nonnuclear and that nuclear weapons are relegated in theory to a strict deterrence-only role. The hue and cry over U.S. contingency plans to use nuclear depth charges in Canadian harbors would be nothing compared to what would happen if nuclear-powered and nuclear-armed SSNs roamed the Canadian Arctic archipelago.[22]

External Affairs Minister Joe Clark acknowledged in early 1987 in the House of Commons that his country and the United States were trying to find ways to guarantee Canadian sovereignty while ensuring North American security,[23] but a Mulroney-Reagan agreement was not forthcoming at the Shamrock Summit in April 1987. Ottawa apparently was willing to trade away a formal U.S. recognition of Canada's sovereignty in return for prior notification and approval of American ship movements.[24] In an agreement signed in January 1988, the two governments arranged such a compromise for the passage of ice breakers. The sovereignty claims of both states are deemed to be unprejudiced by this agreement. Such an understanding, which gives Canada nominal veto power over U.S. transits, helps assuage nationalist concerns while allowing SSNs essentially unrestricted passage.

Without agreement (despite negotiations), and should there be another "unapproved" U.S. ship or submarine in Canadian waters, the issue will become more serious. While the notion of placing Captor mines in the three main entrance or egress points[25] was quickly disavowed by the government,[26] the idea may garner support on the next round. Moreover, since the USSR supports Canadian sovereignty claims,[27] failure of the United States to make any meaningful compromises is bound to have a deleterious effect on public relations.

This entire complex of cruise missiles, submarines, security, and sovereignty could simmer for a long time in the absence of some dramatic event. However, discussions on the expansion of NORAD to the sea are continuing, and at least some of the technical arrangements are expected to be in place by 1992.[28] Although this presumably will be done by executive agreement and exchange of letters or memorandums, thus requiring cabinet but not parliamentary approval, two points must be kept in mind. First, the House of Commons insisted on holding extensive hearings on the renewal of NORAD in 1985, which resulted in over 1,000 pages of testimony.[29] The same may be predicted for a maritime NORAD. Second, the Conservatives must hold an election no later than September 1989. Public opinion polls since March 1987 and by-elections in July 1987 indicate that the government is in serious trouble (primarily over domestic scandals but also over perceived toadying to the United States), and, if these trends continue, it is entirely possible that a NDP government, particularly in coalition with the Liberals, may come to power. At the very least, the NDP would form a more significant opposition than it now does. In either event, defense agreements with Washington would probably face more resistance than has ever been the case.

As serious as is the foregoing area, SDI may be even worse. The official Canadian response to Washington's SDI offer in 1985 was that "after careful and detailed consideration, the government of Canada has concluded that Canada's own policies and priorities do not warrant a government-to-government effort in support of SDI research." However, two qualifications were attached: first, that Canada supports SDI research "in light of significant advances in Soviet research"; and second, that its universities and privately owned companies are free to bid for SDI-related contracts.[30] The hesitancy stems from the government's adherence to MAD, its support for the ABM Treaty, and public pressure. Ottawa's stance on the treaty is unambiguous—the narrow interpretation must stand.[31] This follows logically from support for MAD and responds to public fears over Canadian entanglement in SDI and thence in U.S. warfighting plans. Entanglement could arise from three major sources: organization, technology, and strategy.

The fear of organizational entanglement is based on two connections: first, the deputy commander of NORAD is a Canadian; and second, the NORAD warning system presumably would be linked to SDI alert and subsequent use. Given the command structure changes with the advent of Space Command, which, in line with historical precedent, separate warning and offense by providing a distinct command system that links NORAD only through the American commander's multiple hats, the first fear is largely nonfactually based. Only in times of extreme crisis and confusion could the Canadian deputy commander in chief be involved in SDI decisions, and then only on an ad hoc basis. The second linkage is more logical, as almost all existing warning networks (such as DEWs, BMEW, Pave Paws) are channeled through NORAD, and it would be strange if no connection were made to SDI systems. Moreover—and this is the fear of technological linkage—some of the surveillance systems that might be incorporated into SDI also could be used as part of a space-based surveillance for bombers and cruise missiles as a follow-on to the NWS. The U.S. project for this latter purpose, Strategic Defense Architecture (SDA) 2000 and the Air Defense Initiative (ADI), had some early Canadian involvement given the relationship to NORAD. Certain of these assets for future air defense, such as Teal Ruby, arguably have SDI potential.[32]

The strategic dimension of entanglement is premised primarily on the roof-and-walls analogy.[33] This argument posits that building a roof (SDI) if there are no corresponding walls (NWS-SDA 2000) makes no sense; the roof would stop standard trajectory ballistic missiles but not depressed-trajectory submarine-launched ballistic missiles (SLBMs), SLCMs, or ALCMs. Thus, with the deployment of SDI, the concern is that Canada would have to "thicken" significantly its traditional air defense. In addition, some members of the public are worried that land-based SDI systems that would be used for a boost-phase attack might be based in Canada's north. Both of these potentialities would imply Ottawa's direct participation, or at least complicity, in SDI strategy and use.

Given this complex of fears, which are voiced loudly and receive pronounced media coverage, it is not surprising that the government moves cautiously on SDI and insists on strict adherence to the ABM Treaty. Should the United States unilaterally adopt the broad interpretation of the treaty in the absence of negotiated limits on SDI systems, the Canadian government most likely would face strong public opposition to continued participation in any NORAD arrangements perceived to be tainted by SDI and linked to alleged violations of the treaty. Such a situation could provoke a severe crisis in U.S.-Canadian relations and call into question the joint defense of the two countries.

This is not to say that NORAD is in imminent danger of being dismantled. Majority public opinion generally supports the alliance structure, including joint defense of the continent. Despite testimony to the contrary, the review by Parliament did recommend renewal of NORAD,[34] and the Defence White Paper maintains NORAD as an integral part of Canadian defense policy.[35] However, a growing divergence is evident in beliefs about the reality of the Soviet threat and the nature of threats to Canadian security. Even government spokesmen proclaim that nuclear war is the greatest threat to security. Understandably, such a notion has become a kind of rallying cry for the disarmament movement, whose adherents take a sidestep by assuming this means that the superpowers are to be blamed and feared equally. Such reasoning then is mixed with the anti-American nationalistic fervor over sovereignty and fears of SDI, leading to a decided tendency to see the United States as the likely instigator, if not actual initiator, of nuclear war. It follows that the USSR is the more natural ally, since it would be the other victim of Washington's war aims. Mikhail Gorbachev's *glasnost* and his "peace and disarmament offensive" also contribute to these perceptions.

The "truth" is by and large irrelevant; the political pressure is not. For persons untrained in international relations and strategic doctrine, the subtleties of the Canadian government's pro-MAD/pro-ABM and also pro-NORAD/slightly pro-SDI stance are difficult to fathom. The government could and is attempting to do more to educate the public, but that is a long-term, exacting task at best. Only if Washington is seen to be negotiating in good faith is this vocal segment of the public (often backed and led by the NDP) likely to be rendered ineffective on major defense issues.

Negotiations and Problems in Other Forums

The most prominent of the non-NATO, non-NORAD issues is that of a comprehensive test ban (CTB). Since the 1960s CTB has been relatively high on Canada's agenda, and its preference seems to be for a step-by-step approach effected in tandem with cuts in the nuclear arsenals. Canadian involvement in CTB negotiations is mainly through the CSCE's Committee on Disarmament at Geneva and focuses on diplomatic compromise and verification. Once again, the problem in the bilateral aspect is public opinion. Although Ottawa took a position only slightly different from Washington's on the Soviet moratorium,[36] some members of the public believed that a historic arms control opportunity had been lost and urged the government to do more to pressure the United States.[37] Those opposing Ottawa's stance queried how the government could claim to be in favor of a CTB and then not fully support the USSR by publicly pressuring Washington to join in. Since the Soviets now have resumed testing and the U.S. Senate is actively considering ratification of the Limited Test Ban Treaty and the Threshold Test Ban Treaty, this issue has faded for the time being.

Chemical arms control also is high on Canada's agenda, and the country has done a great deal of work both independently and through the United Nations. The main disagreement with the United States occurred in 1985 when Canada voted for a UN resolution urging states to refrain from the production of binary weapons; by May 1986, Ottawa was supporting Washington's NATO deployment plans.[38] The cluster of other negotiations at the Committee on Disarmament or at the United Nations, on such topics as outer space, disarmament and development, military budgets, and weapons of mass destruction, also are relatively noncontroversial, except when they impinge on outstanding issues, as outer space does on the ABM Treaty.

Conclusion

It is naive to believe that any of these arguments would persuade the United States to adopt a different tack on the basis of sheer reasonableness or for the sake of pleasing an ally. If the Reagan administration or Congress finds Canada to be too troublesome an ally, economic pressure easily could be brought to bear. Another way around Ottawa would be through technology, much as is already being done in ADI, thus obviating a pressing need for the use of Canadian territory, and through organizational structures that exclude Canadians from decision making.[39] Ottawa therefore must use ways and means that would contribute to the realization of an enlightened self-interest on the part of Washington. This would include normal political and technical diplomacy at a variety of levels as well as coalition building among like-minded allies. Having been somewhat embarrassed by direct lobbying efforts over acid rain, the government may be somewhat reluctant to engage in that type of activity, but it is probably necessary. Judicious selection of a few congressmen and senators for trips to Ottawa would not be amiss. As Prime Minister Brian Mulroney has noted, Canada must not let its neighbor forget that "arms control is a component of, not a substitute for, a healthy national security policy."[40]

Notes

[1] This is the standard formulation. See, for example, Roger Swanson, "Deterrence, Detente, and Canada," in H. E. English, ed., *Canada-U.S. Relations, Proceedings of the Academy of Political Science* 32, no. 2 (New York: Academy of Political Science, 1976), pp. 101, 103; George Lindsey, "Defending North America: A Historical Perspective," in R. Byers, ed., *Aerospace Defence: Canada's Future Role?*

Wellesley Papers 9 (Toronto: Canadian Institute of International Affairs, 1985), pp. 10–15.

2 Over $1 billion in goods were sold by Canada to the United States under the U.S., UK, and Canada Production and Resources Board set up in 1942, out of a total of $9.5 billion in war production. F. H. Turner, "World War II Defence Production Planning," at the 1983 Symposium *Planning for Mobilization*, Emergency Planning Canada. Morton has somewhat different figures: "By 1943, 1,239,327 Canadian men and women delivered $8.7 billion in industrial production." Desmond Morton, *A Military History of Canada* (Edmonton: Hurtig, 1985), p. 184. Canada's industrial capacity today would be larger, although about the same relative to other countries, and its contribution to an allied war effort therefore valuable.

3 The 22 percent of U.S. trade and the total volume of $120 billion are from "U.S.-Canada Relations," GIST (Washington, DC: Bureau of Public Affairs, Department of State, March 1987). The Canadian import and export figures are taken from *Imports by Countries 1986*, p. 19, and *Exports by Countries 1986*, p. 17 (Ottawa: Statistics Canada).

4 Following the logic of Bruce M. Russett, "The Calculus of Deterrence," *Journal of Conflict Resolution* 7, no. 2 (March 1963): 104–5.

5 C. G. Galligan, "The Economic Impact of Canadian Defence Expenditures, FY 1984–85 Update," Report No. 11 (Kingston: Centre for Studies in Defence Resources Management, Royal Military College, Summer 1986), p. 62, Table 4-3.

6 Information received via author's telephone call to Statistics Canada, Edmonton office, April 13, 1987.

7 John E. Reilly, ed., *American Public Opinion and U.S. Foreign Policy, 1987* (Chicago: Council on Foreign Relations, March 1987), p. 17. Canada is ranked second by leaders behind Japan and West Germany, both at 98 percent; with the public, it is second to the United Kingdom at 83 percent.

8 For a detailed discussion of these and other points see Lieutenant-Colonel W. Alexander Morrison, *Concerns of a Middle Power: The Canadian Role and Interests in Arms Control and Disarmament Affairs*, Paper presented to the University of Manitoba Political Studies Student Conference, February 27–March 1, 1986.

9 Department of External Affairs, *Annual Report 1985–86* (Ottawa: 1986), p. 66.

10 Gallup poll results reported in "Majority of Canadians Reject Military Neutrality," *Ottawa Citizen*, May 26, 1986; also in "Stay in NATO, 56% Say," *Montreal Gazette*, May 26, 1986.

11 Ashton Carter and David Schwartz, eds., *Ballistic Missile Defense* (Washington, DC: Brookings Institution, 1984); esp. Schwartz, "Future Prospects," pp. 356–57, 362–63, and S. Keeney, "Reactions and Perspectives," pp. 413–14.

12 Public opinion polls of Canadian attitudes toward Ronald Reagan are few and far between. A November 1984 poll showed 62 percent having a favorable impression of the president (*Globe and Mail*, March 30, 1985). In January 1986, 47 percent of Canadians believed in the U.S. ability to deal with world problems, but 43 percent had little confidence. "Canadian Opinion Split on U.S. Ability Re World Problems," *The Gallup Report* (Toronto: Canadian Institute of Public Opinion, March 6, 1986).

13 "Facts about the Cruise Missile," pamphlet from Director General of Information, Department of National Defence, Ottawa, 1985. See also Pierre Trudeau, "An Open Letter to All Canadians," printed in *Calgary Herald*, May 10, 1983. A figure of 60 percent opposition is cited in David Francis, "Canadian Ire Grows," *Christian Science Monitor*, February 26, 1987. See also John Barrett and Douglas Ross, "The ALCM and Canadian Arms Control Policy," *Canadian Public Policy* 11, no. 4 (1985): 711–30.

14 *The Canada-U.S. (CANUS) Test and Evaluation Program*, signed February 10, 1983, by Canada's ambassador to the United States, Allan Gotlieb, and by U.S. Acting Secretary of State Kenneth W. Dam. The first test over Canadian territory took place on March 6, 1984.

15 *Christian Science Monitor*, January 25, 1983. Also, both the Yukon Legislature and the Legislative Assembly of the Northwest Territories have voted against continued cruise missile testing. *Globe and Mail*, April 4, 1986, on the Yukon; and March 7, 1986, on the Northwest Territories.

16 "Canada Views U.S.A. Decision on SALT II with Serious Concern," Statement in the House of Commons, November 28, 1986, by the Right Honourable Joe Clark; reprinted in *Disarmament Bulletin* (Ottawa: Arms Control and Disarmament Division, External Affairs, Winter 1986–Spring 1987), p. 3.

17 "Soviet Bombers Intercepted by Jets," *Ottawa Citizen*, September 12, 1986.

18 Drones and other small planes could and most likely will be used to simulate cruise missiles for training purposes, but the real thing is best. This is true not only for the CF-18s but also for the F-15s and F-16s. See, for example, statements by Major L. Rossetto, *Calgary Herald*, January 13, 1986; and "Alberta Cruise Test Delayed," *Globe and Mail*, January 21, 1986.

19 William Winegard (chairman), *Canada-U.S. Defence Cooperation and the 1986 Renewal of the NORAD Agreement*, Report of the Standing Committee on External Affairs and National Defence, First Session of the Thirty-Third Parliament (Ottawa: House of Commons, February 1986), p. 41 (hereafter SCEAND Report); David Cox, *Trends in Continental Defence: A Canadian Perspective* (Ottawa: Canadian Institute for International Peace and Security, December 1986), pp. 18–24; Erick Solem, "Energy, Technology, and Strategy in the Arctic," in R. Byers and M. Slack, eds., *Strategy and the Arctic*, Polaris Papers no. 4 (Toronto: Canadian Institute

of Strategic Studies, 1986), p. 92; W. H. Critchley, "Polar Deployment of Soviet Submarines," *International Journal* 39 (Autumn 1984): 864.

20 Perrin Beatty, minister, Department of National Defence, *Challenge and Commitment: A Defence Policy for Canada* (Ottawa: Canadian Government Publishing Centre, June 1987), pp. 51–55.

21 This goes back to the 1971 White Paper and the subsequent denuclearization of the Canadian forces, which was finally completed in 1984.

22 This was exposed by William Arkin, who later also revealed crisis dispersal plans for B-52s to Canadian bases. See Paul Knox, "Expert on Military Network Stirs International Ripples," *Globe and Mail*, March 19, 1985.

23 Clark statement; broadcast on *The National* (CBC-TV), April 7, 1987; *House of Commons Debates* 129, no. 102 (Ottawa: Government Publishing Centre), 2nd sess., 33d Parliament, p. 4927.

24 That particular position was announced on *The National* (CBC-TV), April 6, 1987, although news reports were less specific; for example, Jeff Sallot and Christopher Waddell, "Irritants Unresolved," *Globe and Mail*, April 7, 1987; and "Talks Made Progress," ibid., April 8, 1987.

25 Cox, *Trends in Continental Defence*, pp. 45–47.

26 Jeff Sallot, "Laying Mines in Arctic Is Rejected," *Globe and Mail*, February 5, 1987.

27 "A Northern Dimension for Canada's Foreign Policy," *Independence and Internationalism*, Report of the Special Joint Committee on Canada's International Relations (Ottawa, June 1986), chap. 10, p. 131.

28 Robert Gordon, "NORAD Link-up Planned," *Halifax Chronicle-Herald*, February 14, 1986. The year 1992 coincides with the projected completion date of NWS. See also SCEAND Report, p. 74.

29 SCEAND Report.

30 Official text of the prime minister's statement and the letter from Defence Minister Eric Nielsen are in *Disarmament Bulletin* (Autumn 1985): 7. See also discussions in Michael Clugston, "A Polite 'No' to Star Wars," *Macleans* 98, no. 37 (September 16, 1985): 10–11; also in Fred Langan, "Canada Wants Free Trade with the U.S. But Spurns 'Star Wars,'" *Christian Science Monitor*, September 18, 1985.

31 Statement by Secretary of State for External Affairs the Right Honourable Joe Clark in House of Commons, January 23, 1986, as reported in Jeff Sallot, "Canada to Continue...," *Globe and Mail*, January 24, 1986; see also Dan Leger, "U.S. Abiding by Treaty," *Globe and Mail*, October 22, 1986. For the full text see *House of Commons Debates* 7, 1st sess., 33d Parliament, January 23, 1986, pp. 10100–102.

32 See remarks by Joel Sokolsky, *Dalhousie Newsletter* 5, nos. 6–7 (Halifax: Dalhousie University Centre for Foreign Policy Studies), p. 28

[33] For example, Lawrence Hagen, "Approaching the Crossroads," *Arms Control Communique* (Ottawa: Canadian Centre for Arms Control and Disarmament, November 1985); Cox, *Trends in Continental Defence*, pp. 27–30.

[34] Winegard, *Canada-U.S. Defence Cooperation.*

[35] Beatty, *Challenge and Commitment.*

[36] The Canadians welcomed the declaration as a step in the right direction but called for a negotiated and verifiable CTB. (Author's interviews.) See also Douglas Roche, *Statement to the 1st Committee at the 24th UNGA* (Ottawa: DEA Communique, October 16, 1986), p. 8.

[37] See the report on the Consultative Group, *Disarmament Bulletin* (Winter 1986–Spring 1987): 9.

[38] On the Canadian chemical weapons position in general see Douglas Roche, *Canada and the Pursuit of Peace* (Ottawa: Department of External Affairs, July 1985). The UN vote discussion is in *Arms Control Reporter* (Brookline, MA: Institute for Defense and Disarmament Studies, 1985), Sect. 704, "Chemical Weapons," p. 704.B.152. The support of deployment was reported in "Canada Backs Chemical Arms Plan," *Ottawa Citizen*, May 23, 1986.

[39] John Hamre, "Continental Air Defence," in Byers, *Aerospace Defence*, pp. 27–29; Cox, *Trends in Continental Defence*, p. 41.

[40] Speech by the prime minister to the Consultative Group on Disarmament and Arms Control, Ottawa, October 31, 1986.

Arms Control and Strategic Surprise

PATRICK M. MORGAN

ARMS CONTROL HAS been proposed and, on occasion, practiced in every system of autonomous states. We can find traces of it in the ancient Chinese and Greek city-state systems, in Renaissance Italy, and in feudal and postfeudal Europe.[1] "Arms control" is a modern term, but the idea behind it is not. However, in the twentieth century there has been a shift in its nature, functions, and importance. Generally speaking, it has become more significant and more elusive. The search for arms control has been far more intensive in this century, especially in the latter half, than in any previous one, but we are not particularly better off as a result. Indeed, our search for arms control has been misguided. To an excessive and harmful degree, the search has been set within the context supplied by the weapons at hand rather than being used to shape that context. We have been looking for arms control of the wrong sort and in the wrong way.

Strategic surprise is an equally old idea (remember the Trojan horse?). As with arms control, an important shift with respect to strategic surprise has taken place in this century. It has become distinctly more appealing to military strategists. It also, in a technical sense, has become more feasible—weapons systems now lend themselves better to it than they did in the past. The incidence of strategic surprise has risen sharply in recent decades, and coping with it has become a serious concern for governments. The possibilities for strategic surprise have shaped the development of strategic thought, with effects that have rippled through military procurements, deployments, and warning systems. Strategic surprise, therefore, is the place to start when thinking about and designing strategic arms control endeavors.

Let us explore the relationship, in theory and practice, between arms control and strategic surprise. We have nearly a century of experience with the modern versions of these phenomena as the basis for distilling some lessons. As arms control now is a promising area in superpower relations once again, it is all the more important to perceive it as clearly as possible. The discussion to follow turns on the point that arms control and strategic surprise are fundamentally incompatible. In itself, that is not a very useful statement; many people would readily agree. However, arms control and strategic surprise are incompatible in that they are contrasting and competing solutions to the same problem, and that as a solution to this problem each, in essence, has evaded or eliminated the other. The tension between the two is significant. However, governments consistently find it very hard to choose between them; often they try to apply elements of both of these solutions simultaneously, injecting that tension into the heart of their national security policies.

Definitions

We begin by grappling with terminology. Arms control consists of measures, directly related to military forces, adopted by governments to contain the costs and harmful consequences of the continued existence of arms, with the objective of sustaining or enhancing their security. Elaboration on the elements of this definition can be found elsewhere,[2] so only the following points will be mentioned. First, arms control is not disarmament because it rests on the anticipation that arms will still exist. In fact, arms control frequently is coupled with the view that weapons are necessary and sometimes quite useful and that true disarmament might even be harmful. In contrast, disarmament advocates are moved by opposition to arms, military forces, and their results. When arms control takes the form of cutbacks in weapons, the two overlap. However, while certain reductions, or even the elimination of a category, might be a part of arms control (as in the biological warfare treaty), such steps are functionally distinct from disarmament because the overall conceptions of what is being done and why are quite different.

Second, arms control is very broad; many steps can be taken to make arms more bearable. Here we will be concerned with major arms control measures designed to deal with the most significant forces. The term "forces" calls attention to the fact that arms control deals not only with weapons but also with military strength, and this includes armed forces and the panoply of economic and organizational resources that creates and sustains them. For instance, arms control efforts after World War I included eliminating the draft in Germany. Modern war seemed to require a mass army. Without conscription there would be no reservoir of trained men to mobilize, and without the ability to mobilize a mass army quickly Germany could not decide to attack. In a current example, the Soviet government seeks to ban not only the Strategic Defense Initiative (SDI) as a weapons system but also even the research necessary to develop it.

The other key term is "strategic surprise," referring to a military attack. This is the way most people use it, but it is worth noting that the term can be broader and encompass more meanings. There can be surprise attacks with strategic implications and consequences that are not military in nature. An example is the 1973 Arab oil boycott—certainly a surprise, clearly an attack, and immense in its effect. There are also strategic surprises of a nonmilitary sort that are not attacks, such as the Molotov-Ribbentrop Pact. Our subject is military surprise attack, the most grievous surprise in statecraft and a phenomenon of considerable concern to arms control.

What makes a surprise attack strategic in nature? While there is no precise measure, a surprise attack usually is strategic in terms of two dimensions. In the first, the attack is meant to alter decisively the military situation, to affect greatly the course of hostilities and possibly determine their outcome. In this sense it is the central component of the attacker's grand strategy. The other dimension is the perception of the attack by the defender, his seeing it as a very serious strike at his national strategy. It is this larger purpose that sets it apart from tactical surprise.[3] Strategic surprise can be employed at any stage in a war, but its most familiar application is at the start, and war initiation by strategic surprise has received considerable attention.[4]

There also is the question of what constitutes a surprise. Most obvious is the case where the attack is unexpected, but in many instances the occurrence itself is not the surprise. Instead, its nature or scale may be shocking. The surprise might be in the timing or location of the attack or even in the weapons and methods employed. Finally, the surprise may result from some unanticipated combination of these features.

Arms Control versus Strategic Surprise

In Europe, activities now called arms control were undertaken for centuries in pursuit of two objectives: to limit the incidence of war and to curb its destructiveness once it had broken out. War was seen either as a normal, legitimate feature of international politics or as an unavoidable one. Thus, the idea was to confine outbreaks to appropriate circumstances and suitable goals and then to prevent the fighting from inflicting unnecessary harm. These laudable aims were pursued largely through the development of international law on war as expressed in the standard practices of states, conventions, treaties, or scholarly codifications and elaborations. There were rules for when, why, and how to initiate war as well as restrictions designed to protect civilians and neutrals, curtail needless brutality, and avoid destruction of churches, hospitals, and other civilian property. Eventually, efforts were made to give these objectives an organizational dimension, such as in the creation of the Red Cross societies.

These efforts reached new and important heights in the nineteenth century, only to have twentieth-century warfare shatter the laws and constraints in ferociously brutal ways. The result was a shift in emphasis and a major adjustment in the priorities assigned to arms control. Two bouts of global warfare have made the prevention of such wars the primary objective. Attention still is paid to the goal of limiting wars, but this is shaped by the overriding objective of preventing any further great-power wars. Thus, much of the theory and practice of limiting war concerns how to prevent any small ones from leading to another great cataclysm. As for limiting a great-power conflict should it occur, there has been no consensus of confidence since 1945 that such wars can be limited. In addition, the perceived benefits of seeking ways to limit such wars have been depreciated by the fear that confidence they can be limited will only make them more plausible or feasible in the eyes of decision makers, a pernicious result. It seems clear that, more than anything else, strategic arms control is really in the business of war prevention.

Great states today believe that the critical factor in war prevention is nuclear deterrence. Thus, the maintenance of stable nuclear deterrence relationships is the core subject of arms control in both theory and practice. (By extension, the creation and refinement of deterrence theory would be an arms control endeavor.) The classic theory of arms control emerged at the end of the 1950s as an extension or logical product of deterrence theory and strategy. The relationship is so extensive that elsewhere we have argued that nuclear deterrence is best thought of as a form of arms control (instead of seeing arms control as an adjunct of deterrence). The whole point of having nuclear deterrence is never to have a nuclear conflict or even another great-power conventional war. That nuclear deterrence is arms control means that we live in an era completely dominated by the pursuit of arms control, that ours is an arms control age. This is not the normal way of looking at it. Instead, deterrence is what we use for war prevention, and arms control, it is said, contributes to this by working to curb breakdowns in deterrence. There is no need to pursue the matter further at this point. Our interest here is in the fact that arms control these days definitely concerns war prevention.

The need to emphasize prevention over limitation was driven by the emergence of nuclear deterrence because, for some reason, nuclear deterrence came to be imagined and then practiced in a fashion almost totally incompatible with war limitation. Relatively early in the nuclear age—certainly no later than the mid-1950s—superpower deterrence came to be seen as requiring nothing less than a capacity to destroy an attacker as a viable society. Superpower nuclear arsenals were designed with this in mind. To this day, such a capacity is seen as the minimum necessary for deterrence.[5] In effect, each side deters by threatening to fight a completely unlimited war. Such thinking was encouraged by the fact that nuclear weapons were far from discrete (and they still are). Thus, in a nuclear conflict many of the old limitations on war would be meaningless.

Both in their immediate effects if used and in their ultimate consequences if fully used, nuclear arsenals go far beyond traditional restraints in war. Arms control thinking has considered the idea of a limited nuclear war or of a great-power conflict confined to the conventional forces level. Flexible response as a strategy initially was justified as contributing to arms control in this way, but it was abandoned as a declaratory posture by Robert McNamara because it had consequences that damaged other arms control objectives, including deterrence stability. It also left the Europeans uneasy and fearful that it undermined war prevention. The ultimate in recent war limitation ideas is the zero option for theater nuclear forces and, once again, many European officials are disturbed.

Another shift in the arms control agenda in this century has been an expanded interest in restraining arms races. The idea that states caught in an arms race would do better to cooperate so as to curtail their costs and avoid unnecessary tension emerged in the latter half of the nineteenth century in connection with periodic Anglo-French naval rivalries. It was frequently voiced, with no results, during the general arms race after 1890. The tsar referred to it in calling for The Hague Conference of 1899. After World War I, naval races were curtailed for a time by the Washington and London naval agreements. After 1945 the idea became generally accepted as feasible and finally resulted in the SALT process.

However, the emergence of nuclear weapons has complicated matters in this regard as well. At first glance nuclear weapons seem to offer an excellent basis for halting an arms race. After a certain point, enough is enough. There is no meaningful "superiority" for either side; the race has no winner. With no one able to win the race, there is a strong incentive to stop running it. As we know, events have not turned out that way. Fear that the enemy can exploit politically and psychologically an image of superiority promotes arms racing anyway. So does the fear that a single massive retaliatory option is unusable and incredible—to have "options" requires multiplying nuclear forces and supplementing them with an array of conventional forces. A single large arms competition becomes myriads of little ones. Finally, there is the pressure to play it safe when it comes to one side's assured destruction capability. Redundancy, as in the U.S. strategic triad, is the result, and this fosters even larger strategic arsenals.

Now, let us turn to strategic surprise. The conditions that have led to a much greater incidence of strategic surprise began to emerge in the latter half of the nineteenth century. Leading governments began to develop capacities to wage mass warfare. Greater control over their populations, backed by nationalism, meant that huge armies were possible. The Industrial Revolution and economic development provided the necessary wherewithal and equipment. Organizational innovations in the military, such as the general staff, together with improvements in transportation and communications, allowed these huge forces to be moved, supplied, and directed in a coordinated way. And new weapons made it possible to inflict huge casualties.

The Prussians were the first to exploit these developments and produced a new form of warfare that, in 1866 and 1870, was a strategic surprise. But once other states imitated the Prussian way of war, no premium was placed on surprise. War was a mass endeavor, a vast national effort to overwhelm the enemy in a few great battles. Surprise was not particularly relevant, or so it seemed, yet these developments were to have the effect in the next century of encouraging the use of surprise attacks.

After 1890 (and even after 1870), when analysts contemplated the shape of a future great-power war, the scale of the effort that would be needed seemed impossible for nations to sustain for long. Economically the burden would be too great, with the sheer expense of an enormous army, the demand for arms and equipment, and the absence of young men from the labor force. It would be impossible psychologically as well. Mass armies fighting huge battles with modern weapons would impose unprecedented casualties, soon sapping morale at the front as well as back home. It would even be politically impossible. In the face of such burdens, political support could not be sustained, and the internal political order would crack.

On the eve of World War I, the Germans faced the problem in an acute way. They feared a war on two fronts against the Franco-Russian Alliance. Facing opponents with greater total resources, they were the first to turn to the most natural military solution: find a way to win quickly. To avoid a war that, it was believed, would soon produce exhaustion, it was vital for the Germans to have a strategy that would achieve overwhelming victories in the initial battles and thereby shatter the enemy. Therefore, much attention was paid in Germany and elsewhere to rapid mobilization—get to the battlefield first with the most—so as to take the advantage in early decisive engagements. Plans for victorious initial offensives in a short war proliferated all over Europe. (At sea the German and British navies thought in terms of a decisive sea battle early in any war as the key to control of the oceans.)

Furthermore, the Germans sought to secure the advantage that would accrue from a strategic surprise. France had to be knocked out of the coming war quickly so German forces could be concentrated against the Russians. The Schlieffen Plan rested on surprising the French with the extent of the sweep through Belgium and with the scale and mobility of the forces employed, to achieve a great envelopment. In effect, this was a perverted form of war limitation, using a massive opening blow to enable one's own side to escape the worst burdens that modern warfare could impose.

It turned out that the confidence in decisive initial victories by means of rapid mobilization and great offensives was badly misplaced. The major participants in World War I suffered a grave disappointment in terms of the results of these strategies. Instead of victory, the outcome was stalemate.

Unfortunately, expectations for the staying power of modern states turned out to be equally flawed. As a gigantic war of attrition, World War I lasted not for a few weeks, as was expected, but for years.

If going straight at the enemy was suicidal, then attacking indirectly and employing surprise were bound to get more attention. An intense desire to avoid a repetition of World War I led Basil Liddell Hart to stress maneuver and the indirect approach. Adolf Hitler and his generals moved to put these concepts together with strategic surprise. They turned to the blitzkrieg, which was initially a strategic surprise all by itself, and Hitler eventually accompanied it with attacks by surprise on several occasions. The Japanese resorted to a series of strategic surprises at Pearl Harbor, in the Philippines, and in Malaya. Their goal was to win the resources of a huge empire quickly and then use the natural advantages of the defense to exhaust their opponents' counterattacks.

Inclinations toward strategic surprise of this sort were strongly reinforced after 1945 by nuclear weapons, especially when those weapons were married to long-range delivery systems. Early air-power theorists in the 1920s had claimed that strategic bombing was the way to win wars quickly and cheaply. This turned out to be nonsense until nuclear weapons arrived. The perfect weapons for quick victory, they were ideal either for destroying an enemy's forces or shattering his civilian sector.

A contributing factor throughout this century has been an inclination in military organizations to stress seizing the initiative and going on the offensive as the proper way to make war. This can be traced to the influence of Karl von Clausewitz: war is a contest of wills, and the object must be to break the enemy's will to fight—done best by offensively smashing his forces, not defensively eroding them. Clausewitz aside, an offensive orientation made a good deal of sense as warfare progressively became more deadly. Soldiers had good reason to want to surprise the enemy and defeat him quickly. This inclination also has been ascribed to the bureaucratic interests of military forces since before 1914. An offensive orientation helped to maintain political support, justify large military budgets, and reinforce the services' professional autonomy.

National experience has had mixed effects, but sometimes it contributes to an inclination toward the use of strategic surprise. The British and French came out of the furnace of 1914–1918 wedded to a defensive approach to war that, in the end, left them quite vulnerable to strategic surprise. The German defeat in that long and exhausting struggle, on the other hand, contributed directly to Hitler's search for ways to win quickly and cheaply. To the Russians in World War II, being on the defensive and on the wrong end of a strategic surprise was a bad way to win, which led them to a postwar preoccupation with ensuring that any future war would be carried to the enemy, by surprise where possible, and fought on his territory.

For the United States the fear that a war would pose too grave a burden was slow to emerge. As late as 1949, American military planners still were expecting that the next conflict would be lengthy, and they counted on mobilization as the key to winning.[6] But in the 1950s, Washington moved secretly to an operational strategy of preemption to produce a short war—a strategy that envisioned an attack not, perhaps, completely by surprise but certainly before the Soviet Union had fully prepared for it.[7] The Korean and Vietnam wars brought home just how unacceptable even a limited modern war could be. This helps explain Secretary of Defense Caspar Weinberger's well-publicized view that if the United States uses force, it must be in a decisive fashion to settle the matter quickly.

Finally, there are the heightened organizational and technical capacities of states that invite the use of strategic surprise. Normally, a strategic surprise attack is a highly elaborate endeavor. We already have noted that the organization, transportation, communications, and other relevant capabilities of great states have been vastly increased. Equally important was the growth in their intelligence capabilities, especially in this century's revolution in technical collection. States could not only hit harder and faster, but they also were better able to know what to hit and where it was. (Of course, improvements in technical intelligence have made achieving surprise more difficult, although far from impossible.)

In short, positive and negative incentives have fostered increased interest in strategic surprise. The positive incentives lay in the greatly expanded capabilities that have made it possible to achieve a strategic surprise. On the negative side has been fear of the costs of long wars and, in our day, uncertainty about the durability of one side's forces under a surprise attack by the enemy. Strategic surprise is not the only way to win quickly, but it is certainly an obvious and attractive one.

Now we can turn to the relationship between arms control and strategic surprise. By the turn of the century, war among the great powers was both a distinct possibility and likely to be terrible for all concerned. Those two truths have held ever since. This is the problem. Many ways to get out of or cope with this situation have been proposed and tried, and two broad solutions have received the most attention.

The first solution is to limit a war, not by arms control but by finding a way to win it without any devastating costs. While there might appear to be several ways of doing this, strategic surprise has become the foremost route to such a victory. The other solution is war prevention through deterrence. As with limiting a war, in theory there are numerous ways to achieve war prevention, but great states lack confidence in nearly all of them. The one that best fits their perceptions and inclinations has been deterrence. These two solutions are fundamentally incompatible. But neither, taken on its own, has been consistently successful and fully comforting. Hence, it has been difficult for great-power governments to choose to rely on just one.

The heart of war prevention among great powers in this century has been deterrence. Prior to the world wars it involved alliances and arms racing. At times it rested on a capacity to mobilize for a quick victory, if conflict seemed unavoidable; at others, in the capacity to mount a conventional defense. Woodrow Wilson tried to institutionalize a collective deterrence in the League of Nations. After 1945 the United States and the USSR gradually led the way into the use of nuclear deterrence. In every case the most serious threat to deterrence has been the possibility of strategic surprise. Today, this threat would come in the form of an attack that destroys the defender's weapons and forestalls retaliation.

Thus, we can amend the statement that the heart of war prevention has been deterrence to say that the key to success in deterrence usually has been the ability to frustrate strategic surprise strategies. This is the critical objective of nuclear deterrence: to eliminate entirely the utility of a strategic surprise. Therefore, nuclear deterrence is our foremost solution to the problem or threat posed by strategic surprise.

Twentieth-century arms control efforts mainly have been preoccupied with either preventing the emergence of strategic surprise capabilities or eliminating those that already exist. Such capabilities obviously can erode deterrence. They also can lead to launch-on-warning postures, preemptive-strike planning, and other destabilizing policies. After World War I the victors sought to strip Germany of its ability to mobilize so as to bar any surprise attack. The British moved to eliminate the German navy's capacity for a surprise blow. After World War II, canceling all capacities for a nuclear surprise attack was the point of the Baruch Plan, while the Soviets sought elimination of the U.S. bases overseas precisely because they were ideal for a surprise attack. Dwight Eisenhower's Open Skies proposal was the major new arms control venture of the 1950s, explicitly aimed at preventing surprise attacks. In the 1960s the United States moved to make stabilizing mutual assured destruction (MAD) the basis of strategic arms control, to be achieved by limiting types of weapons that could lend themselves to a strategic surprise. The entire SALT process was driven by this.

The greatest security debate in our day is over SDI, because eliminating vulnerability to someone else's strategic surprise in this way is very likely inseparable from gaining an enhanced capacity to inflict such an attack. The arms control community sees SDI as potentially destabilizing and not, as the Reagan administration had hoped, as opening the way to a different conception of arms control.

We can see the same preoccupation today with respect to arms control for conventional forces. The chief objective for the West in the MBFR and other talks on security in Europe is to curb the Soviet capacity to mount a strategic surprise—through troop cuts, tank force reductions, and related measures. That is also why the Chinese insist that Soviet troop concentrations along the Sino-Soviet border be reduced. Many confidence-building measures proposed in Europe are aimed at this.

Nor is this merely a great-power concern. The Israeli-Arab relationship has been burdened by reciprocal fears of strategic surprise (and by each side having experienced at least one). This arises from each side's inability to sustain a long war. Israel cannot afford to trade either lives or territory for long. Both sides know how modern warfare can swallow even huge arms stockpiles in days. Elsewhere, the Iraqis now know just how awful a war of attrition can be once an initial surprise attack does not bring victory. Iran and Iraq fought in spasms because the costs of actual combat were too exhausting to sustain for long. That war became an excellent demonstration of why surprise attack can be attractive.

However, successfully limiting the capacities of states to inflict strategic surprise has turned out to be very difficult. Deterrence is crucial in our time because states cannot fully defend themselves against modern strategic forces. And the natural superiority of the offense over the defense at the strategic level that makes deterrence vital simultaneously breeds interest in a quick-victory strategy. After all, the essence of strategic nuclear deterrence is the capacity to attack successfully. Deterrence merely promises that the attack will come as retaliation and defines success solely in those terms. But with such an ability to attack, why rely solely on deterrence to maintain national security? It might fail. The enemy has to cooperate for it to work (hardly a comfortable situation), and deterrence offers no consolation if it fails. Instead, why not try to erase the enemy's forces in an initial strike, suffering little or no damage and being in control of one's destiny? Why not exploit the superiority of the offense in this fashion?

In short, deterrence—and the arms control designed to stabilize it—is a response to the same basic problem, the potentially intolerable nature of modern war, that has given rise to strategic surprise strategies. In the nuclear age each solution has arisen from the same military technology. The crux of each can be found in efforts at finding a way to frustrate the other. Deterrence seeks to prevent any kind of attack, but it takes on great importance as our most vital way of eliminating any strategic surprise. A strategic surprise strategy for great states today, in turn, is an attempt to design around an opponent's deterrence posture and not be constrained by the threat of retaliation.

Implications

States are preoccupied with maintaining their security, particularly through military strength. That has led to a terrible dilemma in this century for great powers (and, at times, for other states as well). They have needed military forces in case of war but were not at all sure they could stand the war they feared. We have outlined the two broad solutions that have been most attractive: quick victory by means of strategic surprise versus deterrence stabilized by arms control, as traditionally conceived. We can readily see that the ideal military posture would be to possess the requisite capabilities for both solutions, which each superpower regularly charges the other is seeking.

The most important implication of this analysis is that the key to war prevention did not have to be the threat of assured destruction through nuclear retaliation. What was required was to cancel the utility of strategic surprise strategies, to void the strategic surprise solution to the problem. Nuclear deterrence does this by promising to make the ultimate payoff of a surprise attack unacceptable. The deterrer says, in effect: "You can attack successfully in terms of getting through my defenses and doing awful harm, but you cannot end the war there, and that fact will have terrible results for you." But since the turn of the century, not being able to end the war relatively quickly always has meant terrible results; it did not take nuclear deterrence to produce that. It could be argued that the reason we need nuclear deterrence at the level of assured destruction (and options beyond it) is because only that can convince governments that the game is not worth the candle. There is absolutely no reason to believe this. It is at least as plausible, and even more so, that a state need only convince its rival that the costs will be significant because no strategic surprise or other short-war strategy will be sufficiently effective.

It would be nice if that is what arms control theory said and if the search for effective arms control were aimed primarily at uncovering a functional equivalent to nuclear deterrence as the way modern great powers frustrate strategic surprise strategies. Instead, strategic arms control mainly has been about how to make nuclear deterrence more reliable at the level of assured destruction. Its underlying premise has been that nuclear weapons cannot be eliminated and that we would all be worse off if they were. The anti-SDI literature is filled with assertions of this sort. There are analysts who wish arms control was not aimed at any significant reductions in strategic arsenals because stability lies in huge assured-destruction capabilities.[8]

Arms control should be about how to get the same results as nuclear deterrence without nuclear deterrence. Why? We could simply say that nuclear weapons are terribly dangerous, that governments are too irresponsible to hold human survival daily in their hands, that nuclear deterrence is utterly at odds with civilized existence. Those arguments have been raised for years with no effect. Evidently, they carry little weight. It probably is more useful to call attention to the intrinsic limitations of strategic arms control as practiced now, limitations readily detectable within the analysis laid out above.

The modern theory of arms control as developed in the late 1950s assumed a mutual interest in stable deterrence on the part of the major states. This was taken to mean that, if given the chance, those governments would be able to cooperate and deliberately choose to restrict their arms competition in order to increase the stability of deterrence. If they went after unilateral advantage, as with a first-strike capability, it would be expensive, dangerous, and probably unsuccessful, which the theory of arms control would be able to point out. Strategic arms control obviously was the way to go.

We now can see that such a view seriously underestimates the difficulties to be overcome. Arms control to stabilize strategic nuclear deterrence makes excellent sense if: 1) the only real threat of a nuclear war arises from an unstable situation in mutual nuclear deterrence, and 2) nuclear deterrence is absolutely guaranteed to work when that threat is eliminated. But if neither is true, and if nuclear deterrence should ever fail and nuclear war becomes unavoidable, then the best military resource would be a first-strike capability. The same is true at the conventional level; if war looks unavoidable, it would be nice to catch the enemy unprepared in an initial blow and then make him fight on your terms on his territory.

Such capabilities are the antithesis of arms control. They do not fit with restraints on arms competitions, and to search for such capabilities is to plan a kind of military superiority that provokes alarm in opponents and a competitive response. They do not fit the goal of stabilizing deterrence because, in a crisis, they encourage preemption by each side. They do not fit the objective of limiting wars because if the goal is damage limitation and winning quickly, there is no incentive to hold back.

Proponents of strategic arms control never tire of asserting that it is the only logical response to our modern-day version of the security dilemma, that arms control grows out of the very nature of modern weapons. The trouble is that this is not true. With the offense dominating the defense at the strategic level and with the potential stakes so high, military technology drives military forces to be fundamentally hostile to arms control.

At exactly the time that deterrence theory and the basic ideas of strategic arms control were being developed in the 1950s, Strategic Air Command (SAC) was busy developing a first-strike capability. It sought to obliterate the USSR's military strength, and most of its society as well, before any true Soviet attack on the United States could be launched. Secretary of Defense McNamara later moved to MAD as official doctrine in part because the air force was using Flexible Response as a covering rationale for devising a first-strike strategy and forces. The Joint Chiefs supported SALT I as long as the interim agreement avoided banning MIRVs, which then were used to upgrade sharply the American hard-target-kill capability. MX and Trident II have had the same appeal, and the Pershing II was attractive to the Pentagon as a fine first-strike weapon.

In doing all this, American military planners have been imitating their Soviet counterparts, who for a long time stressed preemption and damage limitation in the design of their strategic forces. In the entire SALT process the one system the Soviets refused to trade or cut was their collection of large, hard-target-kill ICBMs. The Soviets have tried for much the same posture at theater and lower levels with both nuclear and conventional forces. Given the opportunity, U.S. forces do the same. What else is the "maritime strategy" but an attempt to carry the war to the enemy and eliminate military assets with which he can hurt us?

We stress this because military resistance to arms control usually is traced to other factors: the bureaucratic interests of the services, or hawkish images of the enemy. A favorite target is the outmoded way of thinking that is said to afflict us, in which nuclear weapons, and fighting with nuclear weapons, are seen in the same way as other weapons; that is, they can be used, victory is possible, superiority matters, and so forth. These factors are not irrelevant, but citing them does not get to the heart of the matter. Certainly, the services deny that they resist arms control. (SAC's motto is "Peace Is Our Profession.") At times this can be true, and thus it is not irrelevant, either. But neither of these should be allowed to obscure the fundamental structural antipathy between modern arms and arms control.

This means that it is highly unlikely that great states engaged in a serious rivalry while practicing nuclear deterrence will ever agree indefinitely to a MAD relationship institutionalized by arms control. Yet, this was what SALT was trying to bring about. Its failure usually is ascribed to one of the following: the Soviets do not believe in MAD, they want a first-strike, war-fighting capability; the Americans don't want SALT-based parity, they want superiority. There are also those who think SALT was expected to do too much, that strategic arms control cannot overcome an absence of détente. The trouble with these explanations is that they do not probe deeply enough. To practice nuclear deterrence, it is necessary to contemplate being forced someday to have to use the weapons. To contemplate that possibility is to be pressed, under mutual nuclear deterrence, toward a damage-limitation and (better yet) first-strike capability, on the one hand, and toward obtaining multiple options (nuclear and conventional), on the other. Neither is compatible with serious arms control.

Arms controllers constantly lament that arms control is not better integrated into national security policy, and therefore too many weapons and policies emerge that pursue capabilities that are destabilizing to deterrence, foster proliferation, and the rest. The truth is that the armed forces cannot pursue their mission of protecting the nation and adapt to the nature of modern weapons without seeking just such weapons and policies. Arms control is not better integrated into national security policy because it does not fit.

As we have said earlier, strategic arms control should search for a functional equivalent to nuclear deterrence as a means to great-power war prevention by voiding strategies of strategic surprise. (In effect, strategic arms control should be in the business of doing this as a way of promoting nuclear disarmament.) The Reagan administration and the president in particular deserve great credit for having exactly the right instinct about nuclear deterrence—it is loathsome, and arms control negotiations should deal with how we are going to try to get rid of it.

Unfortunately, the administration has proposed that we defend our way out of nuclear deterrence, which is not at all promising. In theory, it sounds fine. To interdict physically any attack, thus canceling the dominance of the offense over the defense, would return great states to the situation that prevailed on the battlefield in World War I. All that would be necessary is that governments be fully convinced of the futility of attacks and the certainty that the resulting war would greatly exceed any level of acceptable costs. We can envision technological changes that might have that effect, which is what SDI research is seeking. But the technological barriers to be overcome now appear far too great to permit a complete defense. It appears that the pace of the necessary breakthroughs will be too slow to outrun the offensive countermeasures that must be anticipated. Therefore, it probably is not possible to eliminate nuclear deterrence via strategic defenses. The odds are much too poor to make this the proper basis of national security policy.

The other problem with SDI is that, in any partially effective form, a ballistic missile defense adds to our strategic surprise capabilities, just as the Soviets charge. In other words, SDI as a program heightens rather than reduces the tension between arms control and strategic surprise that has made life so difficult for national security policymakers. As we noted earlier, a deterrence capability is really an ability to attack. To thwart the quick-victory strategy by means of a truly effective defense is equally to cancel the opponent's deterrence as well. The ability to do this through a combination of strategic surprise and limited defenses is much more plausible, and certainly more feasible, than getting there entirely by comprehensive defenses.

A second way to tackle the matter of pushing nuclear deterrence aside is to start with arms control measures that encourage states to discard and forego strategic surprise capabilities—not to build first-strike weapons, for instance—and then hope that one side can mount a gradual retreat from nuclear deterrence based on this. Initially, this can be pursued to reinforce and sustain deterrence. This was what we attempted in SALT. We now have enough experience to suggest that this approach is fatally flawed. By itself, it will not result in the true elimination of nuclear deterrence and the installation of an alternative way to eliminate great-power wars.

Instead, it has to be accompanied by a marked shift in the political relationship that gives rise to nuclear deterrence in the first place. That means détente, and a good deal more. Strategic arms control always has had a nonpolitical orientation as though it were a technical exercise. In effect, the argument for arms control was that it was relevant and could be achieved with no fundamental adjustment in the political conflicts that affected the great powers. We now know that a truly technical, apolitical approach to strategic arms control cannot work. Myriads of analyses of the erosion of the SALT approach have identified the decline of détente as the single most important factor. What we have not done is to see that, as arms control must go beyond stabilizing nuclear deterrence, so political accommodation must go beyond détente to the point where the mutual fears of attack greatly decline. Only this will permit stepping back from nuclear deterrence.

The prospects are greater now than they have ever been. It may be possible to link the political improvements within Soviet society to political shifts in the international system, leading to the adoption and implementation of the important proposals to reduce nuclear arsenals that have been put forward by both superpowers. Remarkably, the Reagan administration has stumbled into circumstances quite favorable for the pursuit of the president's frequently stated objective of ridding the world of nuclear weapons. This is not of the administration's doing, contrary to its earlier strategic analysis, in violation of its ideological and emotional predilections, and nonetheless there.

Without détente, and more, there regularly will be heard the charge that the reductions in nuclear forces simply make the world safe for conventional war. Linked to the fear of the Soviet Union's superiority in conventional military strength, this leads directly to the kind of uneasiness Europeans are now displaying about the INF Treaty and to the opposition voiced by James Schlesinger to the Reykjavik Summit discussions: how can we reduce our nuclear forces if it is nuclear deterrence that keeps us safe? And unless the pressure to contemplate and plan for war is greatly reduced, military sectors will continue to try to offset the liabilities of nuclear deterrence by devising strategic surprise strategies and forces.

All this finally leads us to a reassertion of the importance of the world's major conventional forces in any attempt to achieve real success in strategic arms control. First, the most obvious way to deal with the fears of a grave conventional imbalance is to insist on strategic arms control measures being tied in with suitable adjustments in conventional forces to ease the fear of strategic surprise at that level. Reductions in nuclear forces can only go so far without this. We must always remember that, for the West, nuclear deterrence grew out of perceived conventional-level inferiority and projections of a Soviet strategic surprise attack that could overrun Europe, much of the Middle East, and elsewhere. Initially, cuts in strategic forces can stand on their own; eventually, they can only continue if accompanied by adjustments further down.

Second, and much more important, it is vital to begin thinking about how to frustrate strategic surprise reliably at the conventional level, not only through arms control measures but also through defensive tactics, strategies, and deployments. There is no way to eliminate surprise itself. We now know enough about why governments get caught by surprise to doubt that much can be done to correct this. What we can do is take away the possibility of quick victory. A deterrence relationship can be based on that, instead. We have to divide strategic surprise into two dimensions— the initial surprise attack and its eventual outcome—and use a satisfactory handling of the latter to detract from incentives to seek the former.

The chief objection today comes from Europe, where it is thought that frustrating a quick Soviet victory cannot be done on the conventional level alone or cannot be done at an acceptable cost at that level, or that (whether it would work or not in a war) it will not sufficiently deter if tried. Let us consider each of these arguments in turn, albeit briefly.

If it cannot be done, one of the following must be the reason: the Soviets are innately superior at conventional warfare, the offense is inevitably superior to the defense in conventional warfare, or the Soviet bloc is clearly superior in its potential (technical, demographic, economic) for conventional warfare. None of these is true, based either on the history of war in this century or on the plain facts. Thus, it is not true that frustrating a Soviet strategic surprise cannot be done.

Can it be done, however, at an acceptable cost? With the help of properly designed arms control agreements, this would be no problem. Without them, there is no reason to doubt that, although more difficult, a robust defense is impossible to pay for. For arms control to make any real progress and have any meaning, important political shifts will be necessary. There is no reason why such an easing of the military competition between East and West should not benefit defensive postures more than offensive ones and make the tasks of the defense easier and less expensive.

What if there is no major breakthrough in conventional arms control, just the elimination of nuclear forces? Would the cost of deterrence through conventional defense then be acceptable? To begin with, it is highly improbable that any great steps to eliminate nuclear weapons could take place without some parallel developments on the conventional level. If this did occur, there would be substantial monies that now go into strategic and other nuclear forces that then would be available to purchase additional conventional strength. Next, it is hard to see why the West cannot afford a sufficient defense in view of its large economic advantages vis-à-vis the East.

Finally, will it deter? The whole idea of deterrence is to let war be so awful for an attacker that no one would wish to start it. Somehow we got hooked on the idea that the only way to put the awful nature of modern conflict at the service of war avoidance was through nuclear weapons, but that effect can be achieved perfectly well at the conventional level. The Europeans are aghast at the thought of a major conventional war in Europe. The Russians have a better memory of how dreadful such a war can be than anyone else on the Continent. The prospect of a robust conventional defense that would mean no short war—rather, one that went on indefinitely—would be at least as effective as nuclear weapons as a deterrent. And it would be reinforced by the distinct possibility that, if it went on long enough, the war would lead one or both sides to build nuclear weapons again. How can the technologically, demographically, economically—even politically—weaker side in the East-West rivalry contemplate World War III under these circumstances?

Conclusion

We need to elevate our ambitions for strategic arms control. We need to see it as linked to progress at the conventional level. A lot of the action on arms control in Europe now should be taking place not only on nuclear weapons in Europe but also at the MBFR talks. We need a stronger push for détente, and we need to try to go further with détente than we have in the past. The United States and the USSR have been embroiled in a rivalry for years that need not be as militarily significant as it has been. Indeed, arms control can help reduce the military dimensions to their proper proportions.

Arms control differs from disarmament in that arms control does not anticipate a world without weapons, an international politics where force plays no role. But the pursuit of strategic arms control has been almost hypnotically focused on nuclear deterrence as the only way to keep the peace, instead of contemplating how we might achieve what nuclear deterrence does for us in some far less dangerous way.

All of this requires keeping in mind the relationship between arms control and strategic surprise. Arms control is not just hard to achieve. It is hard to grasp many of its key features, and a proper understanding is the ultimate prerequisite for achieving much of it. Understanding can come only when arms control is placed within the military history of this century.

Notes

[1] Trevor Dupuy and Gay Hammerman, eds., *A Documentary History of Arms Control and Disarmament* (New York: R. R. Bowker, 1973); and Leon Friedman, *The Laws of War: A Documentary History*, Vol. 1 (New York: Random House, 1972).

[2] Patrick Morgan, "Elements of a General Theory of Arms Control," in Paul R. Viotti, ed., *Conflict and Arms Control: An Uncertain Agenda* (Boulder, CO: Westview Press, 1986), pp. 283–310.

[3] Klaus Knorr and Patrick Morgan, *Strategic Military Surprise: Incentives and Opportunities* (Englewood Cliffs, NJ: Transactions, 1983).

[4] Richard K. Betts, *Surprise Attack* (Washington, DC: Brookings Institution, 1982).

[5] There are those in Britain and France who think we can get by with less than an assured destruction capability, although it certainly helps to be associated with an ally that does have one. There is debate about what "assured destruction" means operationally, but the main disagreements have been over whether assured destruction is enough, not whether we can get by with less.

6 Thomas Etzold and John L. Gaddis, eds., *Containment: Documents on American Policy and Strategy, 1945–1950* (New York: Columbia University Press, 1978).

7 David Alan Rosenberg, "The Origins of Overkill: Nuclear Weapons and American Strategy, 1945–1960," *International Security* (Spring 1983): 3–71.

8 Dagobert Brito and Michael Intriligator, "Non-Armageddon Solutions to the Arms Race," Reprint no. 1 (Los Angeles: UCLA Center for International and Strategic Affairs, 1984).

Making Arms Control Work

Near- and Long-Term Challenges

Verification and Intelligence: Some Interface Issues

CHARLES R. GELLNER*

VERIFICATION IS A sine qua non of viable arms control agreements. U.S. arms control proposals have insisted on the need for verification ("adequate," "effective," "fool-proof ") ever since 1946, when the United States put forward the elaborately structured Baruch Plan for the international control of atomic energy. That and later plans by Washington for verification of arms control and disarmament agreements have been founded on the proposition that the Soviet Union cannot be trusted. The Soviet government, and other governments as well, also has professed a need for verification of international arms control commitments. Governments, especially adversaries, cannot merely trust each other to carry out treaty obligations when national security is at stake. Some tangible assurance of their faithful conduct is required.

Verification depends upon, but is different from, intelligence. "Intelligence" is here used generically to refer to those government organizations and activities that acquire information about an adversary country (primarily the Soviet Union, but other countries as well) usually having a bearing on national security. It utilizes a variety of means (normally secret or classified) to gain information, including human—by

*The views expressed in this paper are the author's and not those of any organization with which he is affiliated.

direct observation or by study of published sources—and technical (national technical means, or NTM) such as satellites, radar, communications intercepts, and aircraft, ostensibly not requiring intrusion into nationally sovereign space. The term also refers to the information garnered by these methods.[1]

The intelligence community conducts a wide range of operations for the acquisition of information. It collects information on the military, political, economic, and other characteristics of other nations, particularly the Soviet Union. In regard to the latter, the fundamental purpose is to assess the actual and potential Soviet threat to the security of the United States. Capable and reliable intelligence is vitally necessary for the security of the nation. Therefore, the nation will pursue it and devote all the resources it can afford to support the intelligence apparatus necessary for safeguarding security.

Verification is a special form of intelligence consisting of several elements. First, it depends on national intelligence operations or international cooperative arrangements to acquire information. Second, intelligence information must be appraised in the context of the provisions of relevant arms control agreements. These are often imprecise or ambiguous, which make the appraisal uncertain and often a matter of artful judgment. Third, a decision by responsible officials, usually but sometimes only partially based on the first two steps, is necessary regarding the compliance of the observed signatory with the subject treaty. Political or ideological considerations often color this judgment, thus introducing nonintelligence factors into the final result.

Evolution of Intelligence in Verification

The overt employment of intelligence methods in the verification process has evolved in three major stages since international arms control negotiations began after World War II. During the first stage (1946–1960s) the United States proposed extensive schemes of arms control and disarmament, including international inspection and intrusive on-site procedures. The Soviet Union usually rejected these peremptorily as covers for intelligence operations ("spying"). To refute this charge publicly, Washington structured its proposed international verification organizations so as to distinguish and distance them as much as possible from its intelligence operations.

During the second stage (1970s to mid-1980s) attitudes on monitoring virtually reversed. The advent of reconnaissance satellites, or "spies in the sky," brought a radical change. In 1960 the Soviet Union shot down an American U-2 plane on a reconnaissance flight over its territory. In the 1970s, however, both superpowers legalized and safeguarded national technical monitoring activities in space to verify the SALT agreements concluded in 1972 and 1979. Although satellites now have been accepted over national territory as monitors of arms control, reconnaissance aircraft are still forbidden as violators of sovereignty.

The transition to the third stage, beginning in the mid-1980s, has been characterized by several trends. First, more prominence has been given to cooperative and intrusive methods of monitoring in arms control proposals. Some such methods were agreed upon in the Threshold Test Ban and Peaceful Nuclear Explosions treaties of 1974 and 1976 and in the SALT II Treaty of 1979. However, these treaties did not go into effect because the United States refused to ratify them. Intrusive methods of monitoring have been stressed by the Reagan administration and by the Gorbachev regime in recent negotiations to limit nuclear and chemical weapons. They have been incorporated into the Treaty for the Elimination of Intermediate-range and Shorter Range Missiles (INF Treaty) signed by the United States and the Soviet Union in December 1987. On-site monitoring also has been accepted by the two governments for a treaty under negotiation for reducing strategic offensive arms.

Second, technical monitoring capabilities, mainly by reconnaissance satellites, have begun to spread beyond the two superpowers to other governments and to nongovernmental entities. This has opened up significant new, independent centers with capabilities of both intelligence and verification. And third, some of these new centers of independent monitoring have manifested a willingness to carry out verification functions for the U.S. and Soviet arms control agreements as well as for multilateral arms control agreements. The full importance of these developments is still only partially perceived and almost totally unrealized.

Proposals Dependent on Verification

Every proposal for arms control made by the United States in a diplomatic forum it has deemed verifiable, or it insists that it should be made verifiable before it can be signed into an agreement. In only one well-known post-World War II instance was the verification factor deliberately left out. The Biological Weapons Convention (1975) prohibiting such weapons contained no such provisions. The United States joined this convention because it considered these weapons virtually unusable and had renounced their use as a matter of policy. The Geneva Protocol (1925) banning the use of chemical weapons in war had no provisions for verification because such use was assumed to be self-evident if it occurred.

Before 1980 and the advent of the Reagan administration, it was the general rule of the U.S. government to work out the verifiability of its proposals for arms control reductions and limitations before they were introduced. All proposals for verification normally are submitted to interagency staffing, including the Joint Chiefs of Staff and the intelligence community. Ralph Earle, who was at one time the chief U.S. negotiator for the SALT II Treaty, has written regarding those negotiations:

> With one or two exceptions (which were to the potential or at least short-term advantage of the United States), there was never a proposal put on the table in Geneva that had not been determined to be adequately verifiable, from the point of view of the United States ... no instructions were sent to the delegation with regard to proposals, either general or specific, to be made to the Soviets that had not been cleared by among others, the so-called "intelligence community" in Washington; this community was and is led by the Central Intelligence Agency, and included the Defense Intelligence Agency, the National Security Agency, and the Intelligence and Research Bureau of the Department of State. Frequently, in the development of a proposal within the United States bureaucracy, considerable negotiation was necessary when one or more of the members of the intelligence community were of the view that a specific treaty provision was not as verifiable as it should be. However ... virtually no instruction reached Geneva without having gained an imprimatur as "verifiable"—at least so far as it impinged on the Soviet Union.[2]

Intelligence-monitoring capabilities, including those approved by the arms control agreement itself, have often, but not always, dictated the limits of arms control proposals; that is, the United States has generally proposed only what it thought it could monitor and verify. For instance, the SALT agreements limited ICBM "launchers" (silos), rather than ICBMs or ICBM warheads as such, because they could be counted by NTM. But some critics argued that the warheads should be counted because they, not "holes in the ground," killed people. The Reagan administration decided to frame its proposals in terms of warheads, and the Soviet Union has accepted this approach. However, there is no way of counting warheads except by using SALT II's counting rules based on launchers.

The political or military desirability of an arms control provision also might outweigh its monitorability. An example is the clause in the SALT II Treaty permitting 5 percent ICBM modernization. This percentage was considered more desirable than a higher one, which could have been easier to monitor but less valuable as an arms control constraint.

As Secretary of Defense Harold Brown told the Senate Foreign Relations Committee during the hearings on the SALT II Treaty in 1979:

> In order to distinguish between new types and modifications to existing types, a line must be drawn between the two. The agreement does this by specifying the amount by which certain features of an existing missile may be changed before it becomes a new type. Any change in the number of stages or propellant type, or any difference of more than 5 percent in launch-weight, throw-weight, overall length or largest diameter qualifies an ICBM as a new type. Over the period of a test program for a new or modified ICBM we could detect significant deviations from these limits. . .
>
> What I would say is that we might have difficulty—in fact we probably would have difficulty—in monitoring the exact percentage of change. We could have made that easier by making this 25 percent, for example. But that would not have advantaged us. It would have disadvantaged us. . .
>
> But, had we gone, say, to 25 percent on the launch-weight and throw-weight numbers, the monitoring would have been easier. However, I do not think the verification would be any better because, in fact, we would not have been controlling Soviet capabilities as well.[3]

Despite the heavy stress laid by the Reagan administration on the need for "effective" (strict) verification, it introduced some proposals for strategic arms reductions and for abolition of intermediate-range missiles without first working out beforehand and laying on the table its proposals for verification. A major criticism of Ronald Reagan's proposal at the 1986 Reykjavik Summit for abolition of strategic missiles was that verification could be difficult. It evidently had not been fully coordinated with the intelligence community.

Intelligence Ambiguities and Verification

Intelligence is frequently uncertain and ambiguous. The impressions gained by NTM or other intelligence methods are graded in degrees of confidence from high to low. For instance, a Soviet test of a new missile might indicate an upgrading of offensive capabilities, but their exact character might be unclear. Certainties about the missile's capabilities might be low initially but improve as additional tests are monitored. When assessments of the threat to U.S. security by an adversary's weapons system or forces are graded by varying degrees of certainty, worst cases are frequently posited, in order to preserve a margin of safety.

Likewise, monitoring, and therefore verification, capabilities for various arms control provisions can range up and down a scale of confidence. Much less flexibility is allowed in determining whether a Soviet violation of an agreement has occurred than in making an assessment of a Soviet threat. The criteria for a threat assessment are more vague and more judgmental than the criteria for a violation, which are molded by the more precise terms, relatively speaking, of an arms control agreement. This difference can make verification more demanding than threat assessment. However, arms control agreements can facilitate and enhance monitoring by special provisions that normally are not present in intelligence operations.[4] Threat assessments can incur large errors, especially when they involve projections into the future. The well-publicized "bomber gaps" and "missile gaps" of past years are examples.[5] Military intelligence appraisals of security threats (for example, a new weapons system) are generally rated to be serious even if later they turn out otherwise. Politically, the penalty is light if threat assessments are incorrectly overstated.

If regular NTM are employed for arms control verification, then the uncertainties resemble those for routine intelligence monitoring. However, if enhancement aids, such as on-site inspection, are authorized by arms control agreements, such as the 1987 INF Treaty, then the uncertainties of verification can be reduced or eliminated. The percentage of uncertainty, moreover, affects the way a suspicious event (that is, a possible violation by a signatory) might be handled by an accuser. Weighing of alternative responses to possible violations is not the subject here, except to say that intelligence factors influence response policy. The degree of uncertainty in those factors could affect whether the aggrieved signatory would take any action at all. It also could affect whether the aggrieved government would go public with its suspicions or its charges of a violation, or just make its representations in private to the other signatory. However, other factors, especially political ones, enter into such decisions and can override intelligence inputs.

Allocating Intelligence Resources for Arms Control Verification

What are the differences between intelligence operations that normally are conducted in the absence of any arms control verification obligations and intelligence operations that must be conducted for the purpose of verification? Intelligence operations are structured primarily to achieve comprehensive military, political, economic, and other objectives and only secondarily to fulfill verification obligations. The latter often coincide with the former. Assuming that policy officials have carefully coordinated arms control proposals with the intelligence community, then the verification task for the community should be manageable, at least in principle. In the absence of such coordination, the task for intelligence could be more difficult or even impossible.

The conclusion of arms control agreements might necessitate some reallocation of intelligence resources to monitoring those agreements. However, their subject matter almost invariably concerns defense resources and military capabilities of the Soviet Union (or some other country), which would be objects of serious intelligence attention anyway. The allocation of resources necessary for the additional effort required for monitoring by NTM generally has made little difference in the overall operations plan of the intelligence community. We must envision the large size of that community and the enormous resources allocated to it by Congress in order to put in perspective the probable additional allocation of resources required for monitoring arms control agreements. The on-site provisions in the recent INF Treaty and those contemplated for other agreements will incur expenses that are not yet clearly calculated. Moreover, there are trade-offs involved. The intelligence community can obtain valuable benefits that it would not otherwise have from verification provisions in arms control agreements. In addition, there is to be written into the balance the increased national security benefits that accrue from these agreements.

Arms Control Advantages for Intelligence

Arms control agreements can afford many valuable benefits to the intelligence community. Among the most eminent examples were provisions in the ABM and the SALT II treaties that facilitated the verification process and thus enhanced intelligence acquisition capabilities.[6] These provisions permitted each party to use "national technical means at its disposal" to monitor the compliance of the other party. Technically, this provision applied only to matters covered by the treaty. Nevertheless, since there was no way of distinguishing the operations of those NTM that are directed at monitoring the treaty and those that are not, this provision in effect gave a totally free hand to each side to employ its NTM, namely, satellites, land stations, ships, and surveillance aircraft, although within the confines of "recognized principles of international law." This, in effect, legalized the orbiting of satellites over sovereign territory but did not permit overflights of aircraft or incursions of vessels into sovereign waters.[7] In both of these treaties the NTM provision was reinforced by two clauses: each party would undertake "not to interfere with" the NTM of the other party and also not "use deliberate concealment measures which impede verification by NTM."

There are various ways in which an objecting government might interfere with NTM, especially satellites. It could employ antisatellite weapons against monitoring satellites, either to destroy or damage them, or it could employ devices such as lasers, which might render their operations ineffective. Obviously, too, there are many ways in which a government might conceal its weapons or other military facilities, if it were not committed to renounce such concealment: by camouflage, by using mobile means, or by disguising weapons. Thus, the two NTM clauses in the ABM and SALT II treaties greatly facilitated intelligence acquisition that might not have been possible in their absence. The U.S. termination of its observance of the SALT II Treaty has not had any adverse effect on the exercise of the restrictions imposed by these clauses, because, although the provisions in the SALT II Treaty have been canceled, the similar clauses in the ABM Treaty are still in effect.

The SALT II Treaty contained many other provisions that helped the intelligence community obtain information on Soviet military activities and weaponry. For example, the numerical ceilings imposed on Soviet military forces or weapons by the treaty were of help in the intelligence effort to track the numbers of such weapons, which the community would be obliged to do even in the absence of the treaty. Another example is the provision regarding advance notification of certain kinds of ICBM test launchings. These notices assisted in the normal intelligence functions of monitoring such tests. Whether the Soviet Union will continue to observe such articles of the treaty now that the United States has renounced them is not clear, but Moscow is legally free no longer to observe those clauses and thus to abolish those particular intelligence aids.

The cooperative measures in the SALT II Treaty eased the way for the precedent-breaking on-site inspection measures in the INF Treaty. These measures are of four main types. First, they call for periodic exchanges of information regarding existing weapons affected by the treaty, which then are subject to on-site confirmation by inspection. Second, they allow firsthand observation by opposite-side inspectors of the actual dismantlement or destruction of affected weapons. Third, they allow for a period of years short-notice inspections of former bases, support facilities, and production centers where the presence of illegal weaponry might be suspected. And fourth, they permit continuous on-site monitoring of production plants where forbidden missiles might be hidden.

As in the earlier SALT agreements, NTM are protected. Thus, the INF Treaty permits an interaction between national technical and on-site monitoring methods that is new for intelligence gathering. It is not now known what synergistic results might occur from the cooperation of these intelligence methods.

Intelligence and On-Site Inspection

To what extent can on-site inspection strengthen verification of compliance of a country with arms control agreements? Some well-known advocates of arms control have tended to downplay the value of such inspection as a means of monitoring.[8] There is some truth in their contention that this inspection sometimes can add little or nothing to information available by other monitoring methods. However, their argument has been motivated in part by their desire to prevent demands— conceivably unreasonable demands—for on-site inspection from impeding the successful conclusion of arms control agreements.

Despite the adverse arguments, there is a widespread belief that on-site inspection or other cooperative arrangements would be the only reliable form of monitoring for certain arms control agreements. It has been proposed for certain kinds of weapons restrictions (for example, limitation of mobile systems) and for constraints on other military activities such as movements of troops or controls on production of various materials or systems. It seems incontrovertible that some forms of on-site inspection would afford opportunities to acquire valuable intelligence information that could not be obtained by NTM or by analysts at desks studying documents. Both the United States and the Soviet Union obviously believe that many proposals for inspection would provide opportunities for espionage.

For many years Moscow contended that Washington's proposals for on-site inspection of arms control agreements were schemes for spying in the Soviet Union. In a certain sense the Soviet position has been correct. The presence of on-site inspectors, or even on-site black boxes that must be serviced by visiting officials from time to time, would permit access not only to more detailed information about the particular activity or object being inspected but also provide opportunities for observation of peripheral or unrelated facilities and operations. So in a certain sense, acquiescence of a government to on-site inspection does provide a license for collateral forms of information gathering, such as observing activities or objects while en route to the main inspection site. The extent and value of this expansion of intelligence acquisition cannot be evaluated except in the context of specific cases.

Moreover, although Washington proposes measures requiring the intrusion of inspectors into another country, as in the 1987 INF Treaty, various groups within the United States, including the military, private weapons producers, and Congress, sometimes react adversely to similar proposals that would apply to this country. They very likely would not agree to them because of fears of espionage. In the INF Treaty, for instance, the two superpowers agreed not to permit inspection of the disposition of the "physics package" of nuclear warheads because of the sensitive intelligence nature of the nuclear technology. However, both the U.S. and Soviet governments concurred in extensive, unprecedented forms of on-site inspection in the INF agreement that will provide access to intelligence data not obtainable by NTM alone, but they reduced opportunities for collateral intelligence gathering by not allowing short-notice inspections "anywhere, anytime." Expectations are that a treaty reducing strategic armaments will require broader short-notice inspection rights.

Nonmilitary Intelligence

Intelligence operations in relation to arms control often are construed solely in terms of acquisition of information regarding Soviet armed forces and military activities related to arms control agreements. However, other important areas of intelligence bear upon the formulation and execution of national arms control policy, including acceptance of verification measures. These areas lie outside of the strictly military categories of intelligence dealing with weapons and armed forces. Many intelligence assessments focus on political developments within other countries that are or could be relevant to arms control negotiations. These developments include the political aims of leaders and parties in other governments that could have a bearing upon their willingness to negotiate agreements and the kinds they would be willing to accept.

Intelligence regarding the economic conditions of a country also would affect the policy aims of its government in regard to motivations either for or against particular kinds of arms control measures. Furthermore, there is more narrowly focused intelligence regarding the kinds of positions that other governments might take in arms control negotiations and what exactly might induce them to either persist in or amend their positions. In short, there are many sectors of intelligence activity that can be useful to the U.S. government in formulating or in carrying out its arms control policy other than just those assessments and information regarding military strength and forces.

Conflicts between the CIA and the DIA

Another significant factor in weighing the intelligence community's role in the verification process is that it is not an ideal homogenous, error-free model of unimpeachable integrity. Although called a community, it is a group of a dozen or so separate organizations that have been likened to warring tribes. There are unifying organizations and other forces such as the preparation of National Intelligence Estimates (NIEs), the annual publication of *Soviet Military Power*, and the president's reports on compliance with arms control agreements, now required by Congress on a regular basis. These exercises compel coordination of often rival viewpoints and conclusions.

In regard to verification and related arms control issues, the two main actors are the Central Intelligence Agency (CIA) and the Defense Intelligence Agency (DIA). The State Department and the Arms Control and Disarmament Agency (ACDA) are lesser actors in decision making affecting verification. There are often disputes among these agencies and others that affect policy and negotiations. For instance, during the interagency meetings on the president's report on treaty compliance submitted to Congress in 1987, there were, according to reports in the press, strong differences of viewpoint among the Pentagon (the DIA), the State Department, and the CIA arising out of the verification process. Those disputes related to such important matters as whether the Soviet Union was preparing to break out of the ABM Treaty by establishing a nationwide ABM defense system.

The Defense Department, in making use of the DIA, has painted a menacing picture of a vast Soviet research program to prepare a breakout from the treaty and to deploy a comprehensive defense of its national territory against ballistic missiles. Secretary of Defense Caspar Weinberger and other defense officials decried the "Soviet SDI." Evidently, they were striving to find justification for the U.S. Strategic Defense Initiative (SDI) and support for a new or broad interpretation of the ABM Treaty that would remove it as a barrier to testing and development of SDI systems. The CIA, on the other hand, is publicly described as adjudging the probability that the Soviet Union is aiming at a breakout from the treaty and developing a national ABM deployment as "low and getting lower."[9] The DIA often judges that the Soviet Union is a more serious violator of arms control agreements than it appears to be in CIA appraisals. In recent years the DIA conclusions seemed more in tune with the political beliefs of Secretary Weinberger and other defense officials and political groups upholding a hard line against the Soviet Union.

Certain attributes of the organization and personnel of the CIA and DIA can affect their assessments. Simple generalizations, however, are subject to exceptions and experiential qualification. First, the organizational rank of each of these agencies in the U.S. government provides a key to its orientation. The CIA is headed by a director who is immediately under the president of the United States. Not only is he the head of the CIA itself, but he also has a statutory base as chief of the entire intelligence community. The director of the CIA thus has a uniquely prestigious and authoritative position. As a consequence he has higher status and a greater measure of independence than the director of the DIA. The latter is merely a subordinate officer in the Department of Defense and is subject to the authority and direction of the secretary of defense, who created the agency. Consequently, the DIA does not have the same status or independence as the CIA, and it is subject to the will, expressed or implied, of the leaders of the defense establishment.

Since the DIA is dependent on the secretary of defense, it is often to its advantage to perceive the Soviet threat in enlarged dimensions. This assists the leaders of the Department of Defense in justifying their budget requests to Congress. An overstated appraisal of the Soviet threat is a standard element in the department's budget briefs presented to Capitol Hill.[10]

Second, the character of the personnel in the CIA and DIA is different. The CIA is composed more of intelligence careerists and professionals than the DIA. The reputation and status of CIA officials and analysts depend in the long run on the most scrupulous respect for the integrity and soundness of their assessments. This unimpeachability or honesty must be preserved from administration to administration, no matter what is the political hue of the president whom the CIA and its director serve. Accusations of politicization have been leveled at the CIA, particularly when Director William Casey served as a member of President Reagan's cabinet, but these accusations are exceptional.

Although the director of the DIA has certain integrating functions, the agency is composed of separate U.S. Army, Navy, Air Force, and Marine components, each with its own parochial outlook. These are staffed to a great degree by military personnel who have their own particular viewpoint and interests. The CIA, on the other hand, is composed of personnel with a variety of backgrounds. The CIA also is a more unified organization that does not have the traditions of separatism found in the military intelligence services. As one authoritative observer has noted: "A military intelligence officer tends to put loyalty to his Service and his organization above support to the intelligence community as a whole. A CIA officer tends to think first of what is good for the CIA."[11]

The goals of the CIA encompass a broader approach to and perspective on intelligence appraisals than is customary in the DIA. The CIA looks not only at narrow military factors, but it also analyzes in depth political, economic, and other kinds of factors that affect the actions of a target country. It has a more comprehensive and profound grasp of the components of a threat to the United States and of the circumstances that could figure in preserving the integrity of an arms control agreement than does the DIA.

Satellite Proliferation and International Verification

As described earlier, a new stage of verification has recently begun. It is marked in part by several trends: 1) the spread of satellite and other technical forms of monitoring to additional countries; 2) the growing acceptance of international verification organizations; and 3) a potential for marrying satellite monitoring to international verification organizations.

Until recently only two governments in the world—the United States and the Soviet Union—had the capability of carrying out high-quality satellite surveillance of military activities around the globe. Now, satellite technology has begun to spread. Within the next decade or two, satellite technology with advanced surveillance capability will be possessed by many governments as well as by nongovernmental entities, including scientific, commercial, and news-gathering organizations. A major revolution in satellite surveillance is under way.

A number of other organizations and governments, including the European Space Agency, China, India, and Japan, either now have or are planning to obtain such a capability. Predictably, additional governments will be joining them in the coming years. In addition, nongovernmental entities have acquired or are planning to acquire satellite-monitoring capabilities. At present there are commercial satellites such as EOSAT and more recently SPOT, a satellite with sufficient accuracy to provide to the newspapers of the world detailed photographs of the Chernobyl disaster.[12] President Reagan's decision in August 1986 to remove commercial missions from the space shuttle has given strong impetus to private and commercial space projects in the United States. Elsewhere on the globe, incentives exist for an increase in privately sponsored space missions.

The concept of an international organization for verification purposes has received growing acceptance. During the first stage of verification in the 1950s and 1960s, there were a number of proposals for elaborate organizations for overseeing various arms control regimes, but these proposals came to naught. One such organization was established, however, that has been successful and has enjoyed growing acceptance: the International Atomic Energy Agency (IAEA), founded to carry out the provisions of the Non-Proliferation Treaty of 1969. A new milestone in its growing acceptance was reached recently when the Soviet Union agreed to open some of its nuclear facilities to IAEA inspectors and also invited agency representatives to view the Chernobyl reactors. (China also is negotiating to permit entry of IAEA officials.) In addition, Euratom, composed of the member states of the European Economic Community, acts as a verification agent to ensure the peaceful nuclear activities of its members. In some respects its inspection capabilities are superior to those of the IAEA. France, a military nuclear power, is a member of Euratom and has opened to some extent its civilian reactors to IAEA surveillance.

The IAEA and Euratom, however, stand virtually alone as successful operating international verification organizations.[13] Some limited cooperation exists among national authorities engaged in seismic monitoring of underground nuclear explosions, but this is ad hoc, although it has had some success in keeping the world informed of testing carried out by the nuclear powers. Agencies that monitor underground nuclear explosions in the United States, the USSR, and in other areas of the world operate in certain neutral countries such as Sweden. These neutral authorities can contribute unbiased information on the conduct of nuclear explosions that, if appropriate, can stand as a corrective to statements issued by the governments conducting such explosions. Six proarms control governments recently have volunteered to monitor, either by themselves or in cooperation with Washington and Moscow, a moratorium on nuclear testing by the two superpowers.[14] Their offer has not been accepted, but it represents a significant potential.

Implications of the Spread of Satellite Technology

What are some of the implications of the spread of satellite technology? This technology will come into the hands of additional governments— some allies of the United States, some adversaries, and some neutral and nonaligned countries. It also will be acquired by nongovernmental organizations of many different types (scientific, commercial, journalistic). Moreover, satellite technology could be provided to or be obtained by international organizations established by governments with missions and resources to add an independent reinforcement of verification activities.

As it stands now, only the United States and the USSR have substantial means of satellite verification of arms control provisions vis-à-vis each other. In this mutual relationship there is not only a cooperative but also an adversarial character. During recent years it has evolved from a somewhat mutually tolerant kind of adversarial relationship to one verging on hostility, even to the point of using verification as a means of political attack on the other side. During the past several years, the Reagan administration and Soviet leaders have directed numerous charges at each other on nonfidelity to the mutual arms control agreements in effect between them. Because of the secrecy of the intelligence data on which such charges have been based and the refusal of the two governments to make public the evidence, it has been impossible for outside observers— whether ordinary citizens of the two countries, third governments, or other authorities—to assess clinically the validity of the charges made by each superpower.

Some information on which the charges are allegedly based has been leaked or disclosed to the public, but such information is often not firsthand and is normally fragmented. It is difficult to determine whether informal disclosures are biased and to what extent they are intended to bolster an informant's political cause. In sum, it is difficult or impossible for the general public to assess fully the merit of the charges made by the two governments. It would be highly desirable to have other independent unbiased sources with the ability to provide reliable intelligence, whereby charges of treaty violations could be evaluated.

Independent centers of satellite-monitoring capability could serve as a reserve or backup in case a national satellite network, for one reason or another, should become deficient. It has been a sad experience for those concerned about the effectiveness of the U.S. satellite-monitoring system to see that it has been threatened by the failures of rocket launches in 1986 and 1987. Slippages and breakdowns have occurred and could recur. They could become even more likely if monitoring is required to become more sophisticated in order to exercise surveillance over more complex provisions of future arms control or arms reduction treaties. Additional monitoring capabilities in third countries, or even better, in a neutral international agency, could instill confidence that a would-be violator would be under adequate scrutiny, even if certain breakdowns in national verification should happen.

Attributes of a Designated International Agency

The spread of satellite-monitoring capabilities to additional governments, the advent of organizations that provide monitoring services for a fee, EOSAT and SPOT, the expected multiplication of different kinds of satellite organizations in the future—all could in one way or another provide information useful for arms control verification. However, in many instances, these satellite-monitoring organizations would perform functions useful for verification only as a by-product of their principal missions. A news service, for example, operating a satellite would be interested in many different kinds of news, only one of which might have specific application to arms control verification.

Consequently, the information provided by these various satellite agencies acting independently would be unsystematic, incomplete, and not necessarily reliable for a full check of the conduct of signatories for compliance. Although information useful for verification could filter out of those sources, it would lack the comprehensiveness desirable for consistent reliability as a verification procedure. The most reliable type of organization for providing consistent and comprehensive information regarding compliance, which could furnish data helpful in resolving disputes, would be an international organization with the proper technological capabilities and a designated verification mission.

What kind of attributes would an international satellite-monitoring organization require? Technologically, such an organization would require access to a satellite-launching capability. It would either have to have its own launchers or, more likely in the beginning, it would need to have access to other launching facilities such as those now offered for sale or lease by national governments, preferably on a dependable schedule.

Such an international organization also would require access to sufficient numbers of satellites in appropriate orbits, with different kinds of sensing abilities (infrared, radar, photographic, and optical) that could carry out comprehensive surveillance. It would have to be assured of having operating time on such satellites adequate to carry out reliable monitoring functions. It could either lease time on satellites launched primarily for other purposes or, more desirably, it could acquire its own satellites tailored to its own needs.

Politically, the organization should be designed and operated in such a way as to command respect for its competence and impartiality. It should be free of taint of bias and instill confidence that its only purpose is to convey the truth regarding compliance, to the extent that this would be technologically feasible. Moreover, it would have to be free to announce its findings and conclusions to the public. Conceivably, there would be instances in which it could carry out its mission best by dealing confidentially with relevant governments, but ultimately it would need the discretionary authority to go public because this would be the ultimate sanction for enforcing its authority.

Legally, the organization would have to be located and set up in such a way that it could not be constrained, influenced, or prevented from carrying out its duties by any government or other authorities.[15] And finally, the personnel involved in such an operation would need the qualities necessary to instill confidence in the effectiveness of the organization. The technicians would have to be highly skilled. The management would have to attract candidates possessing not only administrative talent but also the political know-how to deal with highly sensitive subjects.

An Earlier Plan for an International Organization

The most effective mechanism for a neutral monitoring agency would be an international organization formally established by governments with a mission to verify arms control agreements. A French plan for an international intergovernmental organization to monitor arms control agreements by satellite was proposed several years ago that could be a model for serious examination today, although new technological, political, and other conditions would have to be taken into account.

The proposal was introduced by France at the United Nations in 1978. The concept was overwhelmingly approved by the General Assembly, which commended the contribution that satellite technology could make to the solution of various monitoring problems. Foremost among these problems named by the UN resolution were disarmament agreements.[16] The General Assembly initiated a study by a group of experts on the legal, financial, organizational, and other aspects of establishing an international satellite-monitoring agency (ISMA).

At that time the initiative was not approved by either the United States or the USSR. Essentially, the Soviets opposed it because they would not be directly connected with the implementation of individual arms control agreements. The United States emphasized the large cost of such an agency. It questioned whether the establishment of an agency for disarmament verification before agreements were even concluded would turn out to be suitable for the task. As far as real reasons are concerned, it can be presumed that the two superpowers did not want a third party interfering with their mutual verification arrangements and their monopoly over satellite surveillance. However, that monopoly has now been shattered, and they must deal with a new intelligence reality.

The UN Report

The report completed by the group of experts in 1981 still stands as an extensive study of many of the factors involved in the establishment of an ISMA.[17] It concluded that international law, including space law, did not prohibit an organization such as ISMA from carrying on monitoring activities by satellites. Such monitoring was being performed by national governments over the territory of other national governments and generally was viewed as permitted by international law. Consequently, if an organization of governments decided to perform such monitoring from satellites, there could be no international law impediment.

The report recognized the practical difficulties involved in establishing the structure of an ISMA. It declared that, in general, three kinds of facilities would be required. First of all, there would be the satellites themselves. These should be advanced-technology satellites, perhaps initially comprised of satellites of lesser capabilities but in time advancing toward those of greater sophistication with high-resolution power and rapid-transmission capabilities. The report contemplated that ISMA would have area surveillance systems, close-look systems, and nuclear explosion-detection systems like those now possessed and operated by the United States and the USSR. It conceived that these kinds of satellites might be transferred to ISMA by national governments either from the types already developed, or they might develop new systems especially for the purpose of ISMA. The report also stated that in time ISMA might develop its own satellite system to serve its own purposes.

Second, ground stations would be required to receive and disseminate the data transmitted from the satellites. And third, there would be an image-processing and interpretation center (IPIC) to convert the data received by the system into information useful for the various ISMA tasks. Personnel in this center would employ various kinds of sophisticated interpretive and technological analyses.

The actual installation of these three major components, according to the report, would go in reverse order. In other words, the IPIC would be established first and would avail itself initially of data from currently operating satellites through purchase, leased time, gift, or any practical method. These would include meteorological and earth-resources satellites now operated by various countries, including such systems as EOSAT and SPOT. The center also would receive other data from the national services of various countries such as India and Japan and from the military reconnaissance systems of the United States, the USSR, and other countries.

Second in order of installation would come the ground stations. These would have to be in place in order to convert the data sent by the satellites into practical applications, once the satellites were obtained and placed in operation. The satellites themselves would be the third component to be obtained and placed into operation. These would accord ISMA its own independently programmable data-acquisition capability. The cost of establishing and maintaining these three types of facilities would increase greatly with each step of installation.

Proposed Initiatives

The adoption of the following initiatives would assist governments in achieving effectively verifiable arms control agreements in the current stage of technological monitoring, that is, the stage of internationalized intelligence resulting from proliferated satellite capabilities. A basic premise of the third stage is that the superpowers' monopoly over satellite intelligence-gathering has been shattered. Many independent centers or agencies for acquiring intelligence by satellite on military and other activities relating to compliance with arms control agreements are appearing. The superpowers likely will resist as long as they can the implications of their loss of monopoly. But the sooner they act in accordance with the new technological facts of satellite acquisition of intelligence, the better their own policies and the cause of effective arms control will be served.

1) Any group of interested governments, preferably but not necessarily including the United States and the Soviet Union, should immediately take steps to establish an international satellite-monitoring agency to provide public information on compliance and on crisis situations. (These might include not only political crises but also natural or man-caused disasters.) The initiative could be either inside or outside the United Nations. The first facility to be established might be a data-interpretation unit utilizing available data from any operating remote-sensing satellites. Time on

existing public-service satellites such as SPOT could be purchased, while data acquired by satellites of national governments could be sought by gift or purchase. The organization might design its own satellites that could be launched on boosters furnished by any one of an increasing number of governments willing to provide such a system.

2) The United States should include in its current proposals for strategic and other arms control agreements, in addition to provisions for customary adversarial inspection by the signatories, a commitment for establishing and providing monitoring data to an international satellite-data processing agency. This agency could perform a number of independent verification functions for the signatories, such as backup for verifying compliance and confirming or correcting charges of violations.

3) In any future arms control agreements, the United States and the USSR should pledge not to make any charges of violations without disclosing the supporting evidence, either to the international satellite agency or by making it public in some other way.[18] Insofar as the wall of secrecy surrounding the intelligence information of the two superpowers— on which charges of violations are based—is increasingly being breached anyway by other independent agencies producing data relevant to arms control compliance, it should be to the advantage of Washington and Moscow to publicize the data on which their allegations are based.

Notes

[1] The human faculty of intelligence, as described by psychologists, is a different concept that may or may not be applicable to government intelligence.

[2] Ralph Earle, "Verification Issues from the Point of View of the Negotiator," in Kosta Tsipis et al., eds., *Arms Control Verification: The Technologies that Make It Possible* (Washington, DC: Pergamon-Brassey, 1986), p. 15.

[3] See U.S. Senate, Committee on Foreign Relations, *The SALT II Treaty*, Exec. Rept. No. 96-14, 1979, pp. 209–13.

[4] Such provisions can be found in the ABM and SALT II treaties, both of which mandate no interference with or concealment from NTM.

[5] The "bomber gap" of 1955 and the "missile gap" of 1958 were intelligence projections of Soviet strategic forces that later turned out to be greatly exaggerated. See John Prados, *The Soviet Estimate* (Princeton: Princeton University Press, 1986), pp. 41–50, 80–95, 111–26.

[6] The ABM Treaty was concluded and came into force in 1972. The SALT II Treaty was concluded in 1979, and, although it was not ratified by the United States or the Soviet Union, its terms were observed in practice by the two governments until May 1986 when the Reagan administration announced that it would no longer be bound by it.

[7] Such incursions by ships and aircraft occur for intelligence purposes. They generally are not protested by either party unless they become publicly known.

[8] Herbert Scoville, "Intelligence on Arms Control—A Valuable Partnership," in Alfred C. Maurer et al., *Intelligence Policy and Process* (Boulder, CO: Westview Press, 1985), p. 319.

[9] Michael Krepon, "The New Red Menace," *Washington Post*, March 15, 1987.

[10] Glossy editions of *Soviet Military Power* have been prepared annually by the DIA and distributed by the Department of Defense to Congress and the public.

[11] Gerard Hopple and Bruce W. Watson, eds., *The Military Intelligence Community* (Boulder, CO: Westview Press, 1986), p. 11.

[12] SPOT also has provided photographs of the military facilities on the Kola Peninsula and of the Krasnoyarsk missile-warning spacetrack radar. EOSAT formerly was called LANDSAT.

[13] The Latin American Free Zone has an international verification organization, but it engages in little or no monitoring activity.

[14] *Washington Post*, August 8, 1986. The governments are those of Argentina, Greece, India, Mexico, Sweden, and Tanzania.

[15] Some organizations operating privately with satellites are forbidden to acquire certain technological capabilities necessary for optimum performance. For example, at the present time satellites of a private character such as LANDSAT, which operate from the United States, are forbidden to have photographic resolution capabilities smaller than about thirty feet. U.S. government surveillance satellites have a resolution of about six inches. These restrictions are imposed by Washington for alleged national security reasons.

[16] It also declared that such a satellite-monitoring agency could contribute to resolving international crisis situations.

[17] United Nations, Department of Disarmament Affairs, UN Document A/AC.206/14; report of the secretary general, *The Implications of Establishing an International Satellite Monitoring Agency* (New York: United Nations, 1983).

[18] Over twenty years ago the United States displayed at the United Nations intelligence photographs that backed up its charges of Soviet missiles based in Cuba.

The U.S. Prognosis for Arms Control: A Guarded Affirmative

STEPHEN J. CIMBALA

THE FUTURE OF arms control after SALT is not certain, nor are assessments of the accomplishments of U.S.-Soviet arms control negotiations consensual. Nuclear arms control has seemed besieged by conservatives who object to it in principle and by liberals who are disillusioned with its results. Especially ironical was the successful outcome of superpower negotiations on intermediate-range nuclear forces (INF), culminating in the Reagan-Gorbachev summit of December 1987. Neither conservative supporters of the Reagan administration nor liberal advocates of arms control seemed thrilled by the prospective precedent of actual reductions in whole categories of nuclear weapons. Assessments of superpower arms control efforts are circumscribed by a policy debate that places a higher premium on scoring debating points than it does on understanding what arms control realistically can be expected to do.

The SALT legacy is an important one for the remainder of the 1980s and 1990s. It established over a decade of consultative expectations with regard to the deployment of strategic nuclear forces. It matters less what forces were actually deployed, provided neither side came within range of a credible first-strike capability. And neither side did. The window of vulnerability alleged to characterize American strategic nuclear forces in the early 1980s applied more to vulnerability in domestic policy debate than it did to realistic options for Soviet war planners.

The Reagan administration did more than allege that a window of vulnerability had overtaken U.S. strategic offensive forces. It also alleged that the entire structure of deterrence based on offensive retaliation was shaky and should be phased out in favor of defense-dominant denial forces. This went very much against the grain of previous development in U.S. strategic doctrine, which had evolved from the massive retaliation of the Eisenhower years into a version of flexible nuclear response by the early 1980s. From 1974 through 1982, presidents and secretaries of defense called for flexible nuclear options, including flexible strategic options, in order to provide for essential equivalence in deterrence across the spectrum of possible conflicts. The Reagan Strategic Defense Initiative (SDI), if the Soviets followed suit, would reverse this trend, for limited strategic options (LSOs) might be among the earliest casualties of a primitive Soviet ballistic missile defense (BMD) system. And policymakers of the 1980s apparently had forgotten that LSOs were the substitutes for superior U.S. strategic forces that had obtained, relative to their Soviet counterparts, in the 1960s. In effect, a defense-dominant world could decouple the flexibility from Flexible Response.

A defense-dominant world also might shift the basis of arms control, from its current focus on "bean counting" of warheads, launchers, and throw-weights. A defense-dominant world would involve the preeminence of weapons systems not now deployed and in some cases not yet conceived. Arms control efforts would focus on limitation of qualitative, instead of quantitative, competition, perhaps extending to limitations on laboratory research and intrusive inspections. No one could prove the impossibility of such a world, but the transition strategy for getting from here to there was controversial. How to phase out offenses while phasing in superpower defenses and still maintain stability was a problem with no apparent solution, other than strategic autarchy. One side would begin to introduce new defensive systems, and the other would see a fruitless competition in the offing and thus acquiesce to offensive reductions. It was hard to see how this would come about on the basis of previously stated Soviet doctrine, which emphasized the use of offenses and defenses for damage limitation, should deterrence fail.

In addition, there was a hopeful assumption in the cataloging of missile defenses as "defensive" weapons based upon the probable use of them to thwart a preemptive first strike. Depending on their character, technologies that we thought to be tasked for defensive missions might appear threatening to the opponent and so provoke crisis or war. For example, space-based lasers might be better as antisatellite weapons (ASATs) than they were as BMD systems and thus provide threats to the survivability of the other side's warning and communications satellites. Therefore, some discussions of the defense transition confused defensive *strategies* with defensive *technologies*. Since history cannot be rewritten and given the present baseline, introduction of defensive technology could contribute to the feasibility of offensive strategies. It could do this by making possible the credible first strike that is not now possible, if either side deployed a partially effective defense capable of absorbing the other's retaliatory strike.

It also was not clear that ballistic missiles and missile defenses were the heart of the problem, relative to the future of U.S.-Soviet strategic nuclear deterrence. Without complementary air defenses against atmospheric threats such as cruise missiles and bombers, missile defenses would solve only part of the problem. Cruise missiles and bombers were being modernized by both sides, and more of these missiles were being deployed at sea as well as aloft. Cruise missiles also would become more attractive as future components of a strategic reserve force for use in the postattack phase of a conflict. For arms control, they were a mixed blessing. It would be difficult to distinguish nuclear-armed from conventionally armed cruise missiles by using national technical means (NTM) as authorized by SALT. On the other hand, cruise missiles of the present generation would be poor weapons for a preemptive strike, since their slow flight times made them less obvious candidates for that purpose than the comparatively prompt ballistic missiles. BMD might drive research and development toward cruise missiles of greater range and smaller "observables" for radars to detect. Stealth bombers combined with stealthier cruise missiles eventually might evade atmospheric defenses and BMD, the latter having been deployed at some substantial cost.

Reykjavik and After

In October 1986, President Ronald Reagan and General Secretary Mikhail Gorbachev met in Reykjavik for a summit designed to clear the decks for arms control agreements between the superpowers. The results of this meeting continued to be disputed within the U.S. national security community and among America's European allies, and there was immediate fallout in at least two directions. First, the momentum carried over into 1987 discussions on the reduction and possible elimination of American and Soviet long- and short-range INF in Europe. Second, agreement in principle was reached to pursue drastic reductions in strategic ballistic missile offenses, perhaps by as much as 50 percent within five years and ultimate reductions to zero within ten years.

It was a challenge to American leadership in NATO to bring Europeans along on both these points simultaneously. By the spring of 1987 a remarkable degree of agreement among the principals in NATO Europe had emerged, relative to the "zero-zero" option for removal of U.S. and Soviet INF. Taking the Europeans along on the second issue, drastic reductions in strategic ballistic missile forces, proved more difficult. The proposed reductions raised fears of a U.S. disengagement from its commitment to provide a nuclear umbrella for Western Europe. The umbrella was thought to protect Europeans against both nuclear and conventional aggression, and the issue of conventional deterrence seemed more problematical as theater and strategic nuclear weapons were removed.

Here the United States faced logically inconsistent but very practical continental fears: of decoupling the U.S. strategic deterrent from NATO Europe and of American willingness to engage in first use under conditions of doubtful necessity to the Europeans. Moreover, as the verdicts of the treasuries were heard on the subject of drastic nuclear force reduction and offsetting conventional force improvements, these verdicts were pessimistic as to probable costs for NATO. Whether any improvements in NATO's conventional forces could offset the geographical advantages available to Soviet attackers was unclear, and proponents of the Conventional Defense Initiative proposed to offset Soviet advantages with new tactics and new technology. It seemed likely, however, that whatever improvements NATO could make the USSR could offset, at least in Europe, and attacks on the Soviet periphery outside of the Continent promised little in the way of decisive results on the Central Front.

The prospect of deep strategic offensive reductions thus proved to be problematical with regard to expectations among alliance members. However, these expectations did require rethinking. For years NATO had coasted along on U.S. strategic nuclear superiority or "essential equivalence," and this coasting persisted long after experts recognized disturbing asymmetries in the nuclear balance. Although a rough parity existed between superpower strategic nuclear forces, forces that could be brought to bear in the European theater of operations, without tasking strategic nuclear forces, favored Moscow's planners by the beginning of the 1980s. Of particular concern to NATO was the Soviet LRINF SS-20s, which were mobile and carried three warheads per launcher, with reloads available. At maximum deployment more than 400 launchers presumably were targeted against Europe and Asia. In 1977, then-West German Chancellor Helmut Schmidt suggested that U.S.-Soviet strategic parity required NATO to maintain equivalence in theater nuclear forces (TNF) also. The "572" Pershing II and ground-launched cruise missile (GLCM) deployments on the Continent were to provide visible evidence of the coupling of Washington's strategic nuclear forces to European theater-based nuclear and conventional forces. The visibility was perhaps more important than the capability, since during crises the Pershing II missiles deployed in West Germany might tempt preemption. And the 572 deployments did nothing to improve NATO's conventional forces, which were thought to be more in need of repair than its nuclear forces, either theater-based or based outside Europe.

Spillover from SDI research might contribute to improving NATO's conventional defenses. Deployment of theater BMDs and improved air defenses could protect NATO air bases, command centers, and other important targets from destruction by Soviet conventionally armed ballistic missiles and aircraft. Moscow's strategy for war in Europe would include a plan for keeping the war conventional if the political and military objectives could be attained without escalation. But controlling escalation requires preemptive destruction of NATO nuclear weapons or NATO cooperation in self-imposed restraint, if the Soviets are to fulfill the operational requirements for any viable war plan. NATO therefore must preserve its TNF as survivable against preemptive attack by Soviet conventional forces. The fewer there are of NATO TNF, the more difficult this task becomes. It might be thought that arms control provides a possible way out of this problem, but it does not provide an automatic one. Some conventional capabilities are more difficult to monitor and verify than nuclear ones, and bean counting may tell us less in the conventional instance than an accurate knowledge of doctrine. Still, there is a plausible case for either reduction of Soviet short-range ballistic missiles deployed in Eastern Europe or for improving the defenses of targets against which those missiles might be launched.

NATO is probably deluding itself, however, if it expects to push nuclear weapons, even theater nuclear weapons, out of the picture entirely. The proximity of Soviet conventional forces to NATO Europe ensures that movement of those forces into West Germany will provoke fears of nuclear war, even before an exchange of nuclear weapons. If the TNF are reduced, as both sides now seem willing to do, then NATO is all the more dependent upon the willingness of the United States to employ its strategic forces, including those (such as Poseidon SLBMs) nominally assigned to NATO. This means, to the extent that TNF of all ranges are reduced or even eliminated from arsenals, that Europe faces two types of wars: a conventional one and a strategic one, with few capabilities for graduated escalation. This might be sensible given the low probability of a limited nuclear war under present conditions, but the threat it poses is somewhat different. Instead of a proliferation of nuclear weapons in Europe that might lead to inadvertent nuclear war, deterrence now would rest upon the denial capabilities of conventional forces plus the retaliatory threat from U.S. strategic nuclear forces. If conventional war began, the two sides would think immediately of how to protect their strategic forces against preemptive attack, no matter what was going on in Europe. Indeed, it would not be a conventional war in any sense, but rather a war involving general-purpose forces equipped with nuclear weapons (for not all of them would have been negotiated away), which might escalate into a strategic nuclear war.

This scenario, if it comes about, implies more than the removal of a rung from the ladder-of-escalation metaphor, requiring that NATO declaratory explanations of flexible response be amended. It also affects operational capabilities and net assessments. Soviet attackers might not believe that NATO deliberately would escalate to strategic nuclear war as easily as they would be convinced that such a war could come about inadvertently. NATO would be departing from a heavy reliance upon the "threat that leaves something to chance" in favor of a threat that leaves nothing to indeterminacy. If the United States had either obviously superior offensive forces or an impervious defense which the USSR could not duplicate, then the missing rung might not matter. But such American preeminence is not in the cards, and therefore a war in Europe leaves little to chance. Either NATO conventional forces hold, or both sides lose everything. There are some who argue that this is not necessarily so, and that strategic nuclear war is in some fashion "winnable." We pass over that argument as unwinnable and unnecessary for our purposes.

Technology and Arms Control

The relationship between East-West arms control and the evolution of military technology is not a precise one. Some technologies contribute to the success of arms control, and others to its failure, while some are ambiguous in their implications. There is a great danger in treating technology as an independent variable in these discussions. It tends to acquire a life force of its own, outside of the requirements of strategy or policy. Constituencies then form for or against arms control as an end in itself. Consider, for example, the polarized debate over whether the Reagan administration should or should not continue in the tradition of its predecessors by adhering de facto to the restrictions of SALT II on the deployment of strategic launch vehicles. The administration contended that it was only following the Soviet lead in pushing across the threshold of treaty limitations; critics, in turn, accused the administration of perfidy in exceeding the SALT guidelines and abrogating a commitment to which both parties were still willing to adhere. However, much had taken place since the signing of SALT II, including the recognition by both sides that the appropriate unit of account for strategic arms limitations was not launchers, but warheads, and from the standpoint of strategy, survivable warheads.

This meant that the issue of basing schemes, a relatively marginal concern during the SALT negotiations, could prove to be more important in both superpowers' calculations with regard to a START agreement. The Carter MX/MPS scheme was designed as a "warhead sponge" that would move MX missiles around "racetracks" in a shell game designed to absorb more Soviet reentry vehicles than the USSR would be willing to expend attacking it.[1] In order to offset the U.S. basing scheme, the Soviets could deploy additional warheads on the same number of launchers (fractionation) at the cost of reduced yield for each, although not necessarily reduced accuracy. The Reagan administration was anxious to deploy MX missiles but found domestic political objections to the multiple shelters-racetrack scheme compelling, and so it proposed the "dense pack," or closely spaced basing. This, too, Congress found unacceptable, and the administration was thrown back on the Scowcroft Commission's recommendation to deploy 100 MX/Peacekeepers in Minuteman silos and to begin research and development toward eventual deployment of the small Midgetman intercontinental ballistic missile (ICBM) in the 1990s.[2]

This solution was politically viable in Congress, provided the third leg of the MX-Midgetman-arms control triad remained in the administration's policy agenda. Skeptical Congressmen attempted during Reagan's first and second terms to add amendments to appropriation and authorization bills to ensure that the administration toed the line on arms control and kept development of the small ICBM within congressionally mandated guidelines (such as not growing too big for mobility, thus ensuring survivability). Congress insisted that the Midgetman be a single-warhead missile so that it would not be an attractive target compared to multiple-warhead missiles. The theory of the U.S. Air Force was that, deployed in conjunction with MX, Midgetman would provide additional survivability and hard-target kill capability but not invite preemptive attack. However, the technology (improved accuracy) that jeopardized the survivability of MX and other silo-based missiles also made possible the use of mobile missiles for counterforce targeting.

This raised the prospect of their use in extended or protracted wars, which American advocates of arms control certainly did not want to encourage. Or, single-warhead missiles might be used more readily in a crisis or wartime situation against individual targets, without "wasting" the entire MIRV bus of a multiple-warhead missile. Thus, they might be more credible as LSOs or limited nuclear options (LNOs) to the party being threatened and therefore provocative of preemption. The technology of survivability for mobile missiles, either single-warhead or MIRVed, was not fully understood. Soviet deployment of their SS-25 road-mobile ICBM with a single warhead and their planned deployment of SS-X-24 with an estimated ten reentry vehicles (RVs) was followed by a U.S. Air Force announcement that it would consider rail-mobile basing for the second fifty MX missiles permitted by Congress. Technology seemed to dictate that mobile missiles might have to be attacked in large barrage strikes that indeed could be accomplished, but not without incurring a great deal of the collateral damage to other targets that first strikers allegedly want to avoid.

Improved accuracy also made it possible for both sides to contemplate surprise attack against counterforce targets with later arriving cruise missiles as well as early arriving ballistic missiles. Cruise missiles were slow, but if undetected by air defense systems they could be just as deadly. Either cruise missiles or future generations of ICBMs and submarine-launched ballistic missiles (SLBMs) could be equipped with nonnuclear warheads if their accuracies were great enough to destroy the appropriate target. Earth-penetrator warheads and maneuvering RVs provided other options for destroying targets previously thought to be invulnerable, or nearly so. Stealth aircraft and stealthy cruise missiles would be useful in early stages of a war for surprise attack or in its later stages if air defenses were weakened or destroyed.

On the other hand, new developments in sensor technology, including space-based sensors, would help to prevent surprise attack. Improved radar-warning and attack-assessment systems will do likewise. The superpowers agreed in 1984 to upgrade the Direct Communications Link (Hot Line) by endowing it with facsimile capability, and the United States has proposed that both sides establish direct communication links between national military command centers. Senators Sam Nunn and John Warner have proposed that the superpowers establish "nuclear risk reduction centers" in their respective capitals to monitor and warn against false alarms and crisis misperceptions.[3] There is an apparent need for a definition of rules of the road with regard to ASAT deployments, as very capable ASATs would threaten the survivability of vital communications and warning assets, as noted previously.

Very discerning sensors also will make possible the jump to real-time analysis of intelligence and reconnaissance data on the conventional battlefield. U.S. and NATO concepts of AirLand Battle and Deep Strike are predicated on the development of improved sensors that can detect moving targets well behind the forward edge of the battle area (FEBA) and fix them in memory while they are destroyed by deep-strike air- and ground-launched systems. There is great controversy over whether the larger schemes for NATO's Follow-on Forces Attack (FOFA) provide an adequate basis for conventional defense in Europe. General Bernard Rogers (former SACEUR) never contended that conventional deterrence would hold without the threat of nuclear escalation in the background.[4] Without getting into these broader arguments, it seems a fair supposition that future battlefields on land will be more transparent to electronic intercept and photographic intrusion. This provides some consolation for NATO, which depends upon timely reaction to warning and subsequent mobilization in order to defeat a Warsaw Pact attack on the Central Front.

This good news, however, is balanced by the recognition that if defenses can deploy enhanced technologies, so can the offense. The Deep Strike technologies that could allow NATO to attack Soviet second-echelon ground forces also could attack NATO's rear at the outset of a war, before the defender had fully coordinated its efforts and regrouped.[5] Improved sensors and electronic warfare capabilities (electronic countermeasures, or

ECM, and electronic counter-countermeasures, or ECCM) also would assist the Soviet conventional war plan, which emphasizes speed, surprise, and a rapid encirclement of forward positions together with prompt penetration by operational maneuver groups (OMGs) or other raiding forces into NATO's vital rear sectors.[6]

Improved sensors also could be destabilizing, at least from the Western perspective, in another way. The possibility of improvements in U.S. or Soviet ability to detect strategic ballistic missile submarines (SSBNs) in the open ocean with improved acoustic, or even nonacoustic, sensors has been discussed in the open literature.[7] Expert consensus suggests that American and Soviet SSBNs, for somewhat different reasons, would remain survivable against preemptive attack, although this survivability is guaranteed with regard only to their performance of the assured destruction mission (countercity retaliation). Any technology breakthrough that would allow for preemptive attacks against submarines in the open ocean would favor the USSR, which relies more upon bastions close to its own coasts for the survivability of its SSBN force, whereas the United States favors concealment provided by thousands of miles of open ocean. It would be difficult to trail successfully, let alone to destroy preemptively, most of the U.S. "boomers" even if the entire fleet is reduced to about twenty SSBNs in the 1990s, as has been suggested. However, complacency is not warranted, since roughly one third of the boomers are in port at any one time (and a larger proportion of Soviet SSBNs is in port as well).

A surprise attack would destroy the portion of the force of either side that was in port unless its missiles could be launched "under attack" on the basis of tactical warning, a mission normally thought to be difficult enough for either side's ICBM force to execute. Clearly, both superpowers have something to gain by attempting to cap the technology for SSBN detection or by establishing rules of the road, such as keep-out zones within which SSBNs would not patrol. However, both Soviet and American SSBNs already can strike at targets in the other's homeland from locations very close to their own shores—where, of course, they might be more easily located by enemy antisubmarine warfare (ASW). An ASW-technology breakthrough of destabilizing proportions need not be limited to sensors; improvements in data processing and filtration of noise from proper signals also could lead to higher probabilities of detection.

Command and Control

The idea of SSBN keep-out zones raises the issue of command and control, for one of the arguments for such zones is that a decapitation attack against vital command centers of the opponent would be precluded. This has been a special worry of students of command vulnerability, who have suggested that Soviet SSBNs on routine patrol could take out a significant portion of U.S. strategic command, control, and communications (C^3) targets, including civilian and military leaders in Washington, in a preemptive attack.[8]

There are two basic issues with regard to arms control and superpower command systems. The first is whether arms control can help to prevent accidental or inadvertent nuclear war. The second is the relationship between command vulnerability and war termination, and whether survivable C^3 systems aid deterrence or encourage false optimism about wartime force performance.

The issue of whether arms control can contribute to the prevention of accidental or inadvertent war is a settled one: it has. The Hot Line agreement already has been mentioned, and other markers are apparent in the unilateral measures taken by each side to ensure that its nuclear weapons cannot be fired without appropriate authorization. For both Soviet and American leaders, "appropriate" has meant top-level civilian or military authorities, although in both cases there is a dual chain of command for postattack nuclear operations. In the Soviet Union, this would run from the political leadership through the Supreme High Command (VGK) and the General Staff to the various theater and multitheater commanders. Parallel to this for those Soviet forces that have deployed nuclear weapons, including the uniquely organized Strategic Rocket Forces, is probably a KGB chain of communication with top party leadership.[9] In the American case, there is the formal chain of political succession as specified in both the Constitution and the Presidential Succession Act (1947), and also the military command structure through which orders from the president and the secretary of defense (together the National Command Authority) will flow.[10] In both instances the probability of accidental war—that is, war begun by a faulty computer chip or by a mad colonel—is judged by experts to be rather remote. In addition to the political protections against usurpation of command, the United States has added electromechanical locks (permissive action links, or PAL) to all but its sea-based strategic nuclear forces.

Inadvertent nuclear war is something else again, and there are fewer guarantees in technology or policy that can be given against it. One illustration of how it might come about has been provided in Barry Posen's discussion of the issue of nuclear war at sea. U.S. naval forces engaged in a conventional war with the Soviet Union might trigger nuclear conflict as a result of clashes over control of the Norwegian and Barents seas, and Washington's maritime strategy calls for prompt attacks against Soviet naval aviation and other assets based at the Kola Peninsula on Soviet territory.[11] Some of this is declaratory deterrence, U.S. Navy variety, but the operational end of it does raise concerns about how the successful prosecution of a nominally conventional war can be kept from crossing the nuclear threshold. Nuclear weapons, after all, are widely dispersed among general-purpose forces on land and at sea.

Although much has been made of the possibility that Soviet attackers could destroy the central U.S. nuclear command system and thus cripple any meaningful retaliation, the problem of controlling nuclear weapons commingled with conventional forces is worse, especially in Europe.[12] To avoid having its nuclear weapons deployed in Europe destroyed preemptively, NATO might have to disperse them prematurely and so invite Soviet attack. The obvious contribution that arms control can make here is to remove theater-based weapons that can attack targets of strategic importance; for example, Pershing II missiles allegedly within ten minutes' flight time of destroying important command targets in the western Soviet Union. More comprehensive limitations on U.S. and Soviet long-range TNF have been agreed to as of this writing, and there is every prospect that short-range missiles will be included as well. But short-range ballistic and cruise missiles have somewhat different implications for stability, and thus for arms control, given the short flight times of the former and their capabilities for use in preemptive attack.

By "inadvertent" nuclear war, analysts seem to find at least two distinct meanings: a conventional war crosses the nuclear threshold because the opponent did not take the last chance to avoid escalation; or, the nuclear threshold is crossed deliberately, but at a low level in the assumption that violence can be contained at that level. In the second instance, nuclear war is not inadvertent, but escalation from small- to large-scale nuclear war is. A nuclear war at sea might begin when conventional forces sink a nuclear-armed ship and the victim's superiors decide that this is tantamount to nuclear war, and so respond. Or, a selective nuclear strike against surface or subsurface craft of the opponent might be attempted, on the assumption (ultimately proved to be false) that it could be restricted to a tit-for-tat exchange. So-called battlefield nuclear weapons of tactical range deployed forward in Western Europe have been used in scenarios in both ways: as components of a semiautomatic crossing of the nuclear threshold that the opponent must fear, and as discriminating nuclear weapons whose use (it is assumed) could be limited to discrete targets with minimal collateral damage.

These related but distinct rationales for the role of theater nuclear weapons in Western deterrence strategy create different command and control dilemmas. The first rationale, that of allowing conventional war to slip into nuclear war, puts a cap on NATO's motivation to improve its conventional forces relative to those of the Warsaw Pact, for fear of removing the ambiguously deterring threat. The second rationale, for discriminating use, assumes that intrawar deterrence and reciprocal targeting restraint will be of equal interest to both NATO and Pact commanders. In effect, NATO must credibly threaten a not-very-tight control of its forces, in the first case, and, in the second, an extremely firm grasp by top policymakers. Whether NATO can threaten both autonomous and deliberate risks of escalation at the same time is scenario-dependent. However, it is worth noting that, on the record, the USSR appears disinterested in making threats whose intellectual baseline is a potential loss of control over the process in which their own forces are engaged.

Arms control could contribute here, too, by placing limits on the numbers, yields, and accuracies of nuclear weapons that are based in Europe or targeted uniquely against it. The Soviet SS-20 IRBM with its range, mobility, and MIRV is a system that is not conducive to arms race stability on the Continent. Nor is the NATO Pershing II deployed in West Germany within prompt striking range of the western Soviet Union. Reductions in the quantities and qualities of theater forces with the potential to turn a campaign into a strategic war are welcome from an arms control standpoint, as the superpowers recognized by 1987.

Beyond the NATO nuclear weapons themselves, however, is the further issue of who commands and controls them. In peacetime the United States deploys nuclear weapons on European soil under bilateral programs of cooperation consistent with NATO directives. In wartime, preemptive attacks against NATO command and control could destroy much of its technical infrastructure and kill many of its personnel. Top leaders in NATO capitals might be among the earliest victims of decapitation attacks from specialized units trained for that mission.

Commanders who are aware of these vulnerabilities are not going to wait forever once they receive contingent authority to fire; the constant knowledge that they are subject to decapitation implies that forces are launched on reliable, or even unreliable, warning of an attack.

NATO is less likely to suffer from the physical collapse of its command assets than it is to find coordination difficult among so many different national command systems. Buzzwords such as "interoperability" refer at best to the technical connections between units of different nationalities with responsibility for defending part of the same front. The more important issue is command philosophy. If one national corps decides to stand and fight behind the advantage of defensively prepared positions, and another national corps adjacent to the first specializes in rapid maneuver (encounter) battles, then both will be working at cross purposes no matter how effectively they are wired.

As high-technology initiatives begin to take hold on NATO's Central Front, much sorting out of priorities among C^3 networks and C^3 countermeasures (C^3CM) will be required. The difficult question of command by coalition will present itself at the most inopportune moments. Whoever gets what kind of information, and how fast, will determine the extent to which national corps forces fight a coordinated air and land battle, or separate corps battles. If arms control is to reduce the probability of any war in Europe, as opposed to reducing the probability of nuclear war alone, then it must deal with conventional force imbalances, including C^3 imbalances, which favor the Pact under conditions of surprise attack. If NATO can withstand a Soviet-Pact surprise attack and hold its own near the inter-German border until the USSR is forced to deploy its reinforcements, then it will have denied to the Soviets a conventional war-winning option. If, on the other hand, the Soviets can attain effective surprise against NATO forward deployments near the inter-German border, then they may be able to exploit that surprise to consolidate a permanent gain in territory within West Germany. It would then be NATO's dilemma either to expel them with nuclear weapons (and devastate much of its own territory) or acquiesce.

One contribution that arms control might make in this regard is to have the Soviet Union and the U.S.-NATO sides agree on counting rules for forces deployed in the guidelines area. Another contribution would require both sides to disengage their forces some thirty kilometers or so from the border, creating a demilitarized zone (DMZ) between West Germany, on one side, and East Germany and Czechoslovakia, on the other. This keep-out zone would prohibit modern, heavily armored tanks and armored personnel carriers, comparable to the DMZ in Korea, although the DMZ is much more comprehensive in its restrictions. Inspection teams would be allowed to visit military installations in both camps on demand as well as regularly scheduled military maneuvers.

Resources

The Reagan administration asked for and obtained significant increases in defense spending, relative to previous peacetime baselines, measured either as a proportion of the gross national product (GNP) or of total outlays. There is much controversy about whether these increased defense expenditures have bought increased military preparedness, although the preparedness output is difficult to measure, absent an outbreak of war. In any case, general-purpose forces have accounted for most of this buildup, although SDI research and development may grow into major expenditures in the early 1990s if they follow the president's original projections. The relationship between arms control and defense spending after the Reagan years may be forced into a tighter linkage by the pressure of a Gramm-Rudman fiscal climate.

Examined superficially, the relationship between nuclear arms control and defense spending seems oblique, since nuclear forces account for such a small proportion of the budget. However, this superficial impression is somewhat misleading, since the separation of nuclear and conventional forces is not as clear in practice as it is in theory. U.S. conventional forces deployed in Europe, for example, are equipped with nuclear weapons, without which, according to NATO strategy, they would not be credible deterrents. And in some scenarios the U.S. strategic and theater nuclear deterrent depends for its survivability upon the European and American conventional forces that would go into battle immediately if deterrence failed on the Central Front.

Therefore, conventional deterrence cannot be separated easily from nuclear deterrence when force structures and military operations are dependent upon both. The removal of U.S. general-purpose forces from NATO Europe in order to reduce defense expenditures, for example, is a strategic as well as a fiscal measure, and it affects our nuclear as well as our conventional deterrence.[13] All of the old arguments about NATO conventional forces as "trip wires" versus "denial" forces passed over the unavoidable requirement for both missions, as if one could separate the two objectives in practice. Instead, NATO conventional forces have denial capabilities not because they can hold off a Soviet attack without threatening escalation, but because they can engage Soviet conventional forces long enough to get escalation started.

As in Europe, so it is in the Persian Gulf and Southwest Asia, where American conventional forces would have little expectation of defeating Soviet forces, for example, in an extended war in Iran. Instead, what the United States can credibly threaten to do, albeit with substantial risk, is to interpose its forces between Soviet attackers and their objectives. This compels the USSR to run over them and thus ignite the U.S. nuclear deterrent and a wider war. Now, at the level of wishful thinking—if we could have all the conventional forces that we want—it might seem a shame that the United States cannot field general-purpose forces without nuclear weapons for interventions outside Europe. In the real world of congressional budgeting, conventional forces with that kind of global reach will not be obtained, and there is no better evidence than President Reagan's inability to obtain them. Forces for interventions with less drastic objectives than superpower confrontation may be available, but U.S. airlift, sealift, and prepositioning outside Europe are limited, and host-nation support for American expeditionary forces is not popular. In restructuring the U.S. Army in order to create additional light divisions, the Department of Defense may find that it has obtained additional resources with which to fight the kinds of wars that Congress is most unwilling to support: wars outside of Europe in which the threat to U.S. national security is not obvious or consensually perceived.

These illustrations are arguable in the absence of actual conflicts of the type hypothesized. The point is that there are limited fiscal benefits from nuclear arms reductions unless their implications for the conventional force balances between NATO and the Warsaw Pact, or between U.S. interventionary and expeditionary forces and their probable targets, are considered. On the first balance, that of NATO and the Warsaw Pact, most assessments are probably too pessimistic. NATO has a better than even chance of defeating any Soviet attempt to mount a conventional blitzkrieg in Europe, assuming that it reacts responsively to warnings.[14] U.S. and allied maritime forces make any scenario for Soviet victory in extended conventional war difficult to write.

On the other hand, Reagan officials may be too optimistic about the second balance, between U.S. conventional forces to be used outside of

Europe and their probable opponents. (Grenada was an unfortunate episode in this regard, since the weakness of the opponent encouraged a false optimism about the capabilities of American forces for these kinds of rapid interventions.) No one doubts that the United States could do better at this now than a decade ago, but how much better depends upon intangibles, including the effectiveness of the military chain of command for special operations, which has recently been revised. Indeed, fiascoes such as the ill-fated Iranian rescue operation during the Carter administration have been falsely attributed to insufficient defense resources. Such episodes are more political than military failures, and, as in Lebanon in 1983, involve a politically misconceived mission and a top-heavy chain of command—a combination that is sure to fail when rapid and decisive action is needed.

If the United States cannot do without the nuclear shadow to make viable its threats to employ conventional forces, this does not mean that budgets for forces in either category must rise exponentially and inexorably. And if the history of Washington's defense budgeting shows any pattern, it is one overall of feast and famine, of roller-coaster funding indulgences and withdrawals, considered microscopically (what did *my* service get this year?). However, from a macroscopic perspective, peacetime defense expenditures since Korea, and absent Vietnam, have been remarkably consistent. So, too, have the relative service slices of the defense pie. Where reductions in nuclear forces might have more to do with defense resources is in the research and development sector.

Although nuclear weapons are not the most expensive purchases made by Department of Defense contractors, the requirements of strategic nuclear deterrence often drive the planning process faster than prudence would dictate. A U.S.-Soviet agreement not to deploy MIRV warheads in the 1970s, for example, would have been easier to reach without the pressures of research and development planners to deploy a "sweet" technology. Another illustration is missile defense systems, which are always on the drawing board or in the conceptual design stage. The research and development community, with an interest in the promotion of technology for its own sake without necessarily caring about stability, joins hands with military officers who see program management as a step to promotion. This is undoubtedly what Dwight Eisenhower meant when he referred to the military-industrial complex: not a conspiracy, but rather a coagulation of interest between civilian and military advocates of weapons systems for their own sake, regardless of strategic priorities. If we assume that arms control is among U.S. strategic priorities, then the momentum of the military-industrial complex is an additional obstacle.

It is certainly conceivable that both U.S. and Soviet governments could obtain some short-run savings in defense expenditures if arms control agreements reduced the size of their strategic forces. The long-run savings would be more difficult to forecast. If either or both sides could avoid deploying redundant systems that result from bureaucratic politics, then both superpowers would gain. However, in war, redundancy has an odd way of paying off, so that forces thought unnecessary in peacetime prove to be useful in the event. Military planners are especially conservative in this regard, tending to overinsure against improbable contingencies. But arms control agreements have limited the deployment of systems unnecessary for deterrence stability, as the SALT I and SALT II agreements did, and as future INF agreements may. In the absence of the test of war itself, systems that are unnecessary for deterrence may be considered redundant from the standpoint of strategic requirements. The difficulty lies in knowing where the line of redundancy begins.

One place to draw the line is to avoid deploying forces that are both vulnerable and provocative, provided there are alternatives that are neither. Thus, arms control would do a service to both superpowers if it allowed them to shift the basis of their strategic deterrents to slow counterforce systems, such as bombers and cruise missiles, from reliance upon prompt counterforce ICBMs. It also would contribute to stability and fiscal prudence if, willy-nilly, ASAT and BMD competitions could be treaty limited and, in the case of ASAT, almost totally restricted by mutual agreement. Much of the U.S. debate about verification of such agreements has focused too much on technical issues, relative to the importance of political ones. Washington has the national technical means to verify Soviet cheating at levels of magnitude such that it would make a difference for deterrence stability. It would take a determined Soviet effort and unprecedented American incompetence to change that situation. Here the control of ASATs has a double benefit, not only by preventing another competition in weapons systems but also by providing assurance across the board that each side is aware of any deployments by the other that might change the strategic balance in significant ways.

In the post-Gramm-Rudman climate of the 1990s, then, the United States should have adequate resources to sustain the Reagan programs for strategic offensive force modernization more or less as projected. But SDI is another matter, and at some point in the next decade decisions about the relative priorities of offensive versus defensive technologies will have to be made. As a research and development program, SDI can stay on the back burner only so long, before congressional and other pressures to force a decision will be compelling. This may be one reason why the Reagan administration in 1987 began urging Congress to consider a near-term deployment of a partial missile defense system in the early 1990s, with a commitment to such a deployment before Reagan leaves office. It is unlikely to happen. Congress is not persuaded that the program is conducive to strategic stability. And if Congress remains unpersuaded, then SDI may become expendable in the decade ahead.

INF and Extended Deterrence in Europe

In December 1987, President Reagan and General Secretary Gorbachev signed a historic agreement to eliminate the entire INF category of U.S. and Soviet nuclear weapons. These weapons included the Soviet SS-20, which, according to NATO, had constituted a threat to the European balance of power since its initial deployment in 1977. Both long- and shorter-range ground-launched ballistic and cruise missile INF were to be eliminated during a three-year period, according to the agreement. The United States and NATO would forgo completion of the 572 deployments of Pershing II and cruise missiles based in Western Europe. The Pershing IIs were of particular concern to the Soviet high command, who feared that the very fast and accurate U.S. ballistic missiles based in West Germany could strike at targets in the USSR, including important military command centers, within eight minutes or so.[15] The agreement would eliminate INF worldwide and apparently provided for very intrusive and unprecedented degrees of American and Soviet inspection of the other's production facilities (the details were unclear at this writing).

The INF agreement had a curious political history. In 1979, NATO adopted its two-track decision to deploy Pershing II and GLCMs in December 1983 unless U.S.-Soviet arms control negotiations by then had removed the necessity for the deployments. This meant that President Reagan, upon being elected in 1980, inherited the two-track decision and the politics that went with it. Europeans would expect that the United States, as putative leader of the NATO bloc, would continue the policy of negotiating with the Soviets while planning for the eventual deployments of INF.

The Reagan administration, however, was initially distrustful of any negotiations with the USSR. It preferred to engage in a sustained defense buildup and then to enter the arms control arena from a stronger position, compared to 1980. In fact, much of the Reagan buildup did go into procurement of new weapons systems, and spending on strategic nuclear forces as a proportion of all defense spending rose significantly during the president's second term.[16] It was arguable whether this had much to do with the willingness of the USSR to negotiate, compared to Reagan's reelection in 1984 and the installation thereafter of Gorbachev as head of the Soviet Communist party. During Reagan's first term, NATO Europeans were subjected to Soviet pressure and internal political upheavals that almost deterred their following through with announced plans to deploy INF beginning in 1983. Meanwhile, the Reagan administration held fast and reaped some publicity benefits when the Soviets walked out of arms control negotiations on strategic and theater nuclear weapons as NATO began deploying INF.

All this would change when Gorbachev consolidated his hold. He saw the opportunity to commit to the arms control process the most conservative administration in postwar U.S. history. No treaty negotiated by Ronald Reagan could possibly be attacked on the American home front as a sellout. And especially not a treaty based on the principle of "zero option" as proposed by Reagan in 1981, nor the "double zero" attainable by adding shorter-range INF to the long-range systems. Gorbachev adroitly played back to U.S. negotiators the president's own arms control proposal, which itself had been a hybrid borrowing from European peace movements and conservative hard-liners within the Reagan Defense Department. The zero option had been attacked by administration critics for its apparent nonnegotiability, but it proved to be negotiable in 1987 to the astonishment of many experts on both sides of the Atlantic.

The reasons for the negotiability of the zero option—actually the zero-zero option, once it included shorter-range INF as well as long-range systems—were complex. First, Gorbachev by 1987 had consolidated his grip on the Politburo and felt free to take initiatives on arms control in the expectation that he would not be subject to military opposition in Moscow. His seriousness about superpower negotiation was telegraphed in the minisummit in Reykjavik in the autumn of 1986. There he and Reagan spoke of reducing their strategic nuclear arsenals by as much as 50 percent, within five years, and of the possible elimination of all strategic ballistic missiles within a decade of any agreement.[17] Although the

American side might not have been as sure of where it was going as the Soviet one, nevertheless the declaratory precedent of drastic and unexampled reductions from existing levels of nuclear weapons had been set. And, although it appeared at Reykjavik that the SDI program would prove to be an obstacle to meaningful discussions and eventual agreements, this turned out otherwise in Washington in 1987.

The second reason for the negotiability of INF in 1987, from the Soviet standpoint, was that Gorbachev had more important objectives, including the promotion of "reasonable sufficiency" in military doctrine and the modernization of his country's economy. This had two implications. First, the USSR would fall behind the United States and NATO militarily in the next century unless its industry was modernized. This was especially worrisome for the Soviets with regard to the implications for conventional high-technology weapons. Second, Gorbachev's military advisers felt threatened by the possibility of an early American SDI deployment, perhaps in the mid-1990s. Such a system would be a crude protection of American cities against a comprehensive Soviet attack, but it might thin out a less than comprehensive attack against U.S. missile silos, bomber bases, and other counterforce targets and therefore complicate Soviet war planning.

The Soviets approached the SDI problem in two stages. First, they attempted to deflect the course of U.S. research and development by insisting that both sides adhere to a strict and legalistic interpretation of the ABM Treaty of 1972. The strict Soviet interpretation would preclude advanced testing, development, and deployment of space-based weapons, including those based on new physical principles such as lasers and particle beams. Many U.S. arms control experts and influential members of Congress agreed with this interpretation of the treaty.[18] Second, the USSR soon changed its tactics, when it became apparent that Reagan personally felt committed to SDI and would not give it up as a bargaining chip in order to get INF or START reductions. Thus, the Soviets somehow arrived at a decision in 1986 or 1987—possibly following superpower disagreements about SDI at Reykjavik—to delink the INF and SDI issues (although not, as of December 1987, the START and SDI issues).[19] This opened the way for the Reagan-Gorbachev agreement of December 1987, and, assuming that the INF Treaty would be ratified by the U.S. Senate, for ensuing discussions in 1988 with the aim of significantly reducing strategic nuclear forces.

The Soviet motivation for reverting to the original 1981 American proposals was to remove the U.S. Pershing IIs from their bases in West Germany. The Pershing II represented a time-urgent threat to Soviet military command centers in the western USSR. It was all too reminiscent of the U.S. Jupiter missiles stationed in Turkey decades ago, which had been removed very much to the liking of the Kremlin. The Soviets' reaction might suggest that they in fact do see something to the claim of American INF proponents, that a U.S. nuclear weapon based in Europe could be more credible as a deterrent than weapons based in America. Certainly, the Soviet conventional war plan would have to deal with the Pershing IIs and GLCMs, and the effort to achieve conventional preemption then might lead either to NATO nuclear escalation or to inadvertent escalation on account of the commingling of large-scale conventional and nuclear forces.

Another Soviet motivation was undoubtedly the conviction that the amassing of additional nuclear weapons in Europe, or of those intended for targets in Europe, was superfluous to Kremlin strategy. The USSR already had the capability to target important European ground zeros with its ballistic missiles of strategic (intercontinental) range, frontal and long-range aviation, and sea-based forces armed with cruise or ballistic missiles.[20] Some NATO military strategists already had reached the conclusion that the INF deployments on land had been unnecessary and that NATO could have supplied the same deterrent capability from sea-based systems.

Two departures in Soviet declaratory policy, both dating from the Brezhnev era but carried over to his successors, also provided part of the context within which the INF agreement was ultimately forged. The first was Leonid Brezhnev's speech in Tula in 1977, in which he renounced the aim of nuclear superiority. This was followed by other high-level political and military statements to the effect that nuclear war between superpowers would have no winners.[21] In the Khrushchev era, both of these statements would have caused the speaker to be deposed. Second, among other important departures in declaratory policy was the announcement by Brezhnev in 1981 that the Soviet Union would never be the first to use nuclear weapons. This in turn spurred critics of NATO strategy in the United States and in Europe to call for a similar pledge by NATO, but conventional force imbalances as perceived by the West precluded such a declaration, without shattering the alliance politically. It was thought by some Washington officials that the Kremlin's no-first-use pledge was disingenuous in any event. No first use as seen from Moscow did not preclude the Soviets' preemption of any NATO first use once their warning and intelligence indicators suggested to them that NATO was so prepared.

Officials in the Reagan administration wanted to take credit for standing firm in the face of the Soviet walkout from the INF and START talks in 1983. They also claimed that the president's unyielding stance on SDI helped to push the USSR to the negotiating table. These arguments were not so much wrong as they were one sided. They saw the motivation of Kremlin leaders through the conceptual lenses of American arms race dynamics. The Soviet Union places high importance on having an accurate knowledge of U.S. nuclear weapons deployments and research programs, but it does not set its own development and deployment goals by measuring comparability to those programs.[22] Nor does Soviet doctrine drive its technology to produce whatever theoretically derived weapons systems would fulfill the tenets of Marxist theory.[23] Moreover, Soviet interest in setting a mutually assured destruction (MAD) criterion for the shared vulnerability of American and Soviet cities has never been high.

Instead, as Michael MccGwire has explained, the USSR has among its primary objectives the avoidance of global war if at all possible, and the avoidance of nuclear conflict if global war should occur.[24] The Soviets are not prepared to sacrifice vital interests in order to avoid war. But, paradoxically, from the American standpoint, their growing strategic and theater nuclear military power over the past two decades has given them more confidence that their own nuclear forces can deter American or NATO nuclear first use. If so, then Soviet and Warsaw Pact conventional forces would be matched against those of NATO, which would allow the USSR to attain its political objectives without war, or at least without nuclear war.

This matrix of Soviet objectives does not lead to any justifiable expectation by the West that the Kremlin is going to abandon its efforts to expand its global politico-military influence. Its very political nature compels the Soviet Union to do that; and on this score, its ideology should be taken very seriously. However, the USSR will have to accomplish its myriad aims without war or be willing to run intolerable risks for the survival of the state. In this context, the Reagan SDI, which from Washington's standpoint seems to be just another research and development program, appears threatening from Moscow's standpoint. Some American cynics have argued that the Soviets oppose SDI because they know what the USSR would do with a missile defense system if they deployed one. In this rendition of the Soviet military mind, they would use it as part of a first-strike strategy against the United States, with their missile defenses absorbing a ragged American retaliation. And some high-level Soviet statements have attributed this very rationale in reverse to the Americans, thus fueling the fires of those Americans who are most skeptical of the Kremlin's motives.[25]

Misleading inferences are possible on this issue of motivation if the conclusions are based on mirror imaging of American and Soviet objectives. The U.S. propensity to invent newer technologies, and then to deploy them for their own sake, seems to Kremlin mirror-image theorists as a capitalist plot to deploy forces for a first strike. Similarly, the Soviets' already deployed BMD system and their continuing research efforts strike officials in Washington as factual evidence more compelling than Moscow's complaints about SDI. The Soviet fear is more realistically contrasted to, than it is compared with, the American one, the latter being that the USSR will combine active and passive defenses with an offensive countersilo capability. This is Washington's prototypical style of net assessment, comparing preattack and postattack net assessment capabilities and deriving therefrom a set of probable war outcomes. The Soviet view of war is more holistic; capabilities for war are military, political, social, psychological, and economic, and nuances about the opponent's intentions are as important as are his actual military forces. There is some evidence, for example, that the USSR expects strategic warning, or warning of intentions to attack, well before those intentions are actually carried out, under almost all conditions.[26] During a crisis in which there seemed to be a significant risk of war, especially nuclear war, the USSR would be using its political resources to try to achieve its objectives through diplomacy. Meanwhile, its military forces would be preparing for the worst.

These arguments suggest that the Soviet view of SDI is as dependent upon the atmospherics of superpower political relationships as it is upon the balance of deployed or developed technologies. For example, in December 1987, when General Secretary Gorbachev and President Reagan signed the INF Treaty in Washington, the issue of SDI was very much in the background. Although delinked in government jargon from INF for the moment, it loomed over any future discussions of strategic offensive force reductions. The improved political relations between the superpowers allowed more room for maneuver and compromise on this issue than had been permissible at Reykjavik. In turn, the Reagan position vis-à-vis

Congress softened. Following the signing of the INF accord, Secretary of State George Shultz said that the administration no longer would insist that Congress accept the broad and controversial interpretation of the ABM Treaty. (The "broad" interpretation of the State Department's legal adviser would be more permissive of SDI's advanced weapons testing and development than the narrower interpretation favored by the USSR.)[27] In effect, Reagan and Gorbachev simply agreed to disagree about SDI for the time being, while proceeding with discussions on offensive force reductions. This made less urgent the insistence of Congress that the Soviet interpretation of permissible research and testing was the correct one.

It was a larger challenge to move from particular arms control agreements to an entirely new basis for arms control, embodied in the administration's New Strategic Concept, as explained by Paul Nitze.[28] As contrasted above, the American and Soviet perspectives on the possibility of a defense-dominant world were very different. The American view focused on which technology would be dominant, while the Soviet perspective emphasized which superpower would have the stronger or weaker strategy after deployments and arms reductions had taken place. The transition to stronger defensive weapons and comparatively weaker offensive ones somehow had to be managed so that neither side, in the interim, felt threatened by the innovations of the other. A combination of badly managed transition and first-strike fears could undo the proposed reliance on defenses by making them components of surprise attack. A special fear in this regard was the imminent U.S. deployment of ASATs and the potential for the USSR to upgrade its already deployed system. Space-based defenses that were vulnerable to inexpensive ground- or space-based ASATs would be worse than no defenses at all, since they would invite preemption in a crisis. And the temptation to deploy ASATs in order to offset the uses of satellites as "force multipliers" during conventional war was growing on both sides as the importance of satellites became more apparent in the 1980s.[29]

Conclusion

Until the INF accord of December 1987, superpower nuclear arms control seemed to have failed. Immediately after the conclusion of that agreement, the way seemed open to progress once again. Observers of the process did not always understand that the process was not an end in itself but merely a component of American and Soviet strategies. Thus, the frequently expressed U.S. view that the process itself was valuable represented a common Western view of arms control negotiations not shared in Moscow.[30]

However, the INF, START, and outer space talks between the superpowers did give evidence that the Soviet Union sought to use arms control to achieve certain of its policy objectives—among them the continuation of U.S.-Soviet competition amid a less competitive nuclear arms race. This partial diminution of the nuclear arms competition would not mean the end of the "class struggle" or the advent of a Soviet-American global condominium, but rather that strategic and political realism about the arms race, and about the relationship between political influence and military power, was taking hold.

The fact, not now disputed by even the hawks on either side, is that the two superpowers by 1987 had deployed nuclear weapons far in excess of any rational policy objectives, save for self-annihilation. This, in fact, was the policy objective assigned to American strategic retaliatory forces (following the nuclear devastation of the Soviet Union) at the level of U.S. declaratory policy, and that policy influenced earlier arms control proposals. The coming together at Reykjavik in 1986, Washington in 1987, and (presumably) Moscow in 1988 testified to the triumph of political realism in the face of all the forces that always push against it. That is no small achievement, and those who observe the arms control process can only hope that leaders in Washington and Moscow persevere toward mutually acceptable, and mutually beneficial, agreements.

Notes

[1] Office of Technology Assessment, *MX Missile Basing* (Washington, DC: U.S. Government Printing Office, September 1981).

[2] President's Commission on U.S. Strategic Forces (Scowcroft Commission), *Report* (Washington, DC, April 1983).

3 Barry M. Blechman, "New Technology, Stability, and the Arms-Control Deadlock: Part 2," in Robert O'Neill, ed., *New Technology and Western Security Policy* (London: International Institute for Strategic Studies, 1985), pp. 107–15.

4 Bernard W. Rogers, "Follow-on Forces Attack (FOFA): Myths and Realities," *NATO Review* 32, no. 6 (December 1984): 1–9.

5 François L. Heisbourg, "Conventional Defense: Europe's Constraints and Opportunities," in Andrew J. Pierre, ed., *The Conventional Defense of Europe* (New York: Council on Foreign Relations, 1986), pp. 71–111.

6 John Erickson, Lynn Hansen, and William Schneider, *Soviet Ground Forces: An Operational Assessment* (Boulder, CO: Westview Press, 1986), chap. 3.

7 See Donald C. Daniel, *Anti-Submarine Warfare and Superpower Strategic Stability* (Urbana: University of Illinois Press, 1986), which offers an optimistic assessment of the prospects of SSBN survivability relative to their missions.

8 Bruce G. Blair, *Strategic Command and Control: Redefining the Nuclear Threat* (Washington, DC: Brookings Institution, 1985).

9 Stephen M. Meyer, "Soviet Nuclear Operations," chap. 15 in Ashton B. Carter, John D. Steinbruner, and Charles A. Zraket, eds., *Managing Nuclear Operations* (Washington, DC: Brookings Institution, 1987), p. 492, suggests that the KGB maintains a strategic communications network that is independent of the military communications system.

10 See Paul Bracken, "Delegation of Nuclear Command Authority," chap. 10 in Carter et al., *Managing Nuclear Operations*, pp. 352–72.

11 Barry R. Posen, "Inadvertent Nuclear War? Escalation and NATO's Northern Flank," in Steven E. Miller, ed., *Strategy and Nuclear Deterrence* (Princeton: Princeton University Press, 1984), pp. 85–112.

12 Paul Bracken, *The Command and Control of Nuclear Forces* (New Haven: Yale University Press, 1983), chap. 5.

13 An example is Melvyn Krauss, *How NATO Weakens the West* (New York: Simon and Schuster, 1986).

14 See John J. Mearsheimer, *Conventional Deterrence* (Ithaca, NY: Cornell University Press, 1983), chap. 6.

15 John Erickson, "The Soviet View of Deterrence: A General Survey," *Survival* 24, no. 6 (November-December 1982): 242–51.

16 On Reagan spending for strategic nuclear forces see U.S. Congress, Congressional Budget Office, *Modernizing U.S. Strategic Offensive Forces: Costs, Effects, and Alternatives* (Washington, DC: Congressional Budget Office, November 1987), pp. 2–4.

17 Secretary of State George Shultz, "Reykjavik: A Watershed in U.S.-Soviet Relations," in *Current Policy*, no. 883 (Washington, DC: U.S. Department of State, Bureau of Public Affairs, November 1986).

[18] See "Sofaer's Last Stand," press briefing with Gerard C. Smith, Spurgeon M. Keeny, Jr., John B. Rhinelander, and Raymond L. Garthoff, *Arms Control Today* 17, no. 8 (October 1987): 14–16.

[19] Some of the important political history leading up to the INF agreement is summarized in Strobe Talbott, "The Road to Zero," *Time*, December 14, 1987.

[20] Background is provided in Donald C. Daniel, "The Soviet Navy and Tactical Nuclear War at Sea," *Survival* 29, no. 4 (July-August 1987): 318–35.

[21] Brezhnev's statement at Tula emphasized that the USSR did not seek military superiority with the aim of delivering a first strike. See L. I. Brezhnev, "Outstanding Exploit of the Defenders of Tula," *Pravda*, January 19, 1977, cited in Raymond L. Garthoff, *Détente and Confrontation: American-Soviet Relations from Nixon to Reagan* (Washington, DC: Brookings Institution, 1985), p. 771.

[22] See Fritz W. Ermarth, "Contrasts in American and Soviet Strategic Thought," in Derek Leebaert, ed., *Soviet Military Thinking* (London: Allen and Unwin, 1981), pp. 50–69.

[23] David Holloway, "Doctrine and Technology in Soviet Armaments Policy," ibid., pp. 259–91.

[24] See Michael MccGwire, *Military Objectives in Soviet Foreign Policy* (Washington, DC: Brookings Institution, 1987), for an informative assessment of the evolution of Soviet objectives from World War II to the present.

[25] For background see Raymond L. Garthoff, "BMD and East-West Relations," in Ashton B. Carter and David N. Schwartz, eds., *Ballistic Missile Defense* (Washington, DC: Brookings Institution, 1984), pp. 275–329. A balanced view of the Soviet BMD program appears in the chapter by Sayre Stevens in the same volume.

[26] Stephen M. Meyer, "Soviet Nuclear Operations," pp. 470–534.

[27] *New York Times*, December 14, 1987.

[28] Paul H. Nitze, "On the Road to a More Stable Peace," *Current Policy* 657 (February 20, 1985).

[29] Paul B. Stares, *Space and National Security* (Washington, DC: Brookings Institution, 1987).

[30] Leon Sloss and M. Scott Davis, eds., *A Game for High Stakes: Lessons Learned in Negotiating with the Soviet Union* (Cambridge, MA: Ballinger, 1986), esp. Sloss, "Introduction and Findings," pp. 6–14.

Index